AFRICAN WORLD HISTORIES

Bantu Africa

AFRICAN WORLD HISTORIES

Series Editor:
Trevor R. Getz, San Francisco State University

African World Histories is a series of retellings of some of the most commonly discussed episodes of the African and global past from the perspectives of Africans who lived through them. Accessible yet scholarly, *African World Histories* gives students insights into African experiences and perspectives concerning many of the events and trends that are commonly discussed in the history classroom.

Titles in the Series

Published

Cosmopolitan Africa, 1700–1875
Trevor R. Getz, San Francisco State University

Transatlantic Africa, 1400–1800
Kwasi Konadu, City University of New York, and Trevor Getz, San Francisco State University

Colonial Africa, 1884–1994
Dennis Laumann, University of Memphis

Sovereignty and Struggle, Africa and Africans in the Era of the Cold War, 1945–1994
Jonathan T. Reynolds, Northern Kentucky University

Africanizing Democracies, 1980–Present
Alicia Decker, Pennsylvania State University, and Andrea Arrington, Indiana State University

Bantu Africa
Catherine Cymone Fourshey, Bucknell University, Rhonda M. Gonzales, University of Texas at San Antonio, and Christine Saidi, Kutztown University

Forthcoming
Authoritarian Africa
Nic Cheeseman, University of Birmingham (UK)

Bantu
Africa

3500 BCE to Present

Catherine Cymone Fourshey

Rhonda M. Gonzales

Christine Saidi

Foreword by Patrick Manning

New York   Oxford
OXFORD UNIVERSITY PRESS

Oxford University Press is a department of the University of Oxford. It furthers the University's objective of excellence in research, scholarship, and education by publishing worldwide. Oxford is a registered trademark of Oxford University Press in the UK and certain other countries.

Published in the United States of America by Oxford University Press
198 Madison Avenue, New York, NY 10016, United States of America.

Library of Congress Cataloging-in-Publication Data

Names: Fourshey, Cymone, 1970- author. | Gonzales, Rhonda M., author. |
   Saidi, Christine, author.
Title: Bantu Africa / Cymone Fourshey, Rhonda Gonzales, Christine Saidi.
Other titles: African world histories.
Description: New York : Oxford University Press, 2017. | Series: African
   world histories | Includes index.
Identifiers: LCCN 2017017181 | ISBN 9780199342457 (pbk.)
Subjects: LCSH: Bantu-speaking peoples—History. | Africa,
   Sub-Saharan—History. | Africa, Sub-Saharan—Civilization.
Classification: LCC DT16.B2 F68 2017 | DDC 967.0049369—dc23
LC record available at https://lccn.loc.gov/2017017181

9 8 7 6 5 4 3 2
Printed by Webcom, Inc., Canada

CONTENTS

Maps and Figures *vii*

A Note on Spellings *viii*

Acknowledgments *ix*

About the Authors *xi*

Foreword *xiii*

Introduction *xvi*

Chapter 1: RECONSTRUCTING BANTU EXPANSIONS *1*
Who Are the Bantu? 2
Phases of the Bantu Expansions 3
First Phase: 3500 BCE–3000 BCE 5
Second Phase: 3000 BCE–2000 BCE 8
Third Phase: 2000 BCE–1000 BCE 11
Fourth Phase: 1000 BCE–500 CE 13
Fifth Phase: 500 CE–1800 CE 21
Methods Used to Reconstruct Early Bantu History 24
Words as Historical Evidence 25
Genetics as Historical Evidence 31
Archaeology as Historical Evidence 32
Oral Tradition as Historical Evidence 34
Ethnography as Historical Evidence 37
Conclusion 39
FEATURE: *Capoeira* 41

Chapter 2: HISTORICIZING LINEAGE, BELONGING, AND HETERARCHY *43*
Lineage and Religion 46
Belonging: Lineage, Clans, and Affines 56

Moving Up: Aging, Elders, and Life Stages   74
Conclusion   84
FEATURE: *A Kaonde Oral History*   85

Chapter 3: EDUCATING GENERATIONS   *89*

Performance as Education   90
Traditions and Transitions   97
Advanced Learning   104
Communication in the Bantu
    Historical Tradition   109
Conclusion   113

Chapter 4: CREATING TECHNOLOGY AND ART   *115*

Food Production   116
Bananas   120
Ceramics and Iron   126
Homesteads, Architecture, and Engineering Technologies   133
Clothing and Body Art   137
Carving Spirits: Wood Work   141
Rock Art Production   142
Conclusion   142
FEATURE: *African Arts, Museums, and Picasso*   143

Chapter 5: NEGOTIATING HOSPITALITY   *145*

Greeting and Welcoming Guests   146
Hospitality in Material Culture, Proverbs, and Greetings   148
Insufficient Hospitality: Oral Traditions of Migration   150
Heterarchies of Hospitality and Social Bonds   153
Close Encounters: Interactions with Non-Bantu   155
Honoring Ancestors: Religious Observance as Hospitality   159
Across the Seas: Non-African Foreigners   160
Respectability and Antisocial Acts: Hospitable and Inhospitable
    Categories   162
Conclusion   163
FEATURE: *Hospitality, Hostility, and Refugees*   165

Index   *169*

Maps and Figures

Maps

1. Political map of Africa   xviii
2. Bantu ethno-linguistic groups   xx
3. African language families circa 1500 CE   xxi
4. Bantu expansions: first phase, 3500 BCE
   to 3000 BCE   6
5. Bantu expansions: second phase, 3000 BCE
   to 2000 BCE   9
6. Bantu expansions: third phase, 2000 BCE
   to 1000 BCE   12
7. Bantu expansions: fourth phase, 1000 BCE
   to 500 CE   14
8. Bantu expansions: fifth phase, 500 CE–1800 CE   22

Figures

1.1. Schematic Tree of Select Niger-Congo
   Descended Languages   xxii
3.1. Kuba raffia cloth   105
4.1. Luangwa pot   127
4.2. Tabwa carving   139
5.1. Anthropomoprhic three-legged stool   152

Tables

1.1. Glottochronology derived dating estimates   29
2.1. Shifting Ancestor and Lineage Concepts in Linguistic Data   86

A Note on Spellings

PREFIXES:

Bantu languages classify all nouns into classes marked by prefixes. Prefixes are separated from word roots by a dash (-), for example *mu-lungu*.

Bantu languages are marked by prefixes–ki-, isi, ci For example, kiSwahili is the Swahili language.

People are marked in Bantu languages by prefixes M-for singular and Ba- or Wa- for the plural. For example, *mtwa* is a Twa person (s.) whereas *Batwa* are Twa people (pl).

SYMBOLS:

* indicates a root reconstructed to a proto-language.

DIACRITICS:

There are several Bantu languages that have seven vowels rather than five. These additional vowels include a super closed high vowel /i/ represented in various sources as /į/ and in others as /I/. This text employs /I/. The second is a super closed mid-vowel /u/ represented in various sources as /ʉ/ or /U/. This text employs /ʉ/.

TONE:

Some Bantu languages have high and low tone represented by diacritics above the vowels. High tone is represented by accent *aigu* /´/. Low tone is represented by accent *igrec* /`/.

Acknowledgments

Writing a history of Bantu-speaking people covering more than 5,500 years in fewer than two hundred pages, and making it accessible to undergraduate students, required the support of many people. And because the research for this book rests on knowledge many people have had a hand in producing across more than twenty-five years, we apologize in advance to all scholars and public intellectuals whose works shaped this work but whose names may not appear here.

Bantu Africa was Trevor Getz's brainchild. As series editor for African World History, he recognized the critical need for a text centered on early Bantu history, a history that has relevance to the continent and beyond. He approached us with an opportunity to write this book, and he has astutely shepherded this project from beginning to end. We are grateful for the commitment of editor Charles Cavaliere and Oxford University Press to this project.

Too many Africanist colleagues and institutions have contributed to our thinking and ability to carry out our work to name them all. To list the obvious, we greatly appreciate Edmond Keller and Muadi Mukenge for their support and leadership of the UCLA James S. Coleman African Studies Center, as we undertook our earliest research in the 1990s. We also recognize the UCLA History Department, Ned Alpers, Karen Brodkin, Christopher Ehret, Afaf Marsot, Boniface Obichere, Merrick Posnansky, and Brenda Stevenson for arming us with the skills, methods, and types of questions necessary to complete the sort of interdisciplinary scholarship reflected in this book. We are grateful to Ruby Bell-Gam of the UCLA Charles E. Young Research Library for her work in accumulating an impressive collection of African sources that have positively bolstered our work in general and this book in particular. Our thanks must also be extended to librarians and archivists—across Africa, Europe, the United States, and México—for their intellectual partnerships in our individual and collective research over the years.

We thank scholars for research that has inspired and challenged us in writing this book. They include Nwando Achebe, Jean-Pierre Chrétien, Edda Fields-Black, J. Desmond Clark, Steve Feierman, Karen Flint, Blandina Giblin, James Giblin, Joseph Greenburg, Malcolm Guthrie, Sondra Hale, Hillary Jones, Nicholas Katenekwa, Kairn Klieman, Neil Kodesh, Bertram Mapunda, James McCann, Joseph Miller, Deogratis Ngonyani, Onaiwu Ogbomo, Akin Ogundiran, Oyèrónké Oyěwùmí, Victoria Phiri, David Lee Schoenbrun, Lorelle Semley, Rhiannon Stevens, Jan Vansina, Adria LaViolette, and Pamela Willoughby. Although this book rests on the work of a cadre of Africanist scholars who over the last half a century have focused research on the Bantu populations across Africa, two eminent scholars in particular must be acknowledged. We thank Christopher Ehret for sharing his expansive knowledge, intellectual courage, and supportive guidance, which continues to inspire our scholarship on underresearched areas of early African history. We also thank Patrick Manning for his emphatic support and enthusiastic encouragement on the importance of doing big history, as well as for graciously preparing the Foreword. We are grateful to Esperanza Brizuela-Garcia, Tyler Fleming, Dennis Laumann, Patrick Malloy, and Troy D. Spier for reading chapter drafts and to anonymous readers who provided critical insight and suggestions to improve the text overall.

To our students and friends who have listened to us discuss Bantu people and their history, in both broad and specific ways, we hope that you enjoy reading this text. Our families have been incredibly understanding and encouraging as we took many hours away from them to collaborate and write this book. They patiently put up with the voices of two extra people in the house during our weekly Skype calls. Finally, we would like to thank Bantu-speaking people—living and ancestral—for producing the histories that inspire our research.

About the Authors

Catherine Cymone Fourshey is Associate Professor of History and International Relations at Bucknell University. Fourshey's published research focuses on agriculture, hospitality, migration, and the intersections of environment, economy, and politics in precolonial Tanzania. She has conducted research and published on gender in Africa both in precolonial and colonial spaces. She has published articles in the *African Historical Review, International Journal of African Historical Studies, JENdA,* and *Ufahamu.* She is completing a book manuscript titled *Strangers, Immigrants, and the Established: Hospitality as State-Building Mechanism in Southwest Tanzania, 300–1900 CE.* Additionally, Fourshey has been conducting research on the history of immigrants/refugees in Tanzania who are known in international aid and development circles as "the Bantu Somali." She has been a recipient of research grants and fellowships from the American Association of University Women, the Fulbright Foundation, the National Endowment for the Humanities, and Notre Dame University. She is from Marin County, California, and holds a B.A. in political science and an M.A. and Ph.D. in history from UCLA.

Rhonda M. Gonzales is a Professor of African and African Diaspora History and Associate Vice Provost for Strategic Initiatives at The University of Texas at San Antonio. The National Endowment for the Humanities, Andrew Mellon Foundation, Ford Foundation, and the American Historical Association have supported her research on women and their roles in sustaining and transforming society through religion, medicine, and economy in precolonial Africa and in the African Diaspora in Mexico. As a first-generation college graduate, she is passionate about envisioning and implementing programming and best practices to support the diverse representation of underrepresented minorities, first-generation, transition, low-socioeconomic-status, and science, technology, engineering, and mathematics student retention through graduation in higher education. She is the recipient of a $3.25 million Department of Education

Title V grant to build four student success programs at The University of Texas at San Antonio: F2G&G, RTE, Alamo Runners, and Math Matters. She is from Long Beach, California. She holds a B.A. in sociology and an M.A. and Ph.D. in history from UCLA.

Christine Saidi is an Associate Professor of African and World History at Kutztown University (a state university serving first-generation students). Saidi is the recipient of three prestigious Fulbright fellowships, a Social Science Research Council grant, a Woodrow Wilson Women's Studies grant, and a National Endowment for the Humanities fellowship. She was instrumental in establishing the Center for the Study of Gender in Africa at the African Studies Center at UCLA. She conducted research in Somalia and in The White Fathers' Archive, Rome, and later in Zambia and the Congo, as a Senior Fulbright Scholar. She has command of written French, Italian, and Bemba. She has authored many scholarly articles, a book, coauthored a book, and is currently writing a coauthored textbook on the history of African women. Christine Saidi is from Los Angeles, California. She received a B.A. in history, an M.A. in African Area Studies, and a Ph.D. in history from UCLA.

Foreword

This concise and comprehensive introduction to the history of Bantu Africa breaks new ground in several ways. It is a brief but rich history of a region as large as the United States, extending across several thousand years. It provides detailed and valuable information on African societies, addressing several areas of their culture in a coherent narrative. It addresses an unusually long period of time for a history book—it tells this story not only because of the skill of the authors, but also because of the long history of development and interaction in the Bantu lands. In addition to the book's strength in portraying space, time, and society, it also conveys in a useful and understandable fashion the methods used to reconstruct Bantu history, including linguistics, archaeology, anthropology, and other fields.

Although it covers a wide region and a long period of time, the work is factually precise and stimulating in its presentation. It is well prepared for general readers in that it presents them with a clear statement of the interactions of various regions and ethnic groups; it shows the evolution of society over time. It provides some well-dated links of these Africans to people from other parts of the world, such as the Austronesian mariners who brought bananas to eastern Africa and the Portuguese mariners who brought Catholicism to Kongo.

After a brief but comprehensive Introduction to which readers will wish to return, chapter 1 provides the detailed framework of the book. Here readers will need to study the concept of worldview and the geography of the Bantu region. The maps (see chapter 1 maps 4-8) have the advantage of emphasizing river valleys as geographic markers, and the authors return to river valleys and lakes as place markers throughout the book, a wise move since national boundaries were established only very recently (see page xviii Map 1). Readers will also study the stages of Bantu migration and learn about five relevant types of historical evidence: words, genetics, archaeology, oral tradition, and ethnography. The reward for learning this framework is that readers will be able to see the past as if through Bantu eyes.

The next two chapters focus on social values and on knowledge. Social values include ancestral Bantu religious conceptions and then showing how ideas changed as Bantu migrants encountered communities with different religions. In addition, this chapter gives a fine overview of matrilineage as the basis of a social system of many Bantu speakers. The chapter on knowledge is very effective in showing the life course of people in Bantu societies and the types of things that they learned at each age.

The final two chapters focus on inventions (in technology and art) and on the Bantu practice of hospitality. The inventions reveal the precise control that Bantu peoples had over fire, yielding excellence in their pottery and iron tools, plus the social relations that sustained the work. Other remarkable skills arose in textiles and architecture. Agricultural innovations included shifts from the original Bantu agriculture, relying on yams; they changed considerably as groups gradually took up bananas, millet, and sorghum. The final chapter shows how the system of hospitality served as the social glue enabling communities to focus on peaceable exchange rather than dominance, at least until recent times.

There are many exciting historical lessons that are conveyed in this book. Although there are now many good books conveying aspects of African history at a general level, this one has the advantage of coherence in telling the story of the unfolding of Bantu society through expansion of a single group that managed to make its imprint on a huge area of Africa. In particular, the book gives useful and interesting detail on times and places often neglected or avoided in courses on world history. The authors are experienced in teaching about history with emphasis on what one can learn from language, and they convey their lessons skillfully.

The significance of Bantu-speaking peoples and their history has only gradually come to be understood. There were empires in the Bantu world, but they were small on a global scale and gained little attention from historians. It was the remarkable similarity of Bantu languages that gradually brought forth the great significance of Bantu speakers in world history. Early Portuguese mariners visiting the African coast recognized the great similarity of languages from Cameroon to Somalia. In the nineteenth century, German linguists Wilhelm Bleek and Carl Meinhof coined the term "Bantu" in their linguistic studies. From 1932, British scholar Malcolm Guthrie began his studies of Bantu languages, beginning with Lingala in what was then Belgian Congo, and later researching in British east and central Africa. He published two comprehensive books on Bantu languages, in 1948 and 1967, positing Bantu origins in the middle Congo valley. But American linguist Joseph

Greenberg, working on his own with fieldwork in northern Nigeria, published in 1963 a classification of all African languages that has been accepted in its outlines since then; an important part of his argument was that Bantu languages had formed and expanded from a homeland at the boundary of Nigeria and Cameroon. Greenberg's 1972 article confirmed his point on Bantu origins—and Greenberg then went on to classify other language groups worldwide. Thereafter, Jan Vansina and Christopher Ehret stood out among those analyzing Bantu languages—Vansina based on field research in Rwanda, Kuba, and the Congo valley, Ehret based on field research in eastern Africa. Though they debated, their debates led to today's understanding of the process of Bantu expansions. Numerous scholars, especially students of Ehret (who include the authors of this book), expanded impressively the specialist knowledge of Bantu languages, social life, and history. But the explanation of Bantu history to the broader public advanced slowly. World history textbook writers were able to fill the interior of their maps of Central and East Africa, previously blank, with arrows labeled "Bantu." But that was hardly enough.

The big step forward brought by this book is the presentation of Bantu history for nonspecialists and with a clear connection to other trends in world history. The authors of this book are path-breaking analysts in the social history of the Bantu expansions; they are also experienced teachers in world history, comparing human experiences across time and around the world. Christine Saidi, Catherine Cymone Fourshey, and Rhonda M. Gonzales have each published on multiple issues over long stretches of Bantu history, each centered in regions of east and central Africa. They are clear on the way in which the linguistic documentation of the Bantu expansion, over five thousand years, gives a remarkable and (so far) unique view into the development and transformation of an ancestral tradition—that of the northern edge of Cameroon forests. The result was the rise of differentiated traditions in many different ecologies, as Bantu-speaking migrants expanded persistently across space, encountered new peoples and various traditions, and incorporated them into Bantu ways. For the period from five thousand to one thousand years ago, this is the single most coherent and sustained narrative we have of social change on the planet. Only the well-known history of the Yellow River traditions of China can meet it in terms of the consistency and detail of its social history.

PATRICK MANNING

Andrew W. Mellon
Professor of World History, Emeritus
University of Pittsburgh

Introduction

Human history began on the African continent, and from earliest times human migration has been central both within and beyond Africa. *Bantu Africa* covers one part of that history that is significant to world history because of the influences Bantu speakers have contributed across the globe. Their history teaches us about a range of ways that people have created enduring yet pliable social and material institutions in which hierarchy, heterarchy, relationships with outsiders, and power dynamics were present and contested. In studying Bantu education, family, hospitality, gender, and more, readers may question what it means to name and be a civilization. For more than five thousand years, speakers of Bantu-descended languages established communities across the majority of sub-Saharan Africa. This is among the largest sets of migrations—in scale and time depth—known anywhere. Across vast and varied landscapes, linguistically related Bantu-descended people developed unique economies, political systems, religious ideologies, and cultural practices. Yet they also maintained a range of cultural continuities. It was through the vehicle of language, as well as their geographic expansions, that both diverse and shared knowledge and practices were transmitted across generations and geography. These migrations helped to transform economic practices, politics, and social organization through cross-cultural interactions and a set of values rooted in hospitality and incorporating ideas from other societies. As such, Bantu-speaking populations have been incredibly important in African and global histories precisely because the implications of their contributions are so instructive and illuminating on both the contingent and processual nature of history. In other words, historical contingencies of circumstances, environments, resources, and interactions make the difference, and history is not merely events, but rather the unfolding of processes.

Writing Bantu history is an awesome task due to its scale, scope, and time depth. Furthermore, this topic has a history of healthy debate among scholars who have differing perspectives about what "Bantu" means and how the languages classified as Bantu came to be dispersed over such a large region of the African continent, a history that is commonly called the Bantu expansions. Over the last 125 years, linguists, archaeologists, and historians have all weighed in on how, when, and why Bantu-speaking people managed to populate such a large part of the continent, especially considering that speakers of non-Bantu languages already inhabited much of the landscape. The debates center in part on methodologies that are employed to reconstruct the Bantu past, but they also emerge from the specialized and regional studies that individual Africanist scholars conduct. Africanist historians commonly take a regional and period-focused approach to reconstruct the histories for groups of Bantu societies closely related both in terms of linguistics and geography. Yet, while they research, learn, and teach about local Bantu histories, scholars always are cognizant that their regional studies contribute to building a much bigger picture of the Bantu past. Deliberation over the details of the many twists and turns of Bantu history over the longue durée are ongoing. Presently, there remain opportunities to fully flesh out regional and localized studies that will add to comprehensive coverage of the full expanse of Bantu history. In regard to competing theories regarding Bantu expansions, Botswanan linguist H. M. Batibo expressively notes, "In fact, most of these views are not contradictory but rather complementary in dealing with the complex patterns of historical events, as shown in the analogy of the three blind people who thought that an elephant was like a trunk, a big banana leaf and a large suspended rock. All of them were right in so far as their experiences were concerned."[1] Bantu history is complex, and differences of opinion and debates among scholars will persist as new evidence continues to be uncovered.

---

[1] H. M. Batibo, "Comments on Christopher Ehret, 'Bantu History: Re-Envisioning the Evidence of Language'" *The International Journal of African Historical Studies* 34, no. 1 (2001): 68.

Given the growing body of local and regional histories about particular Bantu communities written in the last two decades, this overview of Bantu history is both important and timely.[2] This project brings knowledge about Bantu scholarship to a broader audience of young scholars, who will be at the forefront of the next phase of scholarship on Africa. This book captures a history of fluidity in migrations that is not reflected in the static boundaries of modern day political map (see Map 1), which is included to give readers a sense

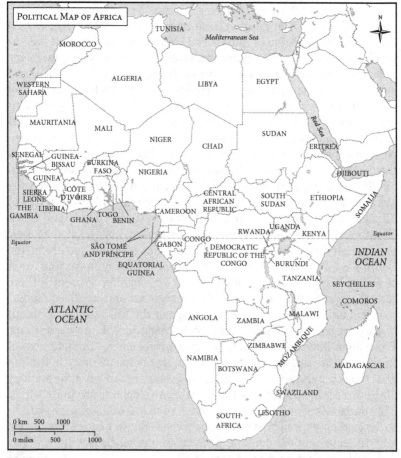

MAP 1

[2] David Schoenbrun, "Representing the Bantu Expansions: What's at Stake?" *The International Journal of African Historical Studies* 34, no. 1 (2001): 1–4.

of locations discussed in earlier eras. The political map above will be useful to readers as a point of reference for locating historical sites and events discussed throughout the text. This is a history in many ways similar to other familiar histories; it is one filled with migration, exceptionalism, innovation, entrepreneurial spirit, and the accompanying failures.

The challenge before us was to write a five thousand–plus year history of people who cover one-half of Africa, the world's second largest continent, and completing it in so few pages is a formidable undertaking. In setting out to write this text, there were important questions to consider: What should be included? And, more important, what should be left out? We had to decide how to capture the debates in the field, present important themes, explain the chronology, and provide detail on region-based microstudies, while also providing readers with an overarching representation of Bantu history. To do this, this book emerges from the foremost scholarship to present a narrative overview, context, and examination of salient themes.

In particular, readers of *Bantu Africa* will be introduced to the technological, epistemological, educational, cultural histories, and lived experiences of Bantu-speaking peoples from 3500 BCE to the present. The book begins at 3500 BCE, the period when speakers of the proto-Bantu language lived in an area of western Africa adjacent to forests between the Niger and Congo Rivers. Today, there are nearly five hundred Bantu dialects and languages, a number of which are discussed in detail are noted in Map 2 (see page xx). Eachs descends from proto-Bantu, a subgroup of Niger-Congo (see page xxii Figure 1.1[3]), a language family whose history dates back to as early as 10,000 BCE. The breadth and depth of linguistic history on the African continent is prodigious. In Africa there are approximately two thousand indigenous languages and dialects spoken. Each language belongs to one of Africa's four major language families. They are Nilo-Saharan, Afrasian, Khoesan, and Niger Congo (see page xxiv Map 3). The primary focus is Bantu people and their interactions with people of other linguistic backgrounds, which shaped the diversity of the continent.

---

[3] Christopher Ehret, *The Civilizations of Africa: A History to 1800* (Charlottesville, VA: University of Virginia Press, 2002); Kairn A. Klieman, *"The Pygmies Were Our Compass": Bantu and Batwa in the History of West Central Africa, Early Times to C. 1900 C.E.* Portsmouth, (N.H.: Heinemann, 2003); Kay Williamson, "Niger-Congo Overview," in *The Niger- Congo Languages*, ed. by John Bendor-Samuel, (Lanham, MD: University Press of America, 1989), 3–45.

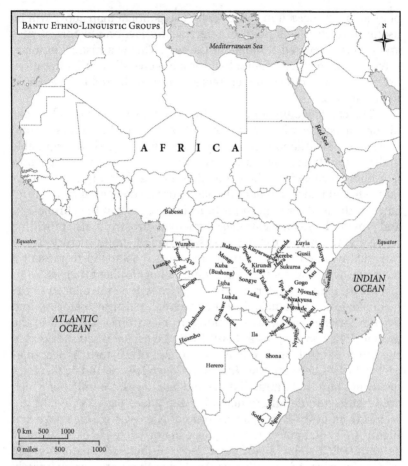

MAP 2

Because of length limitations, we had to leave out a great deal on Bantu forbearers, who include the Niger-Congo (also referred to as Niger-Kordofanian), Atlantic, Atlantic-Congo, and Benue-Kwa (Benue-Congo). It is important, however, to recognize that Bantu speakers are part of a larger and deeper tradition that is connected to people in West Africa proper. Early on, Bantu was merely one small sub-subbranch of Niger-Congo. Other Niger-Congo branches, Mande, Kordofanian, and Volta Congo subbranches, Kru, Kwa, and North Volta spread into more compact regions north, northwest, and northeast of the Niger River. Their lands extended in the end from

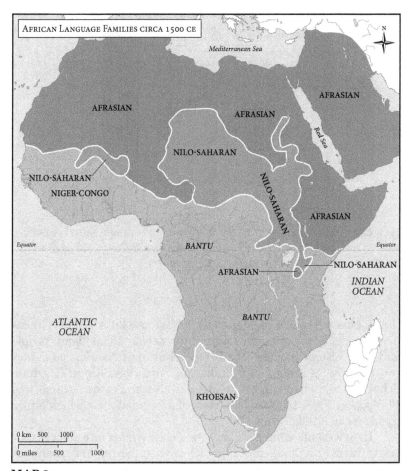

MAP 3

the equatorial rainforest of Africa through the south and southeast of the Congo Basin to the Central Africa grasslands, as well as the East African Great Lakes region, the highlands, savannas, and coastlands of eastern Africa, and the steppes, grasslands, savannahs, and woodlands of southern Africa. In other words, this one small branch of Niger-Congo moved into a territory adjacent to larger expanses of geographically open, though occupied, woodland and forest that abutted further east onto savanna.

As early as the nineteenth century, scholarly debates took shape on the history of the Bantu and the nature of their expansions through

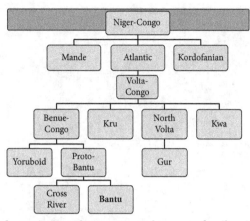

Figure 1.1 Schematic tree of Niger-Congo language family with three well-studied branches: Mande, Kordofanian, and Atlantic-Congo. Adapted from Williamson 1989, Ehret 2002, and Klieman 2003.

the linguistic studies of Meinhoff, Johnston, Guthrie, and Greenberg. In the later twentieth century, the debate about Bantu people and their history included the perspectives of archaeologists deMaret, Denbow, Huffman, and Phillipson; historians Ehret, Klieman, Schoenbrun, and Vansina; and linguists, Bastin, Bostoen, Nurse, and Philippson. These scholars have created a foundation on which future scholars can build.

In five theme-centered chapters, *Bantu Africa* introduces readers to varied methods and approaches to gathering and analyzing data to write the histories of people and societies whose deep pasts were not often preserved in written documents. Thus, the reconstruction of early Bantu history must rely on the use of multiple methodologies and approaches. Evidence is drawn from linguistics, genetics, archaeology, oral traditions, art history, and comparative ethnography.

Chapter 1 presents the distinguishing elements of the five phases of Bantu expansions. Additionally, it lays out the multiple methodologies employed to reconstruct the phases and details of Bantu histories elaborated in this text. The goal of this chapter is to provide a framework for understanding the idea of and hypotheses about Bantu origins and expansions. They moved along riverways, through and out of rainforest niches of western and west central Africa into woodlands, savannahs, arid territories of eastern Africa, and along the coasts of both the Atlantic and Indian Oceans.

Chapter 2 discusses the epistemological assumptions and worldviews of Bantu-descended people. This chapter narrates the dynamics and fluidity of kinship and lineality central to many Bantu-speaking communities. It examines the relations and networks Bantu people built with both non-Bantu and other Bantu-speaking peoples. It also introduces readers to the concepts of heterarchy, belonging, and lineage—ideologies that informed Bantu people's decisions and their development of social, political, and economic practices.

Chapter 3 introduces readers to Bantu approaches to teaching, learning, and transmission of ideas, practices, and concepts. Knowledge was conveyed and reconstituted through public performances, theater arts, storytelling, initiations, and apprenticeships. These prepared people for practical, professional, and intellectual endeavors that were important in their communities. Educational models reveal the ways Bantu-speaking communities valued the production, reproduction, and preservation of history.

Chapter 4 surveys Bantu production, innovation, and invention of science, technology, and art in a historical context. In the larger arc of Bantu worldviews, science, technology, and art were necessarily interconnected and complementary human activities that brought together the material world and humanistic expressions of the spiritual and emotional dimensions. This chapter considers a range of sciences, industries, and aesthetics that include agriculture, ceramics, iron production, textiles, beautification techniques, and architecture.

Chapter 5 brings together an array of Bantu perspectives and practices under the theme of hospitality. It contends that within Bantu societies hospitality was an early, dialectic principle. It shaped and was shaped by social, economic, and political realities. Hospitality was an important ideology and system of ethics that informed people's decisions and choices they made toward outsiders and guests. It rested on principles of circulating reciprocity, which regulated social relations, created social security, and facilitated people's efforts to develop their societies. Many Bantu-speaking communities saw the value of welcoming outsiders and acknowledging firstcomers.

The book's five chapters draw on regional examples from across Bantu-speaking Africa. It introduces historical evidence using categories that align with Bantu worldviews in time and place. *Bantu*

Africa underscores the intersectionality and pliability of historical categories reflected in Bantu languages and cultures. In so doing, it challenges common Western traditions' discrete and often rigid political, economic, religious, and social categories. This book encourages readers to be attentive to the ancient and modern nuances of Bantu tradition. Ultimately, this book underscores the critical roles Bantu speakers have played in the shaping of African and world histories.

Our aim is to give students an understanding of the long-term history of the Bantu world in areas that readers might identify as cultural, political, religious, economic, and social. However, in this text we rarely use these particular categories because we argue that Bantu epistemologies (worldviews) did not get divided into such strict categories. Bantu-speaking populations are located in countries from Cameroon to South Africa, which are over 6,000 miles apart. The 300 million speakers are primarily located in the modern-day countries of Angola, Botswana, Burundi, Cameroon, Central African Republic, Comoros, Democratic Republic of Congo, Gabon, Kenya, Lesotho, Malawi, Mozambique, Namibia, Republic of Congo, Rwanda, Seychelles, South Africa, Swaziland, Tanzania, Uganda, Zambia, and Zimbabwe, and there are small numbers even as far north as Somalia. In keeping with major themes of the series, *Bantu Africa* is particularly timely because it provides detail and background on a theme and era essential to many college course curriculums, but insufficiently covered in texts to date. Instructors of the first half of African History and World History (and perhaps even AP World History) are likely to find this useful because it will provide foundational knowledge for students and professors on African history with special emphasis on early eras.

FURTHER READINGS

Asombang, Raymond, and Pierre de Maret. "Reinvestigating Shuma Laka: The December 1991–March 1992 Campaign." *NSI: Bulletin De Liaison Des Archéologues Du Monde Bantu*, no. 10–11 (1992): 13–16.

Bastin, Y., A. Coupez, and Michael Mann. *Continuity and Divergence in the Bantu Languages: Perspectives from a Lexicostatistic Study*. Tervuren, Belgium: Musée Royal de l'Afrique centrale, 1999.

———. "Articles—Comments on Ehret, "Bantu Expansions." *The International Journal of African Historical Studies* 34, no. 1 (2001): 64.

Bostoen, Koen A. G., and Jacky Maniacky. *Studies in African Comparative Linguistics: With Special Focus on Bantu and Mande.* Tervuren: Royal Museum for Central Africa, 2005.

Bostoen, Koen A. G., and Yvonne Bastin. *Bantu Lexical Reconstruction.* Oxford: Oxford University Press, 2016.

de Luna, Kathryn M. *Collecting Food, Cultivating People: Subsistence and Society in Central Africa.* New Haven, Conn.: Yale University Press, 2016.

de Maret, Pierre, and F. Nsuka. "History of Bantu Metallurgy: Some Linguistic Aspects." *History in Africa* 4 (1977): 43–65.

de Maret, Pierre, and G. Thiry. "How Old Is the Iron Age in Central Africa?" *Culture and Technology of African Iron Production,* edited by Peter R. Schmidt, 29–39. Gainesville: University of Florida Press, 1996.

Denbow, James R. "Pride, Prejudice, Plunder and Preservation: Archaeology and the Re-Envisioning of Ethnogenesis on the Loango Coast of the Republic of Congo." *Antiquity* 86, no. 332 (2012): 383–408.

———. *The Archaeology and Ethnography of Central Africa.* Cambridge: Cambridge University Press, 2014.

Ehret, Christopher. "Bantu Origins and History: Critique and Interpretation." *Transafrican Journal of History* 2, no. 1 (1972): 1–9.

———. *An African Classical Age: Eastern and Southern Africa in World History, 1000 B.C. to A.D. 400.* Charlottesville: University Press of Virginia, 1998.

———. "Bantu Expansions: Re-Envisioning A Central Problem of Early African History." *International Journal of African Historical Studies* 34 (2001): 5–42.

———. "Bantu History: Big Advance, Although with a Chronological Contradiction." *Proceedings of the National Academy of Sciences of the United States of America* 112, no. 44 (2015): 13428–13429.

Gonzales, Rhonda M. *Societies, Religion, and History: Central East Tanzanians and the World They Created, C. 200 BCE to 1800 CE.* New York: Columbia University Press, 2008 http://www.gutenberg-e. org/gonzales/.

Greenberg, Joseph H. "The Classification of African Languages." *American Anthropologist* 50, no. 1 (1948): 24–30.

———. "Studies in African Linguistic Classification: III. The Position of Bantu." *Southwestern Journal of Anthropology* 5, no. 4 (1949): 309–317.

———. "Linguistic Evidence Regarding Bantu Origins." *The Journal of African History* 13, no. 2 (1972): 189–216.

Guthrie, Malcolm. *Comparative Bantu: an introduction to the comparative linguistics and prehistory of the Bantu Languages* 4 vols. (Farnborough: Gregg, 1967-1971).

Guthrie, Malcolm, and International African Institute. *The Classification of the Bantu Languages.* London: Published for the International African Institute by the Oxford University Press, 1948.

Herbert, R. K., and T. N. Huffman. "A New Perspective on Bantu Expansion and Classification: Linguistic and Archaeological Evidence Fifty Years After Doke." *African Studies -Johannesburg* 52, no. 2 (1994): 53–76.

Huffman, Thomas N. "Archaeological Evidence and Conventional Explanations of Southern Bantu Settlement Patterns." *Africa: Journal of the International African Institute* 56, no. 3 (1986): 280–298.

———. "Ceramics, Settlements and Late Iron Age Migrations." *African Archaeological Review* 7, no.1 (1989): 155–182.

Johnston, Harry H. *A Comparative Study of the Bantu and Semi-Bantu Languages: By Sir Harry H. Johnston. Vol. 1.* Oxford: at the Clarendoess, 1919.

———. *A Comparative Study of the Bantu and Semi-Bantu Languages: By Sir Harry H. Johnston. Vol. 2.* Oxford: at the Clarendoess, 1922.

Klieman, Kairn A. *"The Pygmies Were Our Compass": Bantu and Batwa in the History of West Central Africa, Early Times to C. 1900 C.E.* Portsmouth, N.H.: Heinemann, 2003.

Laman, K. E., and Elin Wilkander. *Grammar of the Kongo Language (Kikongo).* New York: Christian Alliance, 1900.

Nurse, Derek, and Gérard Philippson. *The Bantu Languages.* London: Routledge, 2003.

Oliver, Roland, Thomas Spear, Kairn Klieman, Jan Vansina, Scott Macechern, David Schoenbrun, Yvonne Bastin, H. M. Batibo, Bernd Heine, Michael Mann, Derek Nurse, and Simiyu Wandiba "Comments on Christopher Ehret, "Bantu History: Re-Envisioning the Evidence of Language." *The International Journal of African Historical Studies* 34, no. 1 (2001): 43–81.

Philippson, Gérard, and Serge Bahuchet. "Cultivated Crops and Bantu Migrations in Central and Eastern Africa: A Linguistic Approach." *Azania* no. 29–30 (1994–1995): 103–120.

Phillipson, D. W. "Archaeology and Bantu Linguistics." *World Archaeology* 8, no. 1 (1976): 65–82.

———. "The Chronology of the Iron Age in Bantu Africa." *The Journal of African History* 16, no. 3 (1975): 321–342.

———. "The Spread of the Bantu Language." *Scientific American* 236, no. 4 (1977): 106–114.

Rexová K., Y. Bastin, and D. Frynta "Cladistic Analysis of Bantu Languages: A New Tree Based on Combined Lexical and Grammatical Data." *Die Naturwissenschaften* 93, no. 4 (2006): 189–194.

Saidi, Christine. *Women's Authority and Society in Early East-Central Africa.* Rochester, N.Y.: University of Rochester Press, 2010.

Schadeberg, Thilo C. "Trees and Branches in the History of Bantu Languages." *The Journal of African History* 45, no. 2 (2004): 315–316.

Schoenbrun, David Lee. *A Green Place, a Good Place: Agrarian Change, Gender, and Social Identity in the Great Lakes Region to the 15th Century.* Portsmouth, N.H.: Heinemann, 1998.

Stephens, Rhiannon. *A History of African Motherhood: The Case of Uganda, 700–1900.* Cambridge: Cambridge University Press, 2013.

Vansina, Jan. *Paths in the Rainforests: Toward a History of Political Tradition in Equatorial Africa.* Madison, Wis.: University of Wisconsin Press, 1990.

———. *How Societies Are Born: Governance in West Central Africa Before 1600.* Charlottesville: University of Virginia Press, 2004.

AFRICAN WORLD HISTORIES

Bantu Africa

Reconstructing Bantu Expansions

This chapter introduces readers to a five-phase periodization of the Bantu expansions and the historical methods used in recovering Bantu histories. Though scholars continue to debate methods with regard to recovering Bantu history and continue to collect evidence to refine understandings of details about dates and locations, localized histories suggest collectively that the framework presented here is appropriate and instructive. The first half of the chapter explores key elements of Bantu cultural and social institutions across the five phases. In this depiction, the phrase "Bantu worldview" is used to refer to the way the speakers of Bantu languages oftentimes drew upon a shared heritage to conceive and reconceive the differing historical worlds in which they lived. It insists that understanding the worldviews that shaped people's perceptions, choices, and actions is essential for interpreting their history. In a continual dialectic, experience, environment, education, and beliefs influenced how people formed their worldviews, and their worldviews influenced the way they lived. The second half of the chapter explains how historians use historical methods that include words/linguistics, genetics, archaeology, oral tradition, and ethnography. The entirety of *Bantu Africa* encourages readers to use both analytical thinking and historical imagination to make sense of the dynamics that Bantu people and societies have generated between 3500 BCE and the present.

WHO ARE THE BANTU?

Today, speakers of about five hundred Bantu languages and dialects live in diverse ecological environments on the African continent. How those Bantu languages came to span nearly half of sub-Saharan Africa is a question scholars have long studied and debated. Those researchers have analyzed the evidence from different disciplinary perspectives and weighed in on whether or not people who speak Bantu languages derive from a common ancient Bantu "ethnic" or "cultural" community of speakers. And they have investigated whether or not Bantu-speaking people share common genetic and biological origins. Each position, about who the Bantu were historically and who they are today, carries its own set of assumptions and implications for understanding these histories.

Whether "Bantu" is characterized in linguistic, ethnic, cultural, or biological terms depends on the period, location, community, evidence, and perspectives of scholars engaged in research on the Bantu past.[1] The term "Bantu" cannot be narrowed to a single group. Rather, it is helpful to think about it as a conceptual paradigm that can be termed the "Bantu tradition." It is much like the familiar idea of the "Western European tradition" or "East Asian tradition." Each encompasses societies of variable linguistic, cultural, artistic, historical, political, and religious practices that are commonly discussed together, although it is simultaneously understood that the traditions are heterogeneous. Likewise, millions of people who speak languages classified as Bantu today share key social elements linked to ideas and practices that sometimes are traceable to a common proto-Bantu society and language. The term "proto-Bantu" refers to an ancestral Bantu linguistic community that was primarily economically agricultural and existed nearly 5,500 years ago in the borderland areas of modern-day Nigeria and Cameroon. Because so much time has passed, Bantu societies, similar to the societies of the Western European or East Asian traditions, are thus culturally diverse even as they share common deep, historical

---

[1]   The details of these differences will be discussed in the later section on the Bantu expansions.

roots. Their diversity owes to countless migrations, cross-cultural encounters, and the innovation of new ideas that have collectively contributed to the unfolding of Bantu history.

PHASES OF THE BANTU EXPANSIONS

Population movement and demographic change are familiar themes in ancient and modern history. As noted earlier, scholars have strongly debated the nature of Bantu population movements. However, it is widely agreed that by 3500 BCE the earliest Bantu speakers constituted several small communities in proximate locations at the far northwestern edges of the western African equatorial rainforest. Sometime after 3500 BCE, pioneers among them moved out onto frontiers and unknown territories setting in motion the early dispersals of Bantu speakers into new landscapes. Collectively, researchers call the long and complex history that then ensued by a misleadingly simple name, "the Bantu expansions." Over the course of more than five thousand years, Bantu societies spread out across more than 3 million square miles (almost 8 million square kilometers) of territory, between southern Cameroon in the northwest to coastal Kenya in the northeast, to the eastern Cape and Kwazulu-Natal in the south. The population movements that took Bantu speakers to all these areas initiated sweeping realignments of culture, economy, and peoples across a third or more of Africa. As with all developments of far-reaching impact in history, scholars have vigorously debated who, what, why, where, and how these transformations unfolded. Prominent points of inquiry in Bantu historical research revolve around space and time. This involves answering such questions as where the original Bantu homeland was located and how long ago the earliest Bantu speech communities emerged. Another set of queries concerns the paths and routes taken by the early Bantu as they left the rainforest areas. Many have wondered how so few people—the original small cluster of a few thousand proto-Bantu speakers living in a far northwestern part of the equatorial rainforest, in a remote corner of western Cameroon—could expand their way through a region of dense, tropical forest, to give rise to societies that eventually covered so much territory and commanded such diverse environments. Another point of debate is whether warfare and conquest or amicable interactions characterized these interactions. And were their approaches different in different times and different regions? This book addresses these very questions and debates.

In addition, one has to realize that those lands new to Bantu were already inhabited and used by people of other linguistic backgrounds, cultural traditions, and economies. Linguistic, archaeological, and oral evidence reveals that these encounters produced moments of cross-cultural exchange that included sharing, borrowing, and even imposing ideas, practices, and language. Through these processes, to varying degrees, Bantu and non-Bantu incorporated each other into their respective communities and kin networks.

It is important to consider the nature of these multilinguistic, multiethnic interactions and why people of non-Bantu origins adopted Bantu languages and cultures. People who spoke non-Bantu languages had their own worldviews with their own deep histories, which shaped their economic practices, social institutions, and cultural traditions. They, too, very likely exerted influences, to varying degrees, on incoming communities of Bantu speakers. Though some of the non-Bantu languages are extinct, scholars have uncovered useful linguistic and archaeological evidence pointing toward their existence in the past. Research on non-Bantu languages has been more limited. Some studies have focused on the fact that those present-day communities came to speak Bantu languages. Scholars consistently look for the elements of divergence that might have derived from either local innovation or borrowing from other historical and linguistic traditions. One scholar who has delved into the history of Batwa people who occupy equatorial forests and whose ancestors very likely spoke non-Bantu languages is historian Kairn Klieman. Her work is an informative example of Bantu-focused research that recovers religious and political influences that various non-Bantu communities have had on Bantu of western central Africa. Her work reveals that Bantu societies of these regions maintained a diversity of cultural practices going back to their proto-Bantu ancestry. At the same time, they recombined older ideas with newer customs and practices that they and their descendants invented or had adopted from non-Bantu-speaking Africans.

Scholars such as Rupp, Geschire, Klieman, Moïse, and Wilmsen, whose scholarship centers on the history of the equatorial Africa in which autochthonous peoples lived prior to Bantu expansion, remind us that there are multiple perspectives on the nature of the relations among non-Bantu-speaking indigenous (firstcomers) and Bantu newcomers in the past and present. Whereas most scholars would now argue that Bantu history was almost never one of military conquest and pillage, one must still consider the kinds of competitions, tensions, disputes, and negotiations that surely arose over land use, economic activities, religious practices, political structure, and cultural traditions. The following sections present a narrative and overview of what were at times fluid and overlapping developments in the long history of Bantu expansions.[2]

FIRST PHASE: 3500 BCE–3000 BCE

Beginning around 3500 BCE, proto-Bantu emerged as a distinct society as Map 4 shows in geographic spread. They originated as one of a number of societies speaking languages of the Eastern Benue-Congo linguistic subgroup, who lived in that era in the mountainous region that today is the border between Nigeria and Cameroon. They likely emerged as a distinct cluster of communities that migrated southeast from the Cameroon Mountains into the region around the Sangha and Nyong Rivers. This area was at the edge of dense rainforest. This initial movement of proto-Bantu into the lowlands serves as an example of the kind of geographic and ecological pioneering that, as scholars have argued, descendant Bantu-speaking communities continued to engage in over the next few millennia. Initially, Bantu-speaking people did not inhabit the heavily canopied portions of the tropical equatorial forest where trees blocked sunlight. Rather, most often they utilized lands following riverbanks at the edges of the forest. They did cross the forest, but they would have done so moving along the sunnier riverbanks, where there were major tree breaks, and where they could raise their staple crops, yams and oil palms. They would also have taken advantage

---

[2]   Peter Geschiere, "Autochthony, Citizenship, and (In)security: New Turns in the Politics of Belonging in Africa and Elsewhere," in Z. Gambetti and M. Godoy-Anativia (eds.), *Rhetorics of Insecurity: Belonging and Violence in the Neoliberal Era* (New York: New York University Press, 2013), 40–68; Stephanie Rupp, "Multiangular Identities among Congo River Basin Forest Peoples," in Barry S. Hewlitt (ed.), *Hunter Gatherers of the Congo Basin* (New Brunswick, N.J.: Transaction Publishers, 2014), 277–298; Robert E. Moïse, "'Do Pygmies Have a History?' Revisited: The Autochthonous Tradition in the History of Equatorial Africa," in Barry S. Hewlitt, (ed.), *Hunter Gatherers of the Congo Basin* (New Brunswick, N.J.: Transaction Publishers, 2014), 85–91; Kairn A. Klieman, *"The Pygmies Were Our Compass": Bantu and Batwa in the History of West Central Africa, Early Times to C. 1900 C.E.* Portsmouth, N.H.: Heinemann, 2003.

of scattered patches of intercalary savanna within the forest to grow these crops and also black-eyed peas and African groundnuts. These were not migrations that unfolded rapidly over long distances, nor did a single community of speakers initiate them. Rather, over decades and centuries, cultural and geographic, small settlement groups again and again would have ventured out from previously established villages to new locations, following rivers and clearing small areas of forest and utilizing the intermittent patches of savanna. They often moved small distances from previously settled areas and traversed short stretches of the rivers as they sought new territory.

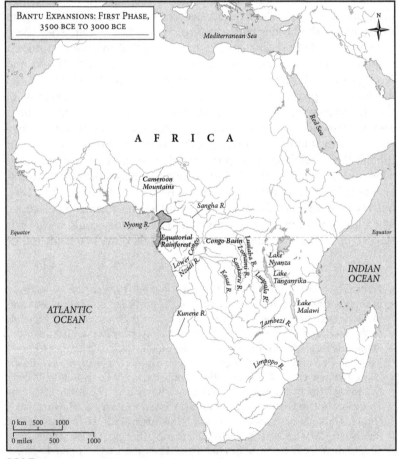

MAP 4

In terms of heredity, the proto-Bantu community may well have been a relatively genetically homogeneous and compactly settled population in southern Cameroon, with little differences of dialect. But as communities moved outward toward the Sanagha River and following that river further south and southeast into the forest, their cultural world increasingly varied and transformed through interactions with a diversity of people. In their new geographies and ecologies, descendant communities who shared a common language began speaking various dialects distinct from their ancestors and related descendant communities. As the centuries passed, these dialects became numerous distinct languages. The evidence of language, genetics, oral tradition, ethnography, and archaeology individually and collectively indicates that Bantu communities encountered and integrated new knowledge, practices, and technologies from people with distinct traditions. In later ages they repeatedly found ways to incorporate people from other cultural and genetic backgrounds into their Bantu-speaking communities. Over a long period of several millennia, they continued to negotiate space, language, and culture as they established many distinct communities.

Early Bantu societies developed in areas of what are today the central African countries of Gabon, the Republic of Congo, and the Democratic Republic of Congo. Imagine many rural communities each with two to three hundred people established close to a tree-lined river or in an area of savanna within the forest. Rain was abundant and the runoff leached the soil, leaving it less than ideally fertile for agriculture. Many areas had lateritic soils, which, if heavily rained upon, hardened, making them difficult to cultivate. Yet early Bantu-speaking farmers innovated the techniques to survive and thrive in this environment. They cleared some forest to create environments for their crops. They did this with polished stone axes. When they planted yams, they left any cut-down vegetation scattered on the ground to protect the soil from destructive leaching and hardening due to rains.

To sustain themselves, they also made extensive use of river environments. For an accessible and nearby source of protein in the diet, they fished with traps, hooks, and fish baskets. The early Bantu navigated an intricate mosaic of waterways in the wooden canoes that specialists crafted. Their use of the resources around them for modes of food production and for transport made their villages sustainable centers. Their practices also laid a foundation for greater expansion, as we know in hindsight.

Practices such as canoe building; fishing with hooks, traps, and baskets; mixed farming; potting; and beekeeping were life-changing and cutting-edge technologies 5,500 years ago. From a present-day perspective, where industrial and digital technologies run people's day-to-day lives, it can be difficult to imagine that developing better ways to grow yams or better methods to catch fish could be called technological innovations. Most of the technologies of the last 150 years, in the industrial and postindustrial ages, were not available to people anywhere in the world prior to the nineteenth century. Well before mechanization, Bantu-speaking people's approaches helped to ensure more plentiful food resources and reserves in the equatorial tropical forest. The most effective and efficient of these technologies, which facilitated the first phase of expansion in ancient times, especially those connected with fishing and yam farming, often endure today.

Although there is some contentious debate among historians on the time depth, directions, means, and categorizing for Bantu history, there is much agreement on early Bantu food production techniques, crops, and even the close-knit family-based units of organizing. In the first phase of the long history of Bantu peoples, similarity and closeness likely continued to predominate. Communities sustained themselves on resources at the edge of the forest and in open areas within the forest and only stage by stage moved into new territories.

SECOND PHASE: 3000 BCE–2000 BCE

Cultural, linguistic, agricultural, demographic, and other such historical changes that took place between 3000 and 2000 BCE mark the second more protracted phase of Bantu expansions reflected in Map 5 and marked by overlapping chronologies and developments. Across this one-thousand-year period, as Klieman's work has shown, Bantu speech communities came to stretch from modern-day Cameroon's coast to the interior of the Democratic Republic of the Congo. Two particularly distinctive Bantu communities emerged in this phase. We do not know what names they gave their languages or communities, so in order to tell the history of the communities of this era, scholars have named these peoples after the rivers and other locations where they most likely resided. In the first major phase, 3500–3000 BCE, Bantu peoples spread into the equatorial rainforests, from the Nyong River region of Southern Cameroon as far south and east as the confluence of the Congo and Lomami Rivers. So historians give the name Nyong-Lomami to this period and its peoples. During the second phase of the early Bantu expansions, which Klieman places broadly in the period from 2500 to 1500 BCE, one major offshoot of the Nyong-Lomami peoples moved south from the confluence of the Sangha and Congo Rivers, into the areas along the Lower Congo River.[3] Because the Lower Congo is called the Nzadi in the languages spoken in that region today, we give the name Sangha-Nzadi to this important offshoot of the Nyong-Lomami. The importance of the Sangha-Nzadi is that they were the forebears of all the Bantu communities who expanded in much later centuries all across Central and eastern Africa as well as large parts of southern Africa.

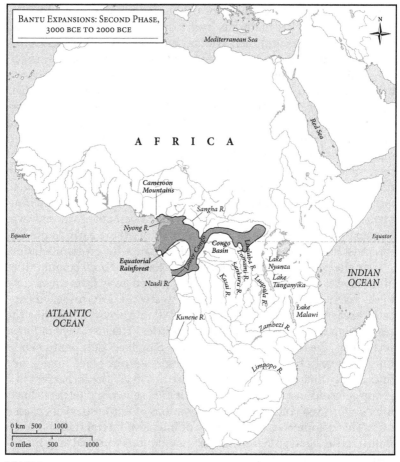

MAP 5

---

[3] Klieman, *The Pygmies*; Rupp, *Forests of Belonging*.

The Sangha-Nzadi settled broadly across a mixed territory of rainforest, woodlands, and savanna between the late third millennium and after 2000 BCE. Their locations along the Lower Congo River and westward along the Sankuru River were flanked by dense forest and wetlands covered in red clays along with areas of sandier soils. These soils lacked nutrients beneficial to crop production, though they were excellent sources to procure potting clay and eventually would also be used to collect iron ore for smelting. Similar to earlier phases, specialists among the Bantu-communities fashioned canoes from great forest trees. In this environment, their watercraft would have been advantageous tools for fishing expeditions, traversing the forests, and carrying materials longer distances. Rowing and poling canoes along rivers and their tributaries, pioneers and scouts in this era of expanding Bantu settlement could cover significant distances.

Although the people of the Nyong-Lomami period appear to have remained in environments quite similar to those settled by their early Bantu ancestors, the Sangha-Nzadi pioneered into much different environs that included savannas. Certainly, there was a good deal of social and economic continuity, for the Sangha-Nzadi maintained many traditions of ancestral Bantu communities. The combining of their older agriculture knowledge with new crops and cultivation practices probably took generations to perfect. They would have had to test new techniques and innovate practices in a mix of drier environments. The fact that Bantu speakers came to populate savannas over the next two millennia attests to the ingenuity these early communities must have deployed as well as their openness to experimentation.

In the period around 2000 BCE, the Sangha-Nzadi communities of the Lower Congo region increasingly moved away from areas close to the rivers. Several settlements went westward into the heavily forested areas between the Congo and the Atlantic coast. Occupying the rest of equatorial forest took many centuries. The last stage of forest settlement, the expansion of a particular Sangha-Nzadi Bantu people into the heart of the Congo Basin rainforest, took place finally only in the early first millennium CE. These are likely the forbearers of a group referred to as the Mongo people. These various settlers slowly filled in forested lands previous generations of Bantu speakers passed over. This commences a new phase of intensive interactions between Bantu settlers and gatherer-hunters populations who had long inhabited and used the forest environments.

The Sangha-Nzadi retained many of the key words relating to economy and culture of their earlier Bantu ancestors. Based on this linguistic evidence, it is known that they continued to cultivate yams, oil palms, gourds, black-eyed peas, and African groundnuts. They kept goats and guinea fowl for food. Their cultural evidence, comparative ethnography, and oral traditions all suggest that Bantu speakers strategically integrated local religious ideas of healing and territorial spirits with their own.

Their spread into the forest-savanna mosaic environments south of the rainforest proper offered both an economic advantage and a potential life threat because of the greater presence of large animals, which were a source of protein but also competition in terms of safety for humans, domesticated animals, and crops. The most southerly Sangha-Nzadi communities around 2000 BCE most likely had to think strategically and develop new hunting techniques to manage and coexist with the less familiar and more varied and numerous large animals of the savanna. Successful hunters could bring a great deal of meat protein to the community, but hunting was a time-consuming, arduous, and risky endeavor. Living in an era before the development of iron technologies, the Sangha-Nzadi relied primarily, as their vocabulary of hunting reveals, on bows and arrows and the use of arrow poisons. With large animals, the arrow poisons could take a long time to work through the animal's bloodstream, and so hunters probably had to track an injured animal for hours. Additionally, because of the tropical environment, meat from hunted animals had to be preserved in the field or consumed by the hunters on the spot. For this reason, these early Bantu-speaking communities residing in savanna zones rarely relied on hunting as a primary food source. Although farming and fishing produced a consistent food source, hunting could occasionally supplement diets.

As Bantu speakers moved into the savannas, gradually they successfully adapted food production strategies to this new eco-niche. They set in motion new economic and cultural opportunities that would emerge in the next historical phase. These latent potential developments came from several directions, as readers will see in the third phase. Evidence of those developments is revealed in new vocabulary and material culture are datable to the second millennium BCE.

THIRD PHASE: 2000 BCE–1000 BCE

Map 6 shows how in the millennium between 2000 and 1000 BCE, a major division of the Sangha-Nzadi Bantu-speaking communities moved into areas quite different from previous generations. They began to spread eastward across a wide mix of areas, ranging from forest-savanna mosaic to areas of woodland savanna, immediately south of the equatorial rainforest zones. In this later phase, the Sangha-Nzadi were a bridge between the people who shaped phase two and those who would shape phase three. Historians call this grouping of new Bantu societies the Savanna-Bantu. Though little archaeological research has been done to date in this region, the available evidence shows that the forefront of their eastward expansion already reached as far to the east as the northern end of Lake Tanganyika by three thousand years ago.

In this new era of population movement, Bantu speakers continued to encounter numerous small communities of gatherer-hunter peoples with quite different cultural and linguistic backgrounds, long

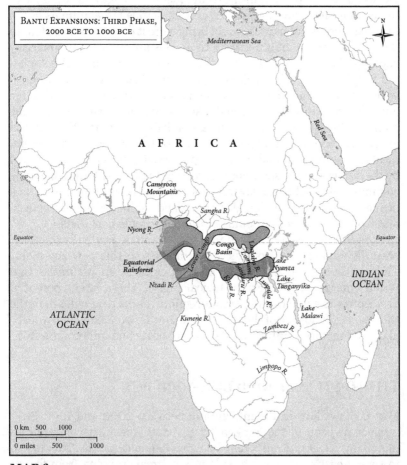

MAP 6

established in the lands of the Congo Basin. Although it is uncertain what these communities called themselves, the Bantu referred to them as *Batwa*, a name which derives from a widespread Bantu root *-*tua*. This ethnonym for gatherer-hunters goes back to the beginnings of the Sangha-Nzadi era of expansions. That so many Bantu languages retained this term across many regions shows that Bantu speakers continued to encounter populations already using the lands into which they moved. But it also means that this term likely did not refer to a specific language or ethnic group, but rather to the idea of the firstcomers or indigenous people who first inhabited the land. There is strong evidence in oral traditions that Bantu speakers initially relied on these populations for their environmental knowledge of the new areas of settlement and often respected them as having spiritual knowledge of those lands, partly because of their aboriginal status.

Between 2000 and 1000 BCE, Bantu speakers and *Batwa* initiated new relationships of regular trade in the different items each produced. This third phase brought about important transformations in food production, settlement patterns, population growth, and cross-cultural interactions. Indeed, Bantu speakers relied heavily on *Batwa*, who had extensive and intimate knowledge of these zones in terms of animals, medicines, foods, and territorial spirits. *Batwa* populations had long known the resources deep in the rainforest, whereas the Bantu speakers had primarily to that time utilized lands along the major riverbanks and not in the forest interior.

The early Savanna Bantu, as they spread eastward across the southern savanna fringes of the rainforest, gave rise to five notable subbranches of Bantu by around three thousand years ago—from west to east, Njila (or Western Savanna Bantu), Central Savanna Bantu (or Lubans), Botatwe (Ila, Tonga, Lenje), Sabi (Bemba and related groups), and Mashariki (Eastern Bantu). Most Bantu languages spoken today in sub-Saharan Africa belong to one of these five subbranches. This implies that languages from other subgroups died out while these five survived.

FOURTH PHASE: 1000 BCE–500 CE

Around 1000 BCE at the far eastern corner of the forests of modern-day Congo, bordering the western edge of the Great Lakes region of Eastern Africa, a group of Bantu-speaking people who are the focus of this section set in motion a new era of transformations and expansions, as Map 7 reflects. Some scholars have called them the Mashariki Bantu, which means "East" in modern-day Kiswahili, one of the most well-known and widely spoken of the Mashariki descendant languages. In this historical phase, their descendants moved as far east and south as the Indian Ocean and the southern tip of the continent. A new set of interactions unfolded between Bantu agriculturalists and populations of Nilo-Saharan, Afrasian, and Khoesan they encountered from the Great Lakes to the Cape of Good Hope (see page xxiii Map 2).

The proto-Mashariki-speaking communities had emerged out of those most easterly Savanna Bantu. The earliest Mashariki and their descendant language communities initially, between 1000 BCE and 500 CE, carried on the traditions and ideas they brought with them

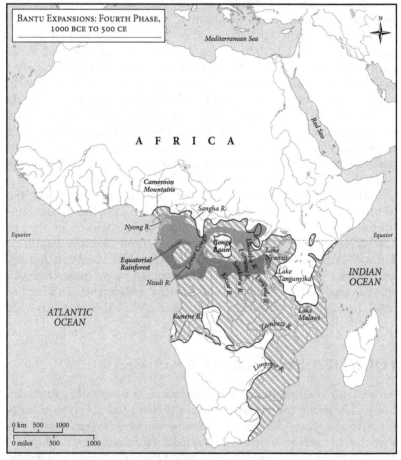

BANTU EXPANSIONS: FOURTH PHASE, 1000 BCE TO 500 CE

MAP 7

from the forest homelands of their Savanna Bantu ancestors. As they began to move after 500 BCE out into the baobab- and acacia-dotted savannas that stretched from eastern to southern Africa, Bantu speakers would have encountered people with practices and ideas they likely saw as exotic, such as grain cultivation, iron smelting, and cattle raising, to name a few. In these locations, the various Mashariki Bantu societies developed their own unique cultural syntheses, in the process adopting many new "exotic" features of material and non-material culture that they saw as beneficial from the populations of Nilo-Saharan, Afrasian, Batwa, and even Khoesan speakers they encountered. Interethnic contacts contributed to the diversity found across Bantu histories, languages, and cultures.

At the beginning of this phase, Bantu-speaking communities met up with Central Sudanian people, who spoke languages descended from the Nilo-Saharan language family. Central Sudanians most likely used lands in the westernmost parts of the Great Lakes region. The evidence of both reconstructed Central Sudanic vocabulary and borrowed Central Sudanic words in Mashariki Bantu languages shows that they were adept cattle raisers and cultivators of grains.

Central Sudanians introduced Bantu speakers in the Great Lakes region to their cattle- and grain-based economic complex. Bantu added these elements into their economic knowledge of tuber cultivation and goat herding. Cattle and grain raising required different techniques, skills, tools, and methods of processing than Bantu producers previously relied on for subsistence and trade. Over the course of the next few hundred years, some Mashariki Bantu speech communities seem to have rather successfully adopted aspects of this Central Sudanian economic strategy and lifestyle. The language evidence reveals as well that they combined their heritage of West African agricultural with Central Sudanian crops, notably sorghum and pearl millet. Over the centuries, they continued to develop techniques to successfully grow yams in many kinds of environments quite different from those occupied in earlier eras.

From the Central Sudanians came also a new technology, the smelting and forging of iron, a manufacturing art that must have been life changing and culturally transformative. People speaking Mashariki languages gained access to enough knowledge of this highly technical process around three thousand years ago that they began to produce iron themselves. The direct adoption into proto-Mashariki of key words from Central Sudanic languages for the bellows used in smelting and forging, for the smith's hammer, and for several iron tools shows that some individuals in the earliest Mashariki communities must have built close relationships with Central Sudanians to learn the skills of iron smelting so technically precise in its requirements. Aside from linguistics, all areas of comparative evidence, from archaeology to oral tradition, reveal that Bantu speakers indeed did garner this knowledge, and specialists who spoke Mashariki Bantu languages mastered the art and science of smelting and smithing.

A number of the early Mashariki terms for ironworking spread westward across the savanna and rainforest toward the Atlantic coast through word borrowing. The close analysis of language data reveals that this east-to-west diffusion of iron is accurate. Early adoption of iron technology came first to the proto-Mashariki Bantu and then spread from them westward to other Bantu societies. Whereas Bantu speakers began in the western half of the continent, it was not until contact was initiated with non-Bantu in eastern Africa that Bantu speakers gained access to this technology.[4] When later Mashariki Bantu communities spread in subsequent centuries to the rest of eastern and southern Africa, they managed to carry the knowledge and practical skills of ironworking along with them.

The proto-Mashariki, like many Bantu-speaking communities before, diverged over the course of the early first millennium BCE into two sets of daughter communities. The northern set of communities some scholars refer to as Kaskazi, which means "North" in Kiswahili. Kaskazi spread at first farther east into the areas along the eastern and southern sides of Lake Victoria. The second grouping of daughter communities, the Kusi, which means "South" in Kiswahili, moved into areas even farther to the south along Lake Tanganyika.

In the later first millennium BCE (between 500 and 100 BCE), Kaskazi and Kusi branches of the Mashariki Bantu began move out from the Lake Tanganyika regions, with their descendant communities over the next several centuries settling in distant parts of eastern and southeastern Africa. These expansions into new lands both accelerated the scale and frequency of cross-cultural influences and enhanced the need to adapt to new environmental niches in the easternmost regions. This shaped a good deal of the unique elements

---

[4]   Although there was an independent invention of iron in western Africa by Niger-Congo descendants in the heartland of proto-Bantu origins, this invention only emerged about two millennia after Bantu had already began to disperse out of the lands between Nigeria and Cameroon. Bantu access to iron came primarily from the east African iron tradition.

their cultures manifested. Although these groups were expanding, they were also assimilating peoples of quite different backgrounds already living in these territories. Kusi speakers moved into the areas of modern-day Malawi, Mozambique, and South Africa between 300 BCE and 200 CE. During the same time span, several groups of Kaskazi settled away from the western region of the African Great Lakes far east into coastal plains, while other Kaskazi peoples moved into forested highlands environments in Kenya and northern Tanzania and also in southern Tanzania.

Kaskazi speakers encountered people speaking southern Cushitic languages from the Afrasian family. Like the Nilo-Saharan populations in the Great Lakes, Southern Cushites operated economies centered on cattle keeping and cattle wealth, which they combined with cultivation of grains for subsistence. Kaskazi-speaking communities learned from their Cushitic neighbors additional techniques of cattle raising, which they appropriated and blended with their other evolving economic activities. In the highland areas of southern Tanzania, people who spoke Kaskazi languages moved into lands previously inhabited in part by gatherer-hunters and in part by cattle-raising Southern Cushites and also Nilo-Saharan-speaking pastoralists. These interactions made for a highly diverse set of economic influences and a multilayered history.

Kusi speakers who settled further south encountered peoples who spoke languages of still another major African language family, Khoesan. Kusi communities who settled farthest south, in northern and eastern parts of modern-day South Africa had strikingly different historical experiences than Kaskazi communities of East Africa. Although each entered into complex economic relations with people of different linguistic backgrounds, Kusi speakers engaged both with numerous small gatherer-hunter Khoesan bands and with the Khoekhoe, who spoke a Khoesan language but were cattle and sheep raisers. Kaszaki and Kusi speakers of the early first millennium CE both engaged with groups of gatherer-hunters and cattle raisers, yet they adopted very different elements from those communities. This manifested as unique balances of economic practices resulting from those encounters tempered by individual choices and the environmental factors at play.

In the first millennium BCE, situated in the savannas south of the equatorial rainforest just west of the Mashariki-speaking communities, several other distinct Savanna Bantu societies developed. Two societies of note were the Sabi and Botatwe speakers. In those centuries, they inhabited parts of Central Africa known today as the

Katanga Province of the Democratic Republic of the Congo (DRC). Further west of the Sabi and Botatwe, another Bantu-speaking Central Savanna Bantu subgroup settled in and developed. These communities were ancestral to Luban and related peoples of later centuries. They settled lands between the middle Kasai and upper Lomami Rivers.

It is worth taking a moment here to point out that Bantu movements were not unidirectional. Bantu speakers did not leave the earliest homelands with a single-minded desire to flee from where they had come. Thus, not all movements of the Bantu expansions were north to south or west to east. Furthermore, although the focus here has been to reflect on history as the Bantu moved out of the original homelands, in fact significant innovations, inventions, and cross-cultural interactions were unfolding in the forests to the west during these periods.

In East Central Africa, the Sabi, Botatwe, and Central Savanna-speaking populations discussed earlier provide a useful example of Bantu-Bantu cross-cultural interactions. They moved in the first millennium CE in a manner that seems to have ignited encounters among Bantu speakers whose ancestors had separated from each other many centuries before. These encounters could be thought about as Bantu-Bantu cross-cultural interactions. Around 1,500 years ago, Luba populations embarked on major new movements eastward and southeastward across the Lomami and Lualaba Rivers. They probably moved into regions of modern-day Katanga province that had previously been settled by Sabi speakers, as the archeological and linguistic examples in later sections will demonstrate. Some Sabi speakers remained alongside Lubans. Around the same time, 500 BCE, other Sabi and many Botatwe-speaking people moved further south and east into areas of modern-day Zambia in which Mashariki Bantu speakers had previously established themselves in the very late first millennium CE. These processes of movement were complex, multi-layered, and overlapping. In essence, subgroups descended from Savanna Bantu were moving into areas already inhabited a millennium earlier by other groups speaking distantly related Savanna Bantu languages.

Far to the west, Savanna Bantu communities belonging to the Njila subgroup began, during the last few centuries BCE, to scatter out across parts of what are today Angola and the western portions of Zambia. Initially they may have settled in narrow stretches of land along rivers, with wetter soils suited to their crops. Between 200 BCE and 300 CE, the most southerly of these settlements reached the Kunene and upper middle Zambezi Rivers, where Khoesan-speaking people who kept sheep lived. From Khoesan herders Njila Bantu groups learned about and began to adopt sheep raising. Early in the first millennium CE, knowledge of cattle, goats, and the African grains, sorghum and pearl millet, spread to them from Mashariki-speaking communities who had moved into the region east of them, in what is today southern Zambia. These food products, though new to the region, were well suited to drier savanna climates. They transformed the economies. Equipped with these newly acquired crops and domesticated animals, Njila-speaking peoples spread out all across Angola and even into northern Namibia between 200 and 500 CE.

The last one thousand years BCE and the first few centuries CE suggest a time of growth across space and increased populations over time. Archaeology for some of these centuries does reflect the emergence in several areas of larger villages and new cultural developments relative to previous eras. In the rainforest of equatorial Africa, river routes of trade facilitated the emergence of long-distance transport of goods along the rivers. Towns and populous villages, often located near the confluences of major rivers, functioned in later times as individual nodes in wider circuits of exchange. The sparse archaeological evidence available suggests that larger population centers of this type had begun to emerge already in the first millennium BCE.

Ironworking, as the diffusion of the various words for ironworking and iron tools reveal, spread multidirectionally along several trade routes westward from Mashariki Bantu in the African Great Lakes region and around Lake Tanganyika.[5] We know from archaeological evidence that ironworking had reached west to the Atlantic coast by 400 BCE, and southwestward across the southern savannas as far as Njila peoples by the beginning of the first millennium CE. These westward spreads of iron provide strong evidence that the movements of ideas, technology, and people were not unidirectional among the Bantu societies. Along with the spread of grain crops west across the southern savanna, these developments hint at the possibility that some Bantu further east maintained connections with the west via technology exchange and possibly even maintained links with ancestral homelands and networks.

---

[5] C. Ehret, "The Establishment of Iron-Working in Eastern, Central, and Southern Africa: Linguistic Inferences on Technological History," *Sprache und Geschichte in Afrika* 16/17 (1995/96): 125–175.

With the hindsight that our knowledge of these slow developments and varied contacts allows, it is possible to understand how, from one single small ancestral community of proto-Bantu speakers concentrated in the northwest, a far-flung and diverse array of Bantu-speaking societies emerged. They practiced different and varied economic activities and followed unique combinations of inherited, borrowed, innovated, and adapted cultural ideas and practices. The various Njila-speaking peoples predominated in the southern savanna belt west of the Kasai River and the upper Zambezi. Luban and other Central Savanna peoples occupied the areas from the middle Kasai River eastward toward the Lualaba River, while the early Botatwe and Sabi peoples occupied lands East of the Lualaba itself. The northerly Mashariki societies, Kaskazi peoples, had settlements reaching as far as the Indian Ocean coast from northern Kenya to northern Mozambique, to the tip of southern Tanzania, and to eastern Zambia as early as the third century BCE. The southerly Mashariki, Kusi people, spread in the same period southward from Lake Tanganyika into the eastern parts of the southern savanna belt and into the farther southeastern parts of the continent.

Bantu speakers, stage by stage over many generations, carried their settlements into areas where the vegetation and climate were sharply different from the riverine and forest margins with which their ancestors were familiar. These early Bantu speakers chose to live in humid areas that sustained torrential showers almost daily through most of the year, typical of rainforest regions. In contrast, early Mashariki Bantu and their Kaskazi descendants settled territories with a long dry season and two rainy seasons each year, one short and mild and the other long with torrential monsoon showers. The lands that Kusi, Central Savanna, Sabi, Botatwe, and Njila peoples inhabited tended to have one dry season and one rainy season. They took advantage of plant and animal resources. They collected materials from the grass fields, acacia bushes, and baobab trees. They also had pockets of woodlands to draw on within these savanna lands. These environments were often rich in native wildlife such as giraffe, lions, warthog, elephants, and both forest and savanna buffalo. In this environment the Savanna Bantu innovated a variety of technologies that included iron tools. With such a rich environment, these communities had opportunities for hunting and the pursuit of other kinds of economic specializations focused on savanna resources.

There were deep and lasting effects that resulted from encounters among Bantu-speaking settlers and peoples already utilizing the areas.

It is interesting to think about how and why the Bantu were so experimental and persistent in expanding their knowledge base, incorporating the unfamiliar in terms of ideas, technologies, and people. As subsequent chapters will show, the accommodations they made to the economic and cultural worlds into which they moved paved the way for a great variety of new inventions, political and social ideologies, and political structures to emerge.

FIFTH PHASE: 500 CE–1800 CE

The African continent, in comparison to parts of Asia and Europe, has been relatively underpopulated throughout human history. Aside from major urban centers, land has been available for settlement in most regions. Though Bantu-speaking populations were growing in numbers over the many centuries of their history, there long remained lands where new communities could be established. Map 8 illustrates that between 500 CE and 1800 CE, speakers of Savanna Bantu languages and the languages of other subbranches of Bantu continued to fill in even more niches, often locations with more challenging environments for the livelihoods that Bantu societies pursued. Perhaps people deemed those environments less suitable for settlement based on their knowledge and skills for agricultural production and natural resource procurement. Their forebears had chosen not to settle into those lands in earlier eras because they found other opportunities more promising.

In the more recent phases of expansion, Bantu speakers moving into new lands would have certainly encountered populations who already used those territories at least part of the year for trade-product gathering, hunting, fishing, or cattle grazing. As population densities increased, individuals in the growing communities may have felt less comfort and autonomy. Those who pioneered new communities, in this fifth phase, would have settled into the most severe niches and would have had to develop innovative economies suited to the resource base. This fifth phase was thus marked by consolidation and further elaborations of economic specialization.

This is the one era for which a substantial body of written documents is available to supplement archaeological, linguistic, oral, and ethnographic data. Through these various sources we know that Bantu-speaking populations encountered new frontiers and opted in many cases to draw upon transregional and transoceanic resources.

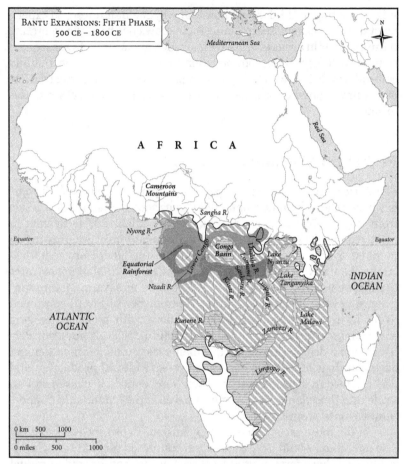

MAP 8

In this phase, Bantu speakers continued to incorporate ideas and practices of non-Bantu peoples. The distinguishing characteristics of this era were settlement in areas passed over by previous generations, urbanization, the rise of several notable centralized political entities, and a kind of cultural hybridity not witnessed in other eras. Certainly, cross-cultural interactions had long characterized Bantu history, but people pursued very different opportunities and enacted new kinds of intensive cultural synthesis in phase five.

Between about 800 and 1200 CE, in response to the opportunities of Indian Ocean trade, two groups of Mashariki Bantu descendants created centralized and urban societies. The first were the Sabaki speakers. One group of Sabaki settled on the Indian Ocean littoral, the Swahili, created at least seventy-five city-states along the coast. They built up a system of long-distance trade up and down East Africa's coral reefs and across the Indian Ocean.

The second peoples, descendants of Kusi, were Shona who inhabited the Zimbabwe plateau and parts of the lowlands between the plateau and the Indian Ocean. The first major Shona kingdom arose along the Limpopo River in the eleventh century. A second and much larger empire arose on the Zimbabwe plateau in the thirteenth century, with its capital at the massive stone-wall structure of Great Zimbabwe. Many of the subordinate kings and chiefs of this empire built their own smaller "Zimbabwes" modeled on the structures displayed at the capital. The power of this state and its kings rested on the control of gold and ivory, two major commodities of luxury trade all around the Indian Ocean world. They traded these two products to the Swahili merchants at the coast, who transported these goods into the wider Indian Ocean trade networks.

The rulers in Great Zimbabwe commanded a powerful religious ideology with ancestors, territorial spirits, and *Mwari* (God) that undergirded and bolstered their temporal power. This large urban center with it monumental buildings was not something that emerged unpredictably or suddenly. In fact, scholars believe that this entire political-religious complex expanded and contracted over several hundred years. Further, it took the *Mwene* (rulers) of the region consistently building upon the work of previous generations to create the physical structures that served as sites of memory in this more encompassing politico-religious urban center. A series of masons worked successively over a two-hundred-year period, starting probably in the late twelfth century, building and updating Great Zimbabwe. The growing sophistication of the building techniques over the next two centuries mirrored the slow processes of political development. Evidence suggests that the political elites of Great Zimbabwe built up their authority and expanded their state into an empire only in the thirteenth century. The implication is that power and authority were not to be commanded, but rather had to be built. Rulers used trade to accumulate wealth to facilitate prosperity and well-being to build the empire. The collapse of their authority came about in the early fifteenth century due to a variety of factors that included environmental degradation in the urban center and social dissatisfaction with the leadership. The political elite struggled as traders pioneered an alternative and a competing trade route cut off the Zimbabwe Empire's access to gold resources of the interior and their connections to Indian Ocean trade at the coast.

Other centralized states emerged further north and west of Great Zimbabwe in the same time frame. The Bunyoro (thirteenth-century) and Baganda (fourteenth-century) kingdoms emerged in this phase among Kaskazi Bantu peoples of the African Great Lakes region. In Central Africa, Luba in the sixteenth century and the Lunda in the seventeenth century created centralized political entities, while in West Central Africa the Kingdom of Kongo was founded in the fourteenth century. What each of these centralized states shared was control of long-distance transoceanic, transcontinental, or intercontinental trade products and privileged access to these networks. Additionally, each of these states contended for power but managed to capture the loyalties of large groups of people either based on a religious principle, economic needs, or social ideology. Although a number of states became more centralized after the turn of the second millennium CE, readers should see this not as an inevitable evolution from small, local to large, global entities. Rather, these examples should be considered in the context of both the many communities and states that chose to remain noncentralized, small-scale entities and the fact that centralization was a dynamic process that often collapsed. Indeed, Great Zimbabwe, as an idea that leaders and community members imagined and implemented, had a rise and a fall.

How do we know who the Bantu were and are? How do we know about their various encounters and the spread of these languages to people of many backgrounds and locations? The short answer is through evidence. The following sections explain in detail the methods and sources used to reconstruct the outlines and details of the many Bantu historical dramas that have unfolded over the millennia.

METHODS USED TO RECONSTRUCT EARLY BANTU HISTORY

Historians who focus on early eras are trained to use methods and approaches to research that provide avenues for reconstructing narratives that are not preserved in written records. This section introduces readers to some of these methods and comparative approaches. In this discussion, the term "comparative" will be used. Making comparisons, sometimes called a comparative approach, can be a useful initial step in the research process, because it gives investigators a chance to identify and compare sociocultural similarities (and differences) across distinct societies. Initial observations of extant similarities are deemed typological.

Researchers commonly use similarity in typology to aid in categorizing data and, from these categorizations, to begin formulating research questions and hypotheses. However, simply observing that societies share particular cultural features at the level of typology is not sufficient evidence by itself of a shared history. The similarities may indeed derive from a shared earlier history or they may have been the results of separate but parallel developments. This problem leads to the second and more significant way that researchers use the comparative approach. They first apply to their comparative evidence the long-established analytical tools of the several relevant disciplines— among them, historical linguistics, archaeology, and comparative ethnography—for distinguishing shared old cultural retentions from parallel developments. Finally, they assess and correlate the evidence and findings of the different disciplines so that their conclusions rest on a growing body of evidence.

This book uses a comparative approach. The narrative it offers is the outcome of analyzing, comparing, and synthesizing the evidence and findings of Africanist scholars from the fields of history, art, linguistics, archaeology, biology, and anthropology.

WORDS AS HISTORICAL EVIDENCE

Each language has a history. The words of a language are the essential tools and medium for people to express and impart their cultural knowledge and to carry on their life activities and their cultural and social relations with people both inside and outside their own society. Human history and language history are fundamentally entwined. To uncover the history of a language and its words, a practice pioneered in the academic field called linguistics, is to uncover a very large body of evidence useful for reconstructing the history of past times and places. A great deal of what we know about the early Bantu past has come out of the research that historian linguists have spearheaded.

Like all languages, therefore, Bantu languages hold clues about their history in the words comprising their vocabularies. The reconstruction of the history of words falls under an approach called comparative historical linguistics, a field that uses language evidence to understand the relationships among distinct languages. For this kind of study, the linguist collects vocabulary sets as well as comparative grammatical and semantic data from related modern-day languages in order to systematically establish their relationships to each other and to reconstruct the phonology, vocabulary, and other aspects of the ancestral language from which those modern-day languages descended. Historian linguists apply the same systematic methods, but with a further ultimate goal—to gain insight into the human-driven changes in past societies.

People use words to name and describe what they know and do. Because words usually persist in use across many generations, changes over time in the meanings and usages of those words reveal past changes in how people carried out the activities or understood the ideas depicted by those words. It is in this line of study researchers especially examine the histories of those parts of the vocabularies of languages that are of cultural significance and interest both historically and to the modern-day speakers and societies. The histories of these kinds of vocabulary reveal the ways in which past people developed new ideas and shared established ideas. And they also shed light on the ways that languages have changed, persisted, or innovated to suit new historical contexts.

Because history is fundamentally about change over time and the processes involved, it is important that historian linguists establish a timeline, or chronology, so that we can offer a periodization for historical developments. This provides a framework for historians to suggest how people who spoke those languages conceptualized and transformed their worlds and to establish chronologies through comparative historical linguistic methods. The chronologies of divergence are a tool to establish family trees that reflect the ways and periods in which these languages diverged. Although the trees reflect the divergences, they do not preclude the re-convergence or later encounters among language communities that moved in different social and/or geographic directions.

The linguistic method used for proposing the approximate chronology of the successive period in the history of a language family is called glottochronology. This method has roots in the provocative work of linguist Morris Swadesh (1909–1967), who developed a standard for estimating when languages divergence occurred. He called it lexico-statistic glottochronology, because it used lexis (vocabulary) to create a chronology. This became the most contested part of his theory and approach.[6] Yet the method has permitted scholars to do two things.

---

[6] W. P. Lehmann, *Historical Linguistics: An Introduction*, 3rd ed. (New York: Routledge, 2013), chap. 9; O. Fischer, "What Counts as Evidence in Historical Linguistics," *Studies in Language* 28, no. 3 (2004): 710–740.

One is that using statistical comparison of the rates of replacement, in pairs of diverging languages, of old words by new words for each meaning in a core set of one hundred very basic words—called basic or core vocabulary—researchers can propose estimates of about how many years before the present (BP) the divergence between the languages began. The other is that illustrations of the way languages diverged over time were possible once relationships and date estimates were estimated. Swadesh theorized that language divergence develop gradually over decades and centuries as communities of people speaking a common language moved further apart socially and quite often geographically. Furthermore, he maintained that as speakers of a language have decreasing or increasing contact, over long spans of time influences and similarities would be captured in the way language changed. Following this reasoning, continued cohesion within a community of speakers would result in the maintenance of mutual intelligibility and, when change in a word for a meaning in the core vocabulary took place, the change would be adopted everywhere in that community.

Conversely, reduced contact among speakers leads to increased dialect difference. The adoption of new words for core vocabulary meanings would spread primarily to nearby communities who spoke the language and not to communities farther away. Communities in different areas tend to develop different ways of pronouncing what were originally the same vowels or consonants. Slowly over time and space, these lexical and pronunciation variances accumulate, and the emerging dialects become more and more distinct from each other, eventually becoming no longer mutually intelligible. When mutual intelligibility finally breaks down, linguists and linguist historians speak of those dialects as having evolved into distinct languages.

The methods of lexicostatistic glottochronology involve a number of steps. When two or more related languages preserve the same old root word going back to their common mother language, or protolanguage, as already noted, sound changes usually will have taken place. As a result, the word will be differently pronounced in each language. So, first, the scholar must identify the phonological components of the modern-day cognate words in the different languages and, then, determine the systematic sound correspondences that explain those differences. One characteristic of language history makes this kind of reconstruction possible is the regularity of sound change. Linguists have called these regular rules sound laws. Usually when people change the way in which they pronounce, for example, a particular consonant in their language, they do not change its pronunciation in just one word, but in every word in which that consonant occurs. If a word can be traced back to the proto-language of a family, the modern-day forms of this word found in the daughter language are what the historian linguist calls the "reflexes" of the ancient root word of the proto-language. These reflexes will show fully regular sound correspondences in all its consonants and vowels and its tonal or stress features. In the case of the Bantu languages, more than one hundred years ago, linguist Carl Meinhof began the systematic reconstruction of their sound change histories.

The next step requires determining the percentage of core vocabulary that languages share. Core vocabulary is commonly captured in a one-hundred-word list. One-hundred-word lists hold terms spoken in nearly every language. Examples included the words: "all," "bone," "foot," "night," "nose," "person," and "water."[7] Such words tend to be more resistant parts of the vocabulary to change. The idea is that because they express universally recognized things and actions, people do not easily give up or replace such words for those of a distinct language unless they are compelled to, or it is advantageous to do so. For this reason, core vocabulary is more resistant to change over time. An example of a 5,500-year-old Bantu core vocabulary word that speakers of the hundreds of Bantu languages and dialects have scarcely replaced with a word from a distinct language is *-ntu*. This root means "person." It is the root for the word *Bantu*, which, with the Ba- prefix, is the ancient proto-Bantu word meaning "people."

Swadesh premised that the rate at which language changes is relatively constant over long periods of time. Table 1.1 offers a time-depth chart that conveys just how that change might look over time. It represents the expected retention rate for a one-hundred-word vocabulary list between related languages over time. For instance, if two languages diverged from a common linguistic ancestor around five thousand years ago, it can be expected that their descendants will share approximately 22 percent of their one-hundred-word core vocabulary.[8] The larger the percentage of core vocabulary that languages share between them, then the more recently they are hypothesized to have diverged from an ancestral language.

---

[7]   Lehmann, *Historical Linguistics*, 180–181.

[8]   Lehmann, *Historical Linguistics*, 175.

Table 1.1 Glottochronology Derived Dating Estimates

ROUGH MEDIAN DATING IN YEARS BEFORE PRESENT (BP)	MEDIAN COMMON RETENTION PERCENTAGE RATES BETWEEN RELATED LANGUAGES
500 BP	86%
1000 BP	75%
1500 BP	64%
2000 BP	55%
3000 BP	40%
4000 BP	29%
5000 BP	22%
6000 BP	16%
7000 BP	12%
8000 BP	9%
9000 BP	7%
10000 BP	5%

Source: Christopher Ehret, "Testing the Expectations of Glottochronology against the Correlations of Language and Archaeology in Africa," in A. McMahon C. Renfrew and L. Trask (eds.), *Time Depth in Historical Linguistics*, vol. 2 (Cambridge: McDonald Institute for Archaeological Research, 2000), 395.

Though exact dates for when languages diverge from an ancestor cannot be definitively claimed, glottochronology makes it possible to propose the chronological order of language divergence and the broad time ranges in which a language diverges and becomes its descendant languages.[9] Once historians understand the relationships among languages and their likely movements and paths of divergence, it is possible to look at the geographic distribution of modern-day language communities and propose the possible ways in which speakers of those languages may have expanded across the landscape.

Although glottochronology's reliability remains a topic of debate, historian linguists find it useful as a tool to establish a relative timeline and framework for the unfolding of historical processes. Still, they

---

[9] Glottochronology is not universally accepted by linguists. It is highly contested because there are languages which prove to be exceptions to each principle Swadesh established. Yet historian linguists have found that lexicostatistic glottochronology is consistently effective in sequencing changes in Bantu languages and that comparing findings against dates provided by archaeology (including archaeobotany) have almost always yielded firm corroboration.

utilize it with an acute sensitivity to its imprecision and pay focused attention on the value of finding correlations and contrasts in other fields of research. That is why it is important to historian linguists that their proposed language divergence dates be tested, whenever possible, with dates and results from other fields and methods.[10] As will be detailed later, archaeology, comparative ethnography, biology, and ethnobotany have been particularly useful in this regard. Having proposed chronologies and dates of language divergence with glottochronology, historian linguists must then test these proposals against the dated changes in recovered material culture in order to validate, refine, or revise those approximate dates.

The historian linguist aims to determine what words in a language's vocabulary reveal about the speakers' history. This includes determining whether the words are old and inherited, newly innovated, or borrowed from the speakers of other languages. We call this kind of investigation etymology, the study of word history. Understanding the history of words helps researchers to understand how a word's structure and meaning can be changed to take on new figurative representations. It is also a way to understand how speakers in different communities adapt a word's meaning over time to fit new contexts and to communicate their changing social and culture practices and worldviews.

Bantu religion offers an example for thinking about this kind of word history. Around 500 CE the proto-Sabi, a Bantu-speaking people living in the region of modern-day Eastern Democratic Republic of the Congo, began to use a new word to name God, *Leza*. The concept of God or Creator had been an aspect of the Bantu worldview from earliest times, ca. 3500 BCE. This is something we know because the proto-Bantu root for Creator God was *Nyàmbe*, from the verb *-amb-* meaning "to begin." *Leza*'s etymology reveals the

---

[10] Christopher Ehret, "Testing the Expectations of Glottochronology against the Correlations of Language and Archaeology in Africa," in C. Renfrew et al. (eds.) *Time Depth in Historical Linguistics* (Cambridge, 2000), 373–399. Kairn Klieman, The Pygmies Were Our Compass, D.L. Shoenbrun, A Green Place, A Good Place 46–47; Rhiannon Stephens, *A History of African Motherhood: The Case of Uganda, 700–1900* (Cambridge: Cambridge University Press, 2014). For critiques of glottochronology, see Lehmann, *Historical Linguistics*, 175–176; C. Renfrew, "Introduction: The Problem of Time Depth," in C. Renfrew et al. (eds.) *Time Depth in Historical Linguistics* (Cambridge, 2000), ix–xiv.

appearance of a distinct new idea about God. Its derivation was from a proto-Bantu verb *-ded-* "to nurture" in the way parents or communities care for children. People transforming the old Bantu verb root word *-ded-* into a term for "Creator" has a history that was the outcome of several linguistic steps. An early development before the coining of the new noun was change in phonemes whereby the sound /d/ became /l/. Then came the addition of a causative aspect suffix *-i,* yielding a verb *-dedi-.* While the initial /d/ shifted to /l/, the second consonant /d/ followed by the vowel /i/ shifted to /z/. Finally, a noun-forming suffix was added to the verb. The result was *Leza,* a word that signified the idea of God as one who nurtures.

This etymology implies a shift in worldview among those Bantu-speaking people. *Leza's* etymology suggests that among the proto-Sabi and proto-Botatwe, the quality of God as a more involved nurturer of creation supplanted the ancient Bantu idea of God as a distant Creator of the cosmos. The glottochronological estimate of the proto-Sabi and proto-Botatwe societies at around 500 CE, and the correlation of that society with a new archaeological culture dating to that era in the areas around the copper belt of Katanga and central northern Zambia suggest that this shift in the worldviews of a particular Bantu-speaking people on the essence of God's nature took place probably not long before the middle first-millennium CE in Central Africa.

Linguistic continuities and changes will be a recurring topic throughout *Bantu Africa,* because they help convey historical knowledge. These features of language history reveal times when speakers continued to use words inherited from recent and distant ancestors—indicating that they continued to find value and meaning in the objects and concepts conveyed by those words. Conversely, linguistic change can demonstrate when innovation or deletion of older concepts occurs, shedding light on significant historical transitions. Across the hundreds of Bantu languages, word retentions, subtractions, and reinventions certainly occurred innumerable times.

GENETICS AS HISTORICAL EVIDENCE

Recent genetic studies of people speaking Bantu languages map a history of Bantu spread congruent with the cumulative historical picture we can draw from the comparative linguistic, comparative ethnographic, and archaeology records. These findings, like those of linguistics, place the beginnings of Bantu divergence and spread at around 3500 BCE. They depict a history of genetic divergence that followed much the same geographical and chronological courses as the language evidence depicts, with the early Bantu expansions passing from the far northeast of the equatorial rainforest, south and eastward through the forest zones. The genetic findings agree as well with the linguistic evidence that the Mashariki Bantu arose out of the eastward spread from the forest of the proto-Mashariki, with the peoples of the Kusi subbranch of Mashariki then breaking off southward to move into southeastern Africa.

The genetic evidence also provides clear signals of the assimilation of non-Bantu peoples into Bantu societies. The Batwa of the rainforest appear to have remained mostly distinct; they formed perhaps too sparse a population to have left more than a relatively small genetic imprint on the Bantu populations of those region. But across the eastern side of Africa the picture is quite different. The demographic contribution of Khoesan peoples to Kusi societies of southeastern Africa is strongly evident in the genetic makeup of those societies. Similarly, the Southern Cushitic and Nilo-Saharan contributions to the genetic makeup of Bantu societies of East Africa are clear in these data. The Central Savanna Bantu and the Njila peoples of the western savanna regions probably similarly have assimilated significant numbers of the previous populations of their regions into their societies. But their genetics have yet to receive the depth of investigation that would resolve the issue in their case.[11]

ARCHAEOLOGY AS HISTORICAL EVIDENCE

The material artifacts that archaeologists recover, analyze, and date are invaluable to reconstructing early history. Historian linguists long have looked to archeologists' findings to compare against independent conclusions reached using linguistic evidence. When correlations for social and cultural changes align with archaeology, the research in each field is bolstered. Although archaeological objects from western, central, eastern, and southern Africa rarely have decipherable written information on them prior to the 1800s, archeological layers can hint at who inhabited a region not in terms of an exact ethnicity, but certainly in terms of

---

[11] Sen li, Carina Schlebusch, and Mattias Jakobsson, "Genetic Variation Reveals Large-Scale Population Expansion and Migration During the Expansion of Bantu-Speaking Peoples," *Proceedings of the Royal Society*, September 10, 2014. DOI: 10.1098/rspb.2014.1448.

continuity or discontinuity of object types, aesthetic, and style. Language evidence provides words that archaeologists can use to interpret material culture, and material culture provides historians with physical evidence to show correlations with linguistic or other data sources.

Archeologist Pierre de Maret contributes an example of linguistics and archaeology working together. His research centers on archaeological sites in the Upemba Depression, in the southeastern part of what is today the Democratic Republic of the Congo.[12] The historical significance of these sites lies in the dated layers of pottery and in the correlation of the periods in the Upemba archaeological record with historical periods and dating derived from the linguistic record.

The Upemba site findings provide historians with important evidence for reconstructing Bantu history in the region. The lowest, oldest level, which dates to about 400 CE, held pottery similar to that Bantu-speaking Sabi group of peoples produced somewhat later and further east in Zambia. Its prevalence at Upemba from around 400 CE suggests that a particular early Bantu-speaking people, linguistically and culturally ancestral to the later populations in Zambia, likely lived in the region.[13] The next three levels show, first, a break with the previous period and then a continuous development down to Luba people, who inhabited this area and the whole surrounding regions in more recent centuries. The archaeology correlates with the linguistic evidence for the Sabi group of Bantu, which implies that they spread out from the modern-day Katanga region of Congo across northeastern, eastern, and central Zambia. The glottochronology estimates of the time for the beginning of this divergence and spread is around the sixth or seventh centuries CE, in close accord with the archaeological dates for the beginning of the spread of the types of pottery made by Sabi peoples in later times.

The archaeology also correlates well with the linguistic dates for the spread eastward into Katanga of Luba-speaking communities from the Kasai River areas of the Southern Congo Basin. These dates estimate this spread in the range of the seventh century CE, closely fitting

---

[12] Pierre de Maret and Terry Childs, "Re/constructing Luba Pasts," in Mary Roberts and Allen Roberts, eds., *Memory-Luba Art and the Making of History* (New York: Museum for African Art, 1996), 49–60.

[13] Pierre de Maret, "Archaeologies of the Bantu expansion," in P. Lane and P. Mitchell (eds.), *The Oxford Handbook of African Archaeology* (Oxford: Oxford University Press, 2013), 627–643; "From Pottery Groups to Ethnic Groups in Central Africa", in A. Brower Stahl (ed.) *African Archaeology: A Critical Introduction.* (Oxford: Blackwell, 2005), 420–440.

with the appearance in the material record of the Upemba depression of pottery with significantly different design motifs from the lower level, indicative of the arrival of a new group of speakers. Likely it was the ancestors of Luba speakers who came into the region.

The quantity and quality of the goods in certain graves increased, which probably meant that so did social stratification. The height of the developments coincided with a period of royal burials, suggesting the existence of a state that we can call the Upemba Kingdom, between around 1100 and 1400 CE. A new Luba Empire arose in the 1600s, lasting until 1860. Through these successions from the seventh century onward, a continuous evolution of ceramic styles took place, revealing an ongoing presence of Luba speakers as the prevailing population across those centuries and down to the present. The stratigraphy of the pottery remains thus correlate with linguistic-based histories that show first the habitation of the region before 600 CE by people who likely spoke a Bantu language ancestral to the languages of the later Sabi peoples of Zambia and western and southern Katanga. Then, in the 600s, a new set of Bantu communities, Lubans, were on the move and immigrated into the region. Luba speakers over the next several centuries became the primary linguistic and cultural society of the region.

That the incoming Luba absorbed the earlier Sabi people into their society is evident from a different kind of linguistic evidence. Specifically, they borrowed words from the language of those former Sabi populations. One especially notable example, because it reached into the one-hundred-word list where borrowing rarely occurs, was the Luba-Katanga replacement of their older word for fish with a new word *-sabi, which they adopted from the Sabi speakers of the region. Language evidence of all sorts provides a rich view of past societies from a speech community's own perspective in its words.

ORAL TRADITION AS HISTORICAL EVIDENCE

The study of oral traditions has added detail that has allowed scholars to add nuance to discussions on past societies and their worldviews.[14] Oral traditions inflect the knowledge that scholars cull from linguistic and archaeological data. Societies that best kept oral traditions as

---

[14] Jan Vansina, *Oral Tradition as History* (Madison, WI: University of Wisconsin Press, 1990).

well as family histories, songs, fables, proverbs, myths, and personal testimonies often maintained relationships with trusted, professional oral historians. Today referred to by the French word *griot*, meaning "storyteller," they were responsible for retaining and recounting when necessary historically relevant and valued information with precision. Historian and anthropologist Jan Vansina demonstrated half a century ago that oral tradition and history as a method contribute authoritative information toward reconstructing histories in Africa. They can provide rich cultural perspectives on history stretching back as far as five hundred years. In societies that preserve them, oral traditions are valued and guarded, just as literate societies place value on preserving and protecting written documents. They recount a community's origins, and they preserve genealogies and family histories. And people employ traditions to educate and socialize community members. Oral traditions reveal how people understood their world. Tradition can be equally illuminating in respect to larger meanings behind the words that historian linguists reconstruct and the material culture archaeologists uncover.[15]

Historian linguists apply a comparative approach to oral traditions in order to give contextual meaning and identify the expression of social values in language data. Although individual words and clusters of words reveal what people know, they do not always reveal how, when, or why people used the ideas that the individual words signify. The following Kikuyu tradition provides an example. The Kikuyu are a sizeable community of Bantu-speaking people residing in Kenya. According to one notable oral tradition, there was a period of time when women were much stronger than men and ruled the society. The men grew tired of this situation, so they plotted to shift societal organization. To do this, the tradition claims they held a party and seduced all the women. Each Kikuyu woman who attended the party conceived.

According to the narrative, in the later stage of pregnancy, these women were unable to fight back. Men seized upon opportunity and exploited their pregnant condition to take control. They attempted to change the names of the original clan ancestors from female to male ones in the historical oral record. In response, the women refused to have any more children if the men changed the names of the ancestresses to male names. The counterdemand the women made prevailed. Hence, to this day, although Kikuyu people observe a patrilineal descent and inheritance, the ancestors of the clans of

---

[15] Jan Vansina, *The Children of Woot: A History of the Kuba Peoples* (Madison: University of Wisconsin Press, 1978).

the Kikuyu are remembered as having been women. [16] As this oral tradition indicates, a shift occurred at some historical moment from a matrilineal tradition of tracing descent and inheritance in earlier eras to a patrilineal system of organization, likely due to a change in worldview.

As chapter 2 will explain, the most ancient pattern of descent in Bantu societies was matrilineal. In this case the historical transition of the Kikuyu from the old Bantu matrilineality to patrilineal descent took place before the reach of more detailed Kikuyu oral histories, which began around 1500 CE but was still remembered in a mythologized version.

Certainly changes in historical circumstances of a society can lead people to modify the storylines of oral traditions. Yet a comparative approach is important because it reveals wider spread patterns, tropes, and interpretations of the significance of particular elements in traditions. Across Bantu Africa, several themes reoccur in oral traditions.[17] Notable examples include the roles of individuals in leading migration, strangers as actors in historical change, women as founders of societies, women as political brokers and intermediaries, the close connection between sons and their mother's brother, social relations among nongendered chiefs and dependents, changing gender roles, economic developments, and the acts and roles of ancestors. These repeated themes reveal that, for the early Bantu and many of their descendants, the world was one in which encounters with immigrants and people of other cultural backgrounds were relatively common, women held some social authority, matrilineages were the norm, human capital and social networks were essential, and ancestors mattered.

Oral societies often employ short sayings, proverbs, and riddles to educate. Comparative analysis of such phrases contributes to our broader knowledge of values where orality prevails. For example, the Haya, residing today in western Tanzania, ask their children the riddle, "*Malwa, Maela, Itunga?*" It means, "Which people never get satisfied with beer, money, or wealth?" The verb used in this riddle is

---

[16] Jomo Kenyatta, *Facing Mount Kenya* (London: Secker and Warburg, 1938).

[17] David A. Binkley, "Southern Kuba Initiation Rites: The Ephemeral Face of Power and Secrecy," *African Arts, Ephemeral Art II* 43, no. 1 (Spring 2010): 44–59.

kwiguta, which means "to be sated with food." For a child to answer this riddle, he or she must mentally examine the concept of "eating to fullness." The answer to the riddle is "the greedy one."[18] The purpose of this riddle is to not only teach children critical thinking but also to share a social value that educates children: they should not desire more than they need. This riddle reveals Haya mores concerning acquisitive behavior, which may be rooted in historical experiences concerning the accumulation and redistribution of food and other goods.

Like riddles, proverbs also provide insight into the ways people use words to construct and reflect a worldview. The Bemba proverb *Ubukulu bwa chambeshi: Ukuicefya* reminds audiences that "a real leader is one who makes himself/herself small/humble."[19] This proverb expresses the value that successful leaders should be not authoritarian but rather collaborative. This example is one among many across the Bantu-speaking world that provide insight into worldviews. The idea of smallness connotes humility, not absolute power, and this quality made a leader successful. Many other Bantu communities attest similar proverbs. Proverbs and riddles like oral, ethnographic, linguistic, archaeological, and genetic data are crucial to filling out the details of the Bantu past. They reveal the utility of comparative method and the importance of the interplay between various methodologies and various types of data, which together allow one to construct a clearer view of Bantu histories across time and space.

ETHNOGRAPHY AS HISTORICAL EVIDENCE

Through sustained and careful observation, anthropologists produce detailed descriptions of societies' practices, ceremonies, and beliefs. These are ethnographies. Anthropologists and local informants produced a large body of ethnographic work in Bantu-speaking regions from the late nineteenth to mid-twentieth century. Although many of these studies have been critiqued as static

---

[18] Johnson M. Ishengoma, "African Oral Traditions: Riddles among the Haya of Northwestern Tanzania," *International Review of Education* 51, no. 2/3 (2005): 148.

[19] Hugo Hinfelaar, *Bemba-Speaking Women of Zambia in a Century of Religious Change (1892–1992)* (Leiden: E. J. Brill, 1994), 10.

presentations of societies, they are useful to historians because their observations contain detailed descriptions of society and culture as they were at a particular period in time. Historians use a comparative ethnographical approach in assessing the historical connection of communities and their culture histories. They can then weigh ethnographic evidence and conclusions against archaeological, oral, and linguistic data to identify patterns of cultural activity in various layers of history.

Examples of cultural and ethnographic ideas represented in vocabularies across a majority of Bantu-speaking societies are evidenced across sub-Saharan Africa. The proto-Bantu root *-dĺmù refers to an ancient idea about spirits of deceased persons who lived long ago.[20] Culture and comparative ethnographic data also reflect the enduring importance of ancestors. Strong evidence exists that people who had lived in past times continue to matter in abstract and tangible ways in the lives of the living. The belief is held in a number of expressions related to remembering and venerating ancestors that will be comprehensively introduced in chapter 2. All through the many published ethnographies of Bantu peoples, the preeminence of ancestors is expressed widely. In works on Bioko Island (formerly Fernando Po), off the coast of Cameroon, the Buni, a Bantu-speaking people, recognize ancestors' spirits playing a critical role in guiding newborn children into the lineage from the time of conception.[21] On the other side of sub-Saharan Africa, in modern-day Tanzania, the belief in ancestors intervening on behalf of the living is in play among Bantu-speaking Gogo. Through the assistance of trained diviners, discontented ancestors are supplicated to when children become ill. This kind of ritual exists very widely among Bantu speakers, not just the Gogo, because ancestors, who always remain an active part of the lineage, can both cause and cure illness.[22] In Bantu societies, ancestor spirits are ubiquitous in oral traditions, the arts, masks, sites of memory, politics,

---

[20] Jan M. Vansina, *Paths in the Rainforests: Toward a History of Political Tradition in Equatorial Africa* (University of Wisconsin Press, 1990), 141, 297. Vansina attests this root as *-dímo.

[21] Ibrahim Sundiata, "Engaging Equatorial Guinea: Bioko in the Diasporic Imagination," *Afro-Hispanic Review* 28, no. 2 (2009): 131–142, 468–469.

[22] Mathias E. Mnyampala, *The Gogo: History, Customs, and Traditions*, trans. Gregory H. Maddox (M. E. Sharpe, 1995), 104.

and the like. Comparing the different societies' ideas of the ancestor spirits, as captured in ethnographic records, shows that ancestors were hardly peripheral. They were a central concern everywhere to Bantu societies. Comparison confirms the implications of the proto-Bantu root word *-dImu meaning "ancestor spirit" and that these beliefs trace back to the proto-Bantu society.

Through comprehensive assessment of evidence in language, oral traditions, ethnographies, genetics, and archaeology, historians have reconstructed the broad stories, and sometimes the detail, of transformative change in farming, music, dance, religious philosophies, and technology in the earlier Bantu past. These changes have been central to life across a large portion of Africa during the past five to six thousand years.

CONCLUSION

The five phases of Bantu expansions cover more than five thousand years of history. Over that time Bantu speech communities settled across large parts of the southern half of Africa. They did so at varying paces, probably initially utilizing the extensive webs of rivers and their tributaries in the rainforest and woodland savannas as avenues of transport. In many times and places the incoming Bantu communities interacted with peoples who spoke languages and possessed ideas and cultural practices quite different from their own. From this demographic and linguistic history, it is possible to begin to understand the ways in which an array of widespread Bantu cultures, although sharing a common ancestral beginning in the proto-Bantu society, are both similar in many of their core features of culture and belief and yet also distinct in their economies and in many details of culture, politics, beliefs, and organization. The rapid urbanization of Africa and the parallel migration of Bantu-speaking people to those urban centers during the nineteenth, twentieth, and twenty-first centuries might be considered an extension of phase five or perhaps a sixth phase, 1800-present, of Bantu expansions into urban spaces." Bantu expansions into urban spaces.

As they spread out over a third of the continent (half of sub-Saharan Africa), Bantu societies have each carried on some aspects of culture and language retained from the deeper historical past that made them recognizably Bantu. Along the way they have also picked up words, ideas, beliefs, and practices from the peoples they encountered and assimilated into their societies. The artifacts of these histories—whether words or features of culture retained from proto-Bantu times, or words and features of culture and technology adopted from the historical encounters of Bantu communities with other peoples—are among the data trails that historians follow in studying the history of Bantu peoples. All of this history has become clearer to historians through the clues that remain in the words, material culture, practices, and oral narratives the early Bantu societies have passed on to their descendants and which successive generations have decided are meaningful enough to maintain.

The diversity of environments, cultures, and economic strategies of modern Bantu societies means that it is crucial to consider the phases of Bantu expansions as movements of groups of people into new areas and, in the process, encountering new peoples, new technologies, and new ideas. Continuity is key to sustaining a society. Commonly, a culture's persistence rests on generally agreed-upon central ideas for understanding and coping with the world that community members acknowledge and uphold, whether in their social organization, their religious tenets, or their economic relations. It is people's constant negotiation of these factors in their daily interactions that guides their decisions about just how they will live, behave, and make decisions. But these choices also influence the types of societies to which people want to belong, whether in 3500 BCE near the Sangha and Nyong Rivers in far northwestern equatorial Africa or living one hundred years ago near the Orange River in South Africa, or today near the Rufiji River in Tanzania.

Bantu peoples developed varied economic, social, and political practices to live within these diverse contexts. They established thriving societies that like many others globally embraced innovation, honored firstcomers and those who had arrived earlier, and had a strong ethos of valuing and incorporating outsiders. Loanwords into Bantu for iron technology, cattle raising, and seed cultivation from peoples who spoke languages variously of the Nilo-Saharan, Afrasian, and Khoesan families provide multiple examples of the historical openness of Bantu societies to adopting new elements of economy, technology, and religious and cultural practices and beliefs.

Capoeira

Historically, Bantu-speaking peoples have had a major impact on vast geographic regions, both in Africa and beyond. One powerful example of people who spoke Bantu languages spreading ideas is manifested in the martial art *capoeira*. As historian M. T. J. Desch-Obi has demonstrated, Bantu-speaking people of southwestern Central Africa created this martial art. Originating in Angola among Kimbundu peoples of the Njila subbranch of Bantu, *capoeira* has become a popular sport and art form among people in the Americas from the streets of Brazil to hipster gyms in New York and San Francisco. Though it has had a contentious history in Brazil, it became a nationally embraced sport for that nation late in the twentieth century. *Capoeira*'s arrival in the Americas has roots in the era of trans-Atlantic slave trade. Some of the enslaved individuals from what is modern-day Angola carried the practice with them to the Americas.

Although it is hardly the only idea or practice Bantu speakers brought into the Americas, it is a well-known one. Moreover, it demonstrates the holistic approach that Bantu peoples have tended to take toward the world, which will be laid out in the next chapter. *Capoeira* combines ideology, physical practice, and religious/spiritual expression. This elegant, artistic, physically challenging, and practical martial art integrates the spiritual and the earthly, the living and the ancestral, martial and leisure, musical and rhythmic elements, and the politics of resistance and justice.

Capoeira's persistence is important because it demonstrates that even traumatic ruptures like the period of the Atlantic Slave Trade did not wholly impede continuity in culture. Imagine the reactions that might have ensued if enslaved individuals audaciously rehearsed militaristic defense drills in front of slave masters. With *capoeira*, the enslaved did practice the swaying rhythmic movements that both strengthened them and made them agile right in front of the slave masters. This activity caused little alarm of revolt because plantation managers and slave owners thought it was just a form of African dance, and little connection was made between this body movement and enslaved people's resistance. Bantu-descended peoples continued to utilize ideas they retained from their heritable past, which were expedient to the various circumstances in their communities.

FURTHER READINGS

Desch-Obi, M. Thomas J. *Fighting for Honor: The History of African Martial Art in the Atlantic World*. Columbia: University of South Carolina Press, 2008.

Ehret, Christopher. *The Civilizations of Africa: A History to 1800*. Charlottesville: University of Virginia Press, 2002.

Klieman, Kairn. *The Pygmies Were Our Compass: Bantu and Batwa in the History of West Central Africa, Early Times to c. 1900 C.E.* Portsmouth, N.H.: Heinemann, 2003.

Vansina, Jan. *Paths in the Rainforest Toward a History of Political Tradition in Equatorial Africa*. Madison: University of Wisconsin Press, 1985.

———. *Oral Tradition as History*. Madison: University of Wisconsin Press, 1990.

Walker, Robert S., and Marcus J. Hamilton. "Social Complexity and Linguistic Diversity in the Austronesian and Bantu Population Expansions." *Proceedings: Biological Sciences* 278, no. 1710 (2011): 1399–1404.

Historicizing Lineage, Belonging, and Heterarchy

Fifty-five hundred years ago in western Africa, the speakers of the proto-Bantu language were a small collection of communities living in what is today the eastern part of southern Cameroon. Yet over the course of the next five millennia, their descendants, through a long and complex history of cross-cultural interactions, transformed the economic, social, and political landscapes of much of central, eastern, and southern Africa.

Residing in small close-knit communities, proto-Bantu speakers rooted their identities, security, and worldview in their lineages. They conceived of a lineage as a unit comprised of the descendants—living, deceased, and those not yet born—of a common ancestor who lived from several to many generations back in the past. As their communities expanded outwardly into new niches and grew and diversified—economically, politically, environmentally, and socially—lineages continued to be the institutions for defining and organizing community and for imparting values. The available evidence from across Bantu speaking areas of Africa shows that heterarchy and belonging were key societal ideals that proto-Bantu speakers used to guide their choices and decisions. Heterarchy is a model of power that is horizontal and relational, rooted in networks rather than primarily vertical and hierarchical. People used these networks to connect to others for support and also to create a practice of diffuse power that reinforced a sense of belonging and accountability. Linguistic, oral, archaeological, ethnographic, and genetic data suggest that the descendants of proto-Bantu long continued to draw upon values of heterarchy and belonging. Bantu histories are best understood through the ethics, principles, worldviews, and choices people made within the context of a given era. The continuities and shifts that unfolded—in lineage, in social organizing, in beliefs, in authority, and in economy among Bantu speakers—is the social history that this chapter explores.

Much in the way that democracy and individual freedoms could be described as twenty-first-century values that guide decisions, thinking, and reactions of most members of the American community, lineage, belonging, and heterarchy explain the tenets undergirding Bantu speakers' processes and actions in their societies. As the ideal in Bantu societies, community members were socialized consciously and unconsciously to honor their collective principles. At the same time, no individual member fully lives up to a perfect adherence to all social values in all circumstances. Indeed, some members may even resist or transform those values, and yet even the alteration is rooted in both the knowledge and practice of historical social ideals. In essence, the human imagination is constrained by what it knows and does not know.

Although in a twenty-first-century context some individuals may find the notion that women and men were being prepared for parenthood antiquated and even objectionable, it is important for us to not be anachronistic in comprehending how people in the past comprehended and mastered the worlds they lived in. Understanding the integrated worldview of the Bantu speakers over time in their own context is critical. The lineage was the basis of belonging for everyone and was the center for the expression of fundamental values, not individuality and personal independence so valued in more recent eras. The primary role of lineages was to guide members through the various stages of life from the state of birth to that of ancestor. The social institutions controlled by the lineage involved ceremonies celebrating various stages of "parenting" from the birth of the first child to puberty initiation schools, to acknowledging grandparenthood and then inevitably "ancestorhood"—the state of being a deceased ancestor—whereby souls of the deceased become responsible for guiding newer generations. This emphasis on the birth and raising of children was essential to maintaining the lineage, and in part it may be based on the reality of the low population density of the African continent continuing into modern times.

In this book, lineage signifies the intersection of family, belonging, and spiritual practice. Belonging refers to the way Bantu-speaking people have identified and defined their relationships and attendant responsibilities that connected them to networks of living people and ancestors. Heterarchy depicts the complex mix and interplay of social and political structures that over time and space shaped understandings and practices of power within and across Bantu speech communities. In early Bantu times, individuals, lineages, and social institutions concurrently wielded, negotiated, and influenced authority. Those holding positions of authority participated in heterarchical systems of power that were horizontal, entwined, and diffuse in nature.[1] Unbending vertical, linear, and concentrated power held by a single person or group does not appear to have been typical in the early Bantu historical tradition. Examining lineage, belonging, and heterarchy reveals that Bantu speakers historically viewed the cosmos as comprising inextricably linked temporal and ethereal parts. In fact, early Bantu speakers likely viewed these realms not as parts at all, but rather as interpenetrating complementary realms.

Lineage, heterarchy, and belonging characterized the types of relationships that proto-Bantu people fashioned. Although connections among people are meaningful in all human communities, the varieties of networks, relationships, and systems that communities create differ across time and context.

Learning about the boundaries, as well as implicit and explicit responsibilities that define types of relationships, is important to understanding the way societies inherit, assign, and wield authority. The earliest Bantu were organized into matrilineages—they followed the maternal family line for identity and inheritance. Within the matrilineages, relationships of authority and family were determined primarily by seniority; thus, female and male elders held influence and authority. Language evidence that dates to the earliest Bantu period around 3500 BCE provides evidence of the kinds of relationships, positions of authority, and organizations that early Bantu-speaking people created. From this evidence, scholars can begin to decipher the frameworks and priorities that the proto-Bantu established to deal with specific historical challenges and opportunities.

---

[1] Kathleen R. Smythe, *Africa's Past, Our Future* (Bloomington: Indiana University Press, 2015), 103.

Finally, comparing and analyzing ethnographic accounts and oral traditions from Bantu speakers in more recent centuries helps us to recover continuities and innovations that unfolded in different societies across the Bantu-speaking world.

LINEAGE AND RELIGION

Despite the immense range of change that has occurred within and across Bantu speech communities, lineage membership consistently has been central to social organization, and these ancestral ties have been of primary importance to Bantu religious thought and family formation. It is critical to grapple with the ways that the ideologies of lineage and religion among Bantu speaking communities continued, over the *longue durée*, to impact the moral and social constructs that, in turn, they drew on to develop political, social, and economic institutions. They saw the family and the spiritual as inextricably linked entities. Whereas the family included living, deceased, and future members, the spiritual encompassed a monotheistic Creator, ancestor spirits, and territorial spirits.

Enduring Family Connections: Ancestor Spirits

By the fourth millennium BCE, proto-Bantu people recognized two distinct categories of spirits, *-dímù*, ancestral and territorial. Ancestral spirits were deceased lineage members remembered by the living. Territorial spirits impacted living people, yet they were associated with specific sites. Ancestral spirits were those who had transitioned to the nonmaterial world relatively recently in relation to those still living. In essence, the ancestor spirits were deceased lineage members who were still in the collective memory of the living. Territorial spirits covered a broader field. Some appear to have originally been special, ancient ancestors whose enduring reputation for things they accomplished while living led to their having been enshrined in a physical place. Bantu adopted other territorial spirits from "firstcomers," people who already lived in the territory before Bantu arrived in the region. As populations moved to new lands, the recognition of new territorial spirits may have helped to legitimize their right to settle in areas where their ancestors had not previously lived or been buried.

Because of their understanding of the effect ancestral spirits could have on the living, Bantu peoples' relationships with those spirits were intimate. Ancestral spirits reached into the lives of, made demands on, and also expected communication and offerings from, the living. Proverbs, oral traditions, and family accounts testify that ancestral spirits responded in one of two ways for descendants' actions and thoughts. Ancestral spirits either caused positive outcomes for descendants, or if dissatisfied they could wreak havoc in the lives of their living lineage members.

People recognized that neglect of their ancestors was unwise, because to forget them could result in misfortune. They understood that ancestral lineage members swayed day-to-day existence of living descendants, including community fertility and fecundity. Dissatisfied ancestors might intervene to cause crisis and catastrophe, whereas satisfied ancestors had the power to cause benevolent outcomes and exert protection for the living. Spirit memorialization required intentional communications that included tangible offerings of food and drink, and ephemeral offerings of song, dance, and other expressions. Because Bantu speakers understood that neglect of their ancestors could have disastrous effects for a person, family, or community at large, they worked hard to uphold their various duties to both satisfy and propitiate their ancestors with their actions and words. Yet misfortune or evil sometimes would occur and living people tried to understand and resolve the root cause.

The notion of lineage is closely tied to the spiritual realm through ancestral spirits who continue to be part of the lineage even after passing into the spirit world. As members of both the earthly and spiritual realms, ancestors influence the living, ensuring that people continuously consider their ethereal lineage roots. Perhaps as early as the proto-Bantu period, 5,500 years ago, *-kódò/*-kólò (see pages 86–87 Table 2.1) was a category of social belonging. Three block distributions of this root hold connected but distinct meanings; the first is "grandparent" stretching from central west to central east Africa, and the second is "base of tree" spanning from northeast to central east Africa. A third block distribution meaning "matriclan" exists among Kaskazi and Kusi speakers in eastern Africa.[2] The languages spoken within these block distributions are of Savanna Bantu origin.

The etymology of *-kódò in two branches of Savanna Bantu, coupled with an understanding about the way people develop metaphors,

---

[2]   /d/ became /l/ in some languages due to phonetic shift.

sheds light on histories of belonging, which are are datable to Nzadi-Kwa languages of the early third millennium BCE (second phase). At the point of its earliest proven use, *-kódò signified the "base of a tree" or "grandparent." These are the root's original concrete meanings. However, simultaneously these early Nzadi-Kwa speakers also used *-kódò as a metaphor for "origin" to signify that people belonged to a common base. This explicit concrete meaning of "base of a tree" appears still today in far-flung Mashariki Bantu descended languages. People typically develop concrete meanings before they conceptualize metaphors.

Moreover, the concrete meaning of *-kódò as "leg" in the Central Savanna languages Luba and Songye paves a way to trace back meaning to the proto-Savanna period. This is because in several African cases the word for "leg" has taken on the additional meaning "trunk (of a tree)," or alternatively the original meaning "trunk" led to a person's leg having been understood as the trunk of his or her body, that is, the thing a person stands on just as a tree stands on its trunk.

Two important considerations should frame ongoing research and analysis into *-kódò's antiquity. One is how the reconstructed etymology of the three meanings that trace back to the Nzadi-Kwa period are similarly oriented to literal and metaphorical roots—base of tree, origin, and grandparent. Second is the question of whether the grandparent term specifically connoted "grandmother" in its earliest usage. If that were so, then the other two meanings would point toward a grandmother as the root of a lineage and the metaphorical base of a tree. It is already clear from the data that the more structured social meaning of *-kódò was the word for a matriclan in the last millennium BCE (early fourth phase). Together these three linked meanings would suggest that in the Nzadi-Kwa era *-kólò presupposed female ancestry as founding relationships among living people.

The three block distributions underscore that one's lineage, inclusive of generations, was the central unit of organizing and belonging. This stands in contrast to notions of the nuclear family shaping belonging and the larger state apparatus shaping social-political organization. Although research on this continues, the working hypothesis that considers both language data and comparative ethnography suggests that a scholar, like yourself, may one day be able to reconstruct *-kódò back to proto-Bantu with a meaning related to maternal line or grandmother.

Since the last millennium BCE, *-kólò implies the unity of ancestors and matrilineal social organization. Unlike the general category of ancestor spirit elaborated by the term *-dímù*, the root *-kólò* continued to pinpoint an ancestor spirit affiliated specifically with the maternal line. A semantic change in the meaning and use of *-kólò*, which has been dated to the fourth phase of Bantu expansions, offers an example of the value place of maternal lineage affiliation. In the final centuries of the last millennium BCE, some Mashariki-Bantu speakers—the Kaskazi—applied *-kólò* to mean "matriclan."

The intersections among lineage, the spirit world, and authority in Bantu worldviews discussed earlier with the root *-kólò* are further reflected in the etymology of the root *-simbi*.[3] Based on its geographic distribution, *-simbi* emerged as a term about three thousand years ago at the end of the third phase of the Bantu expansions. This root means either spirit of the dead or a young woman during female initiation. These two meanings illustrate an aspect of the early Bantu worldview in which these spheres were entwined. Like the root *-kólò* may show in the earliest Bantu eras, *-simbi* reflects that while change was underway links between ancestors and the living persisted in the thinking of some communities even two millennia after the proto-Bantu era.

Among the southwestern Bantu, including the Kongo peoples of Angola and the Democratic Republic of Congo (DRC), this term *-simbi* identifies local spirits (*simbi kya nsi*) who are responsible for controlling weather, for technological innovations, and—and here is the gendered connection—for the reproductive capacities of women.[4] In the history of the Kongo, the BaMbwidi-mbodila [Batwa people] are referred to as the *simbi* spirits who are the "owners of the earth."[5] Yet among three other branches of Savanna Bantu the same word means a young girl during female initiation or a dance for female initiation. Often the songs and stories told during female initiation involve

---

[3]   J. Torrend, *An English–Vernacular Dictionary of the Bantu-Botatwe Dialects of Northern Rhodesia*, compiled with the help of Dr. H. S. Gerrard Farnborough (UK: Gregg Press, 1967); Bruce Kapferer, *Cooperation, Leadership and Village Structure: A Preliminary Economic and Political Study of Ten Bisa Villages in the Northern Province of Zambia*. Zambian Papers, no. 1 (Lusaka, Zambia: University of Zambia Institute for Social Research, 1967); J. L. Wright and M. Kamukwamba, *Kaonde Note Book* (London: Longmans, 1958).

[4]   Wyatt MacGaffey, "Oral Tradition in Central Africa," *The International Journal of African Historical Studies* 7, no. 3 (1974): 417–426.

[5]   MacGaffey, "Oral Tradition," 423.

the metaphoric death of the initiate and her rebirth as a potential mother.[6] One Lamba song common at female initiation, which reflects metaphorical death and rebirth in a new form, exclaims *"Wayina-kamwale, inogo yalala, inogo yalala Ngailale! Nakawumba Siimbi! Ukuwumba temilimo!"*[7] which translates to "Oh mother of the *kam-wale*, the pot is cracked, the pot is cracked Let it be cracked! I'll mould another! Moulding is not work! The pot is broken." Thus, *-simbi* links the idea of spirits that control the earth, production, weather, and female fertility with a set of ceremonies—female initiation—that are part of the religious and cultural process to prepare a young woman for motherhood and the creation of new members of the lineage.

Social values rooted in ancestors, lineages, and clans are critical elements in understanding social organization and the attendant institutions that characterized how leaders, visionaries, and common people in the earliest Bantu societies shaped and guided their communities. Matrilineages and maternal ancestors were at the core of origins and social organization. The evidence for this proposition arises again and again in oral and linguistic evidence from Bantu speech communities. The strategies that Bantu speakers drew upon were in many historical situations rooted in both of these foundational ideas, which were certainly melded with newly imagined and borrowed concepts of identity and belonging.

The Religious Landscape: Territorial Spirits

Territorial spirits were instrumental in people's lives and worldviews, and yet they were more removed than ancestral spirits from their daily lives. Territorial spirits were often associated with and memorialized at particular locations that people perceived to hold some spiritual connection. These included not all, but certain water sources, mountains, caves, defined paths, or forested locations. Although territorial spirits were associated with particular landscapes and locations, historian Kodesh has postulated that people found ways to transport these spirits as they

---

[6]   Clement Doke, *The Lambas of Northern Rhodesia: A Study of Their Customs and Beliefs* (London: G. Harrap & Company, 1931), 150; Hugo Hinfelaar, *Bemba-Speaking Women of Zambia in a Century of Religious Change 1892–1992* (Leiden: E. J. Brill, 1994).

[7]   In this song, *siimbi* is a pronoun for 'others' it is not the same *-simbi.*

moved.[8] The comparative ethnography on territorial spirits shows that they had personalities or qualities. Some were temperamental, whereas others were balanced. They could be mischievous, jealous, cunning, friendly, happy, and generous. People paid respect to territorial spirits through seasonal pilgrimages to shrines. The living made offerings and sought additional guidance or assurance of security from them in times of crisis. They sought consent and blessings from territorial spirits when they pursued risky endeavors or to ensure good fortune.

Bantu speakers had dynamic relationships with territorial spirits, which shifted as social contexts changed. Territorial spirits were not bound to lineages and could even be ancestors of unrelated communities. The Bantu expansions meant that people speaking Bantu languages moved across territories and encountered non-Bantu speakers or even Bantu speakers who had settled in an area earlier. Scholars refer to those predecessors on the land as *autochthonous* or *firstcomer* populations. They too influenced the arriving Bantu speakers. It appears that Bantu speakers who encountered previously settled populations in a given territory believed it was essential to incorporate their predecessors into their spiritual narratives.

An example of Bantu adaptation of Batwa concepts is found in Bantu uses of schematic rock art. In eastern and central Africa, some of this art was created as early as eight thousand years ago, well before Bantu speakers came into this region. People produced rock art in concealed spaces of caves, overhangs, and crevices. Ethnoarcheologists Benjamin Smith and Catherine Namono, working respectively in Zambia and Uganda, argue that gathering and hunting inhabitants, ancestors to the modern Batwa, are the most likely creators of these geometric symbols.[9] Though the artwork chronicles spiritual practices and events, the precise beliefs underlying them remain uncertain. This very early rock art is similar to designs Batwa made in the rainforests of Gabon and the northwestern DRC, and it serves as an archive of multiple layers of history.[10]

---

[8] Neil Kodesh, "History from the Healer's Shrine: Genre, Historical Imagination, and Early Ganda History," *Comparative Studies in Society and History* 49, no. 3 (July 2007): 527–552.

[9] Catherine Namono, "Resolving the Authorship of Geometric Rock Art of Uganda," *Journal of African Archaeology* 8, no. 2 (2010): 253–254; Benjamin Smith, *Zambia's Ancient Rock Art: The Paintings of Kasama* (Livingstone, Zambia: National Heritage Conservation Commission, 1997).

[10] Smith, *Zambia's Ancient Rock*, 23.

As Bantu speakers ventured into east, central, and southern Africa as early as three thousand years ago (early fourth phase), they encountered reddish rock paintings facing south and southwest. Hundreds and sometimes thousands of years earlier, artists and spiritual professionals had painted and etched images into rock surfaces. Although previously arrived populations like the Batwa likely produced these spiritual and religious archives, newly arrived Bantu speakers incorporated such sites into their own traditions and beliefs. Bantu speakers included symbols that predecessor populations produced into their own spiritual practices because of beliefs in belonging, territorial spirits, and ancestors; they needed Batwa ancestral and territorial spirit approval in order to belong in and be productive on land previously occupied and used by other peoples.

In both Uganda and Tanzania, Bantu speakers in recent centuries communicated with important ancestor and territorial spirits for assistance with weather, agricultural productivity, and human fertility at sites decorated with Batwa rock art. In eastern Uganda at Nyero, Bantu established large shrines named *nyumba ya misambwa*— house of spirits—near early red rock art images because they were active sites for spirits.[11] At Nyero, individuals continue to crawl into crevices covered with red schematic art to be as close as possible to powerful ancient ancestors represented by the paintings. These actions and rituals aim especially at increasing reproductive fertility. Likewise, oral traditions recount stories of ancestral rain experts buried near these shrines. This is precisely where, in recent history, local Bantu speech communities held rain control ceremonies.

Further south, in Zambia and Malawi, Bantu uses of ancient schematic rock paintings suggest links with firstcomer Batwa and with Bantu female initiation ceremonies. Sabi Bantu speakers have reproduced Batwa schematic symbols in wall and floor art and ceramic items created for female initiation. Scholars have identified over eighty-six symbols that elders of the twentieth and twenty-first centuries used as mnemonic devices in *chisungu*, ceremonies to initiate and educate young Sabi women.[12] The open concentric circles similar to those found in the rock art are painted on the walls of female initiation houses. In *chisungu* female initiation ceremonies, Bemba Sabi

---

[11] Namono, "Resolving the Authorship," 253–254.

[12] Audrey Richards, *Chisungu: A Girl's Initiation Ceremony among the Bemba of Northern Rhodesia* (London: Tavistock, 1982), 104.

women draw a three-dimensional ceramic concentric open circle inspired by Batwa rock art, integrating it as a ceremonial diagram for education.[13] They draw the same circular symbol on the floor in grain to symbolize agricultural and human fecundity.[14] Young women must move gracefully over the floor without disturbing the drawings during the initiation. At the end of the ceremony elders leading the rite shoot an arrow through a spiraled circle image on the wall. Bemba people have adopted these symbols into *chisungu* rituals and use them to bolster female reproductive knowledge and potential fertility.

In Luapula Province of Zambia, where there are at least a dozen Sabi Bantu speech communities, the oral traditions reveal the deeper significance of this link. One tradition recounts that immigrating Bantu groups accidently killed all but two Batwa when they lit a fire on an island in Lake Mweru. This is likely a reference to the need to integrate Bantu *citemene* agricultural practices with Batwa gathering and hunting economies. The two surviving Batwa demanded restitution from the Bantu people. This restitution required the Bantu to bury the dead and to maintain all Batwa customs and rituals, including rain prayers. The Bantu agreed and hence the common theme of Batwa spiritual presence in Bantu practices.[15] A second version of the oral tradition ends with the Bantu and surviving Batwa discovering that they were from the same clan as the Batwa, thus making the two kin with common ancestors and a shared history.[16]

The rock art, the ethnographic studies, and the oral traditions together show that, in East and Central Africa, Bantu speech communities acknowledged spiritual contributions of predecessor populations to their own societies. And this appears to be a much more general historical phenomenon. In West Central Africa, collected oral traditions

---

[13] Frans E. Prins and Sian Hall, "Expressions of Fertility in the Rock Art of Bantu-Speaking Agriculturists," *The African Archaeological Review* 12 (1994): 187.

[14] Richards (1982), 104.

[15] Ian Cunnison, *The Luapula Peoples of Northern Rhodesia: Custom and History in Tribal Politics* (Manchester, UK: Manchester University Press for the Rhodes-Livingstone Institute, Northern Rhodesia, 1959), 35.

[16] Ian Cunnison, "Perpetual Kinship: A Political Institution of the Luapula People," *Rhodes-Livingstone Journal* 20 (1956): 30–35; Saidi observed and videotaped two BaShila women drawing the initiation paintings on a wall of their home in the small town of Nchelenge on Lake Mweru in the Luapula Valley, August 1998.

show that Bantu speakers consistently considered the Batwa to be originators of ancestors and fertility ceremonies.[17] Whether their motivations were Batwa closeness to spirits, Bantu responsibility toward Batwa, or their desire to create belonging through common ancestry, Bantu speech communities adopted Batwa spiritual traditions and incorporated Batwa territorial spirits into their own cosmology.

In recent history, Bantu women initiation experts in Malawi and Zambia have drawn similar designs on walls of initiation houses, rock overhangs, and caves using them as mnemonic devices for teaching young women their history, their spiritual lessons, and practical life lessons. Caves and overhangs have often been sites where territorial spirits are located. The missionary and colonial anthropologists in the early twentieth century observed that the presence of Batwa people was required to bring power to these Bantu spiritual ceremonies. The power dynamics between Bantu and Batwa were contested, but according to Bantu oral traditions, they relied on the Batwa. This resulted in the development of diverse oral traditions that invoke the memory of varied ancestral and territorial spirits. The specific terms for particular spirits have shifted over time, yet it is clear that they impacted living people's actions, experiences, and understandings across the breadth of Bantu history and geography.

Origins of the Universe: The Creator

Lineages were the realm of humans, but the universe and humanity were, in the early Bantu worldview, the realm created by *Nyambe* (see Table 2.1). Through the use of historical linguistics, scholars understand that *Nyambe* is the root that proto-Bantu speakers used, as far back as the first phase of the Bantu expansions, around 3500 BCE, to name the Creator that began the cosmos. The etymology of *Nyambe* derives from an even older Niger-Congo verb root with the meaning "to begin," which dates back to at least around 5000 BCE. This meaning derivation encapsulates the proto-Bantu conception of *Nyambe* as the force responsible for generating the cosmos. In essence, *Nyambe* was conceptualized as a distant Creator, but unlike the Abrahamic creator, *Nyambe* did not require human attention or supplication. In the Bantu communities in the areas of earliest Bantu expansions, all through the western equatorial

---

[17] Kairn Klieman, *"The Pygmies Were Our Compass": Bantu and Batwa in the History of West Central Africa, Early Times to c. 1900 C.E.* (Portsmouth, N.H.: Heinemann, 2003), 162.

rainforest and in western Central Africa, most Bantu societies continue to use *Nyambe* for Creator. During the past three thousand years, among the Bantu societies that spread farther east in east central and eastern and southern Africa, the belief in an original Creator persisted, but new names and new conceptions of the Creator emerged.

Three examples of people reconceiving the Creator occurred during the fourth and fifth phases of the Bantu expansions. Around 500 BCE, some Kaskazi-speaking people innovated the word *Mu-lungu* to name the Creator. They reimagined the Creator as the one who arranged and put in order the cosmos, creating a new word *Mu-lungu* for the Creator God from the old Bantu verb *-lung-* (see Table 2.1) meaning "to become fitting, become straight."[18] Shortly thereafter, between 400 and 300 BCE, several early peoples of the Kaskazi branch of Mashariki Bantu speakers began applying a proto-Bantu word for the sun, *li-uba* (see Table 2.1), to the Creator. This development reflects the influence from nearby Southern Nilotic and Southern Cushitic people, who as result of a common history of interactions around 1000 BCE, before the arrival of the Bantu, had come to share the idea of a divine power associated with the sun. A millennium later around 500 CE in East-Central Africa, Sabi-descended Bantu peoples applied a proto-Bantu root "to bear, take care of (child)" to name the Creator, *Leza*. Chapter 1 recounts a detailed explanation of the linguistic origins of *Leza*. The term reflected a modified conceptualization of a more personal and nurturing relationship with God.

Although linguistic evidence across five thousand years of Bantu history supports the idea that a distant monotheistic Creator existed in the early Bantu worldview, the shift in terms shows that people continued to rethink their notion of a Creator. The history of ancestors and territorial spirits exemplifies the importance of not only the abstract Creator but also relationships that connected the spiritual/ethereal and human/temporal realms.

Calamity in the World: Evil, Jealousy, and Ill Will

Bantu peoples' worldviews also framed the ways they comprehended the logic or etiology of the range of undesirable, adverse, deleterious, auspicious, and promising situations in life and history. Although misfortune

---

[18] Christopher Ehret, *An African Classical Age: Eastern and Southern Africa in World History 1000 BC to AD 400* (Charlottesville: University of Virginia Press, 1998), 166–167.

is universal to the human experience, in the early Bantu worldview, the Creator was not blamed for evil or misfortune; rather, misfortune could result from malcontent spirits or malicious living people. The malevolence of spirits was one way that Bantu-speaking people made sense of and explained calamity and its solutions. Bantu speakers might explain mishaps in life and disastrous community events as the result of people and communities having neglected ancestral and territorial spirits. To neglect those responsibilities invited calamity, disease, hardships, or other such crises. Despite these potential perils, people in fact had great agency in keeping ancestral and territorial spirits supplicated.

A second source of misfortune and evil was associated with living people, over whom one had much less control. Bantu-speaking people viewed malicious individuals as more significant day-to-day threats than the wrath of discontented spirits. Malice originating from jealous, disgruntled, or malevolent living individuals had effects that were unpredictable, numerous, and not easily known. The proto-Bantu society of the mid-fourth millennium BCE named intentional human malice or evil by the term *bu-logi* (see Table 2.1), commonly translated into English as "witchcraft." This fundamental idea derives from the proto-Bantu verb root, *-log-*, meaning "to bewitch."

This five-thousand-year-old concept has widespread attestation across Bantu-speaking Africa. What is more is that the efforts made to stave off or protect from intentional malice is equally ancient. Proto-Bantu society had professional religio-medicinal healers, the *-ganga* (see Table 2.1). This skilled practitioner diagnosed, treated, and even prevented individuals from falling under harmful spells. Since most cases of witchcraft involved envious individuals, to guard against jealousy people tended to redistribute resources they accumulated rather than amassing wealth. People perceived greediness as antisocial behavior, whereas they valued generosity. Greedy individuals by their behaviors invited jealousy and evil. This belief impelled people to redistribute goods. These dynamics supported heterarchical authority, and they also worked toward ensuring good relationships and guarding against antisocial behaviors from jealous neighbors and relatives.

BELONGING: LINEAGE, CLANS, AND AFFINES

If Bantu-speaking communities and individuals have seen family, lineages, and clans as central to their existence, then it is essential for us to make clear sense of these elements. How the early Bantu imagined their place and role in the world historically was shaped by these interlocking concepts. Bantu speakers, in various historical contexts, have verbally, culturally, and intellectually expressed the paramount importance of belonging. Ancient Bantu speech communities, perhaps much like other peoples of their era, assumed that this norm helped to ensure one's security in an uncertain world. Belonging, not independence, was the norm expected of community members. The necessity of belonging manifested itself in how various Bantu societies organized spiritually, economically, and politically around lineages; created a sense of identity; and organized village communities. Individuals continued over a lifetime to be integrated into a community through specific actions and initiation ceremonies based on their life stage.

Linguistic evidence shows that there was a proto-Bantu word for lineage as early as 3500 BCE. Comparative ethnography, oral tradition, linguistics, and even genetic data help to fill in the finer details and nuances of lineal history. Evidence on lineage from the annals of Bantu speech communities suggests that the extended family comprised of blood relatives and *affines* was normative social practice. What is illuminating is the fact that the earliest Bantu found matrilineal descent, rather than patrilineal or bilateral patrilineal as most beneficial to their lives. Individuals organized their world and conceived survival strategies within the social context of lineage relations. Lineage membership determined how one gained access to identity, rights, and materials.

There were several ways that belonging to a lineage played out. One could be born into a lineage and to a larger clan of related lineages that included living people, those not yet born, and ancestors, all of whom aligned with a maternal or paternal line. A group of lineages that have an agreed-upon common ancestor constitute a clan, which was and often still is the largest social organization within most Bantu communities. Adoption, marriage, and initiation were alternative ways one could become part of a lineage and clan. This helped to ensure belonging.

This relationship was so critical that many contingencies were made to ensure people belonged to a lineage. This state of being provided collective security and guarded against vulnerability that was associated with being kinless. Belonging was not merely about structure; it was also a philosophical principle, the spirit of which is captured in many Bantu languages through proverbs, sayings, and oral traditions. It is critical to wrestle with the meaning of lineage from proto-Bantu times through the various phases of expansion precisely because it was something more than biological family. In fact, it went beyond even the social construction of family. It also encompassed the ideology of belonging physically, spiritually, and conceptually. To understand this helps us to better understand the history of Bantu peoples.

Matrilineages

Over the *longue durée* of Bantu history, there are examples of societies that have been patrilineal and others that have been matrilineal. Comparative ethnography and language reconstruction reveal that most Bantu speech communities determined identity and inheritance through only one parent's lineage—they were *unilineal*. This way of determining inheritance and identity through a single lineage does not obviate the fact that individuals maintained relationships with members of both their maternal and paternal lineages. Today there are hundreds of Bantu-speaking societies that are considered matrilineal. The fact that they are matrilineal means that one's identity and access to resources were gained through one's mother's lineage. The largest cluster of regionally adjacent matrilineal societies in the world stretches from Angola through Central Africa to Tanzania and Mozambique in the east. But what is the history of the matrilineages? How far back in time does this form of lineage reckoning go as a societal principle? A well-debated subject within research on Bantu history is whether proto-Bantu speakers were matrilineal or patrilineal from earliest times in their social organization.

As already considered above, the history of *-kódò*, a proto-Bantu root, indicates that the original ancestor, the founder of a lineage, was metaphorically a common grandparent from which a group descended. The accumulation of linguistic data furnishes compelling evidence that matrilineality was well established in Bantu culture already by the proto-Bantu period of the fourth millennium BCE. What the proto-Bantu word for such a matrilineage might have been is as yet unknown. . We do have some idea of what the early Bantu communities called this institution during the second phase of Bantu expansions in the period 3000–2000 BCE. Two ancient Bantu words that specifically meant "matrilineage" go back to that period and will be discussed below.

The earliest term yet traceable in Bantu for matrilineages is *-cuka* (see Table 2.1). It occurs in widely spread languages whose earliest ancestral speakers diverged from each other during the second phase. The word specifically means "matrilineage" among the Wumbu of Gabon; among the Mongo, Tetela, and Bushongo in the central DRC; and among the Lega of Savanna Bantu branch who live in the more eastern part of the country. And far away to the south and east, in the Mashariki Bantu languages of Nyakyusa and Ngonde of southern Tanzania and northern Malawi, the word occurs also. In these latter languages the word has come to be applied to the lineage ancestor spirits rather than to the lineage as a whole. Bantu speech communities, it seems clear, found matrilineal systems to be beneficial and generated ways to make the concept and institution work even as their landscapes and circumstances shifted.[19]

Interestingly, the derivation of *-cuka* opens up avenues for beginning to understand the intellectual associations people made regarding matrilineages. This root word also has the concrete tangible, and probably original, meaning of "termite hill." Termite hills were believed to be stores of various powers related to fertility, ancestors, and iron. Their striking physical form, as they rise up from the earth as large gnarled mounds often several meters high and a meter wide, make termite hills visible across the landscape. They became locations where many Bantu communities honored and communicate with territorial spirits. Klieman demonstrates that Batwa populations saw termite hills as important sites for spirits as well. Bantu speakers may have incorporated termite hills as sites for territorial spirits through their interactions with Batwa. Moving into territory that firstcomer populations inhabited, they recognized a need to honor the ancestors of those communities. With a strong belief in the importance of belonging, the Bantu speakers often appropriated Batwa beliefs and histories into their own systems and oral traditions. The act of adopting Batwa ideas, practices, and at times people into their communities was an effort on the part of Bantu to legitimate their taking up of a new territory and to turn themselves into indigenous inhabitants.[20]

---

[19] Per Hage and Jeff Marck, "Proto-Bantu Descent Groups," in Doug Jones and Bojka Milicic (eds.), *Kinship, Language and Prehistory: Per Hage and the Renaissance in Kinship Studies* (Salt Lake City: The University of Utah Press, 2011), 75–78.

[20] Klieman, 69–71.

Termite hills also serve as an important trope in origin myths and oral traditions of many Bantu-speaking communities. An oral tradition of the Mongo recounts the original female progenitor emerging from a termite hill. This tradition is dually valuable as a historical source because it directly connects the concept of termite hills and matrilineages. In thinking about how termite hills became affiliated with matrilineages, it is important to consider both the association of *-dImu* (see Table 2.1) with outcrops on the landscape but also the practical uses of termite hills. Comparative ethnographic study of Bantu speech communities indicates that while still inhabited, the builders of termite hills were a source of protein for people as termites are edible, nourishing, and flavorful. Women often used abandoned termite hills much like a hearth to cook food. The large structures termites engineered also served as models for iron and pottery kilns, which became important economic and social activities in some communities. Matrilineages included the living and the dead, and thus they included, in people's conceptions, the ancestral spirits who might be affiliated with hearths constructed on termite hills. Termite hills were also affiliated with territorial spirits that had to be honored for the protection of the matrilineages.

A second term for matrilineage, *-gàndá*, dates to the later second phase of Bantu expansions.[21] The etymology of *-gàndá*, attests today in Bantu languages from the forested regions of Gabon south to Namibia and northeast to the Great Lakes, shows that this root word originally referred to a place of settlement of a community. Because the core population of an early Bantu settlement—either a village or a ward of a village—all belonged to a particular matrilineage, the word came soon to be applied to the kin group, the matrilineage, who lived in the village or ward. Klieman places the development of this meaning for *-gàndá* during what she has referred to as the Sangha-Kwa period, in other words, in the later second phase of early Bantu expansions.[22]

About 2000 BCE (third phase), as people moved into east central and eastern Africa, they often continued to apply the root *-gàndá* as a word for the "new settlement" where their matrilineages would

---

[21] Ehret *African Classical Age*, 151–155; Klieman, *"The Pygmies,"* 69–70; David L. Schoenbrun, *The Historical Reconstruction of Great Lakes Bantu Cultural Vocabulary* (Köln: Rüdiger), 1997, 80–81; Vansina, *Paths*, 269.

[22] Klieman, *"The Pygmies,"* 69–71, 90 fn. 12, based on evidence from Bongili, Gikuyu, Rundi, Ruguru, Bemba, Ila, and Nsenga.

reside. This additional meaning, "settlement," linked the older concept of matrilineages with a new place migrants settled, showing importantly that Bantu communities, as they became more numerous and dispersed, continued to value belonging to one's clan or lineage as socially critical even in a new context.[23] Sabi speakers around two thousand years ago began to apply *-ganda* (see Table 2.1) to the space in which women typically and even predominately cooked and maintained the household alters, but with the specific connotation of a hearth or an altar for ancestors honored within the home. The fact that Sabi speakers applied an old root for matrilineages to the space in which women performed certain ritual responsibilities reflects the continued intersection between matrilineages and ancestors.

In more recent history around Lake Nyanza (also known as Victoria), *-ganda* was conceptualized in a different way—as patriclan. This shift occurred in an era when patriclans had begun to eclipse matriclans. This development may date in some areas to as late as around six hundred to eight hundred years ago during a period of social consolidation and political centralization in the African Great Lakes region.

The use of *-gàndá* to also mean "patriclan" in this part of East Africa as well as in a limited number of languages in the western equatorial forest might raise questions about its original meaning. The answer can be found by examining how the Herero, a cattle-keeping people of Namibia, use *-gàndá*. The Herero are unique in the Bantu world because they have dual descent, which means they recognize patrilineage relationships for the inheritance of political office, and matrilineage relationships for the inheritance of cattle. They apply the root *-gàndá* specifically and only to matrilineages. The evidence from the Herero coupled with the continued use over a broad geographic area of *-gàndá* to represent matrilineage indicates that the use of *- gàndá* as a term for patrilineage in the Great Lakes region arose in more recent periods as a response to social, economic, and political changes.

In addition to linguistic evidence, ethnographies from the last one hundred years and oral traditions, along with genetic studies, inform us about how the presence and the social ideas of matrilineage have affected history over broad geographic areas in both ancient and more recent centuries. These kinds of evidence

---

[23] Vansina, *Paths*, 268–269.

provide clues about how people reinterpreted these ideas and practices in changing historical and geographic contexts, and reveal something of the diversity of ways they have played out in family, community, and places of belonging across time. Examining the semantic history of terms exemplifies the value of a multidisciplinary method. The etymologies of *-cuka* and *-gàndá* help us reconstruct the conceptual ideas associated with matrilineal descent, whereas the ethnographic and oral data help us to situate the concrete application of the terms.

Matrilineages were centered on mothers and grandmothers, the very individuals who in these societies controlled food production and the hearth where food was prepared and where ancestral spirits were often honored within families. Iron smelters often reemployed old termite hills in Central and East Africa. Iron smelting was, based on all evidence in comparative ethnography and linguistic evidence, a male activity. Iron smelting is significant to understanding the original meaning of *-cuka*. Abandoned termite hills often were the sites for the creation of iron kilns, which when in the smelting process were likened to a woman giving birth (this will be discussed in greater detail in chapter 4). Thus, this Bantu root, reconstructed back to four thousand years ago, links matrilineages, the original ancestor, key female activities, and the male production of iron through the metaphor of birth or female reproduction.

The wide geographic distribution of both *-gàndá* and *-cuka* implies a deep time depth for matriclans within Bantu Africa. Supplementary evidence supporting the theory that Bantu-speaking people were from the beginning matrilineal is found beyond language and oral accounts in genetic studies. Studies by several geneticists look to two kinds of data revealed in DNA. The first piece of evidence on matrilineal organizing comes from the Y chromosome, which passes from fathers to male children and is not recombined with the mother's genes. The second comes from mitochondrial DNA (mtDNA), which passes from mother to both male and female children and can be used to trace migrations of people. As mtDNA is passed down, minute mutations occur, and if these mutations persist, they become genetic markers that help distinguish one maternal line from another. Recent studies of both fathers' and mothers' mtDNA among Bantu speakers have shown that the fathers' lines have a great deal of diversity, whereas the mothers' lines show much less diversity. A conclusion reached by some historians and geneticists is that in early Bantu societies the mother's DNA is less diverse because females remained in communities with their families while males moved away and married outside of the community.[24] This kind of out-marrying of men fits with the kinship patterns that we find today most closely associated with matrilineality and matrifocal settlement.

Though it is difficult to imagine the kinds of historical impacts that matrilineal compared to patrilineal reckoning might have, specific examples reveal that in fact there were some significant distinctions. For example, the metaphor of unity in one womb encouraged some social equity. In more recent history, Chewa (Kusi/Mashariki) had primarily male rulers, but the nomination and selection of a new ruler were in the hands of a group of female elders. This is in contrast to many patrilineal societies. In those societies the frequent trend has been toward accumulation of wealth by key patrilineages, political centralization, and limitations placed on women's access to authority. Historical evidence from language data layered with ethnography and oral traditions accords well indeed with the conclusion that early Bantu-speaking societies were matrilineal. Elders of the matrilineages, who made many of the major decisions at both the lineage and community level, set the agenda regarding social norms but also created separate and complementary centers of authority for men and women.

Recurrently in social history, matrilineage-based societies have tended to be politically decentralized, and even when organized into kingdoms, their political and social structures give prominent place to women. Members often redistributed resources rather than accumulating them individually. Women very often stayed with their own lineage at least for the first part of a marriage, which gave them a support base and opportunities to develop their authority. Over time, specialized language emerged to distinguish a woman before motherhood, during motherhood, and as a mother-in-law. Adult women maintained their authority through practices of labor control and social rules regulating the reproduction of new lineage members. Combining linguistic data and more recent written documents, scholars have come to better understand how matrilineages shaped societies historically among some Bantu speakers.

---

[24] Sen li, Carina Schlebusch, and Mattias Jakobsson, "Genetic Variation Reveals Large-Scale Population Expansion and Migration During the Expansion of Bantu-Speaking Peoples," *Proceedings of the Royal Society* 10 (September 2014).

Patrilineages

During the Savanna Bantu period (fourth phase), Bantu societies ancestral to those who would begin moving into eastern and southern Africa after 1000 BCE created a new term specifically connoting a patrilineage, a form of social organization and belonging not attested earlier in Bantu history. Readers might wonder what historical processes gave rise to this type of change. That is to ask, why would communities who were for generations predominantly matrilineal innovate a new way of reckoning their identities and relationships? The examination of a few societies sheds light on four plausible reasons that could have inspired this transformation. Among the possible sources of this kind of development were (1) the moving of previously matrilineal communities into new areas where they entered into sustained relationships and intermingling with patrilineal neighbors; (2) the development in the society of more hierarchical power relations, in which men took the lead; (3) movement into new lands in which groups of men were the prime movers and instigators of resettlement; or (4) the rise in importance of economic sectors, such as cattle raising, in which male ownership or men's activities predominated.

Where Bantu speakers built patrilineal societies historically and even where they persist today, it is nevertheless still common to find enduring matrilineal worldviews, ideas, and practices that became essential to patrilineal success. Those ideas and practices often pertained to accessing the maternal-lineal power of ancestral and territorial spirits, who continued to be sources of potential security for patrilineages. Matrilineal and patrilineal forms of organizing were not necessarily diametrically opposed. Most often when a patrilineal form of organizing predominated, matrilineal legacies still permeated the ways that kin relations played out and were vital to their success, notably in the widespread maintenance of the principles of belonging and heterarchy. In addition, the principle of firstcomer precedence continued over the *longue durée* to guide patrilineal perceptions of belonging and legitimacy.

Turning to the linguistic evidence, in the Savanna Bantu period (third phase) Bantu speakers innovated *-lòngò* to name a patrilineage. Its meaning can be glossed as "generations belonging to a sequence' or 'connected lines of partrilineal descendants." This new meaning repurposes a proto-Bantu-era noun root, *-lòngò* (see Table 2.1), "a line of objects." The line of items in this case was the line of descent, the sequence of ancestors leading down from the founding ancestor down to the paternally related descendants who formed the *-lòngò.[25] In this nascent phase, no evidence suggests that the word named any wider group than a lineage. What it does suggest is an increased emphasis on identifying one's paternal belonging, a relationship that early Bantu-speaking people may have acknowledged in only informal ways. It also brings attention to the way that historians can track back through word histories the various layers of historical change, including in this case clues about the Bantu matrilineal past and about when patrilineal descent first began to be formally recognized.

A question researchers can ask is, why did this new term of belonging, *-lòngò emerge around three thousand years ago. We know that patrilineages were not at this time prevalent among Bantu speaking societies. Furthermore this was before the era of widespread hierarchical political formations in these regions, and it was not a time affected by major new economic factors, such as the adoption of cattle. A possible explanation, but still a speculative one, is that men may have taken the lead in the movements of Bantu into many new places across the southern savanna belt during this period and that patrilineages may have fostered male cooperation in settling new areas, even though the societies they belonged to, once established in the new lands, continued to be primarily matrilineal.

Over the past two thousand years, the other three factors leading toward patrilineage have become the most prominent. For example, the numerous Bantu-speaking Gogo people, who live in modern-day Tanzania, about 450 km inland from Dar es Salaam, began to emerged as a distinct speech community between about 1200 and 1400 CE. They were linguistic descendants of the matrilineal proto-North-East Coastal Bantu, who first reached the central coast of Tanzania about 400 CE. Gogo history provides an example of a historical shift that likely resulted from cross-ethnic intermingling, including marriage. In the last eight hundred years, people speaking earlier forms of the Gogo language began moving from predominantly matrilineal social organizing to a patrilineal practice. At the base of these changes were

---

[25] Ehret, *Classical Age*, 149; Rhonda M. Gonzales, *Societies, Religion, and History: Central East Tanzanian's and the World They Created, 200 BCE–1800 CE* (New York: Columbia University Press, 2008), chap. 3, para. 40–41 <http://www.gutenberg-e. org/gonzales/>.

Gogo long-term interactions with cattle-keeping, patrilineal peoples, such as the Parakuyu Maasai, Southern Cushitic Kw'adza, and the Njombe. Today a large number of the Gogo clans remember in their oral traditions their Njombe and Kw'adza ancestries. These multiple cross-cultural interactions have resulted in a Gogo-speaking society whose culture had blended together economic practices, food taboos, and other cultural elements from those neighbors. Over time, Gogo relationships with Parakuyu, Kw'adza, and Njombe brought about a societal transformation in which patrilineal social organization displaced matrilineality. This shift did not require the invention of patrilineages. Rather, the *-lòngò, which had been a way of naming a paternal line since the Savanna-Bantu period, was elevated in status in Gogo society. Intermarriage was the likely way this shift occurred.

It is noteworthy that although the Gogo remain patrilineal, there are, even today, distinct ways in which they continue to ensure their lineal security through Bantu-rooted matrilineal precepts and practices. The matrilineal worldview legacy in Gogo society shows that although Gogo women living in patrilineal societies birthed children who belonged to a patrilineage, a mother's success hinged on following matrilineal-rooted maternal practices. When it was time for a Gogo young woman to begin transitioning toward anticipated motherhood, her living maternal lineage elders guided her. Her education included communing with her maternal ancestors to convince them of her readiness for motherhood.

Yet she also was also circumcised, which had not been a practice in early Bantu tradition. It was a custom, on the other hand, among the Kw'adza and the Parakuyu. In the twentieth century, some Gogo described female circumcisions as less invasive than Parakuyu circumcision, as they cut to only draw blood that falls to the sand. A young woman's matrilineal elders used this blood during initiation education that readied her for motherhood. In contrast, Parakuyu historically performed complete clitoridectomies. Gogo oral tradition is emphatic that female circumcision is a relatively new, yet an essential practice, one that their original ancestors had not done. These historical processes and perceptible layers of Gogo history bolster the point that belonging mattered to such a degree that Bantu-descended people were willing to incorporate both salient cultural practices from influential patrilineal neighbors. Furthermore, their history underscores the fact that even within a patrilineal society, authority of maternal ancestors and living lineage members persisted in preparing a woman to reproduce children for the patrilineage, suggesting again the heterarchical nature of power. Gogo-speech communities understood that they could not wholesale abandon their spiritual maternal obligations as they aimed to legitimize their existence with their antecedents and secure longevity in changing historical contexts.

Gogo people believed in and venerated a complex of territorial spirits called *milungu*. This practice calls attention to their incorporation of firstcomer spirits that predated their arrival in the region. From the thirteenth century, and even as they began shifting over to patrilineal descent, Gogo emphasized the critical importance of pleasing such spirits to secure societal well-being. Although Gogo use the older Bantu word, *-lungu*, for the Creator God like the majority of Bantu speakers in East Africa have done for over three thousand years, they also innovated a new use of the root by pluralizing it, *milungu*, to name these spirits. Thus, the pluralization of the root for God suggests that Gogo viewed the territorial spirits as related to the spiritual dimension of the Creator, rather than to the spiritual realm of the ancestors of the lineage and clan. As for many other Bantu-speaking peoples, Gogo sought to insure their security via an ancient Bantu principle that required the veneration of territorial spirits that inhabited the land before they had .[26]

Further west in Zambia, the Bantu-speaking Ila developed a mixed agricultural economy in which cattle keeping was very important. In contrast to the Gogo, the Ila remained matrilineal. The

---

[26] Gonzales, *Societies*, chap. 5, para. 26–28 and fn. 47. For accounts of the complex nature of the *-lungu* spirit, the way it was revered and feared, and its role in experienced mediumship/possession in the early twentieth century, see Gwassa, "Kinjikitile and the Ideology of Maji Maji," 204–207. See also, Alpers, "Towards a History of the Expansion of Islam in East Africa," 173–175. The complexity of the *-lungu* spirit as mentioned in various twentieth-century accounts paints a fairly complicated picture of its nature and impact on communities of living people. Among some communities in recent times, it was broadly conceptualized as the land where the dead dwelled. There was no indication, however, that they thought of *-lungu* as ancestors of the *-zimu* sort. The understood distance between *-lungu* spirits and living people suggests that these spirits continued to be connected to land and untamed space, retaining what we suspect is the way they were conceptualized in the earliest communities that recognized them. In recent accounts, too, there remains a sort of reverence based in uncertainty of the unpredictability of *-lungu* that also reminds us of their having retained a quality of potential ill will that could lead to suffering among people.

reason that addressing this point matters is that an entrenched bias of the Western historical tradition has been to frame societies in which cattle were domesticated and important to economies as being more developed or advanced than those whose economies were primarily plant-based farming or fishing. Such societies were lauded for their increased political centralization and patrilineal reckoning, and these cultural features were taken as signs of progress. In line with such ethnocentric ideas, historians and anthropologists have tended to assume that societies who adopted cattle as their primary indicator of wealth and transitioned to patrilineality would develop hierarchical social and political stratification, and thus be more "advanced." Along with patrilineage came patrilocal living customs, in which a woman moved to her husband's community, the antithesis of matrilineal uxorilocal traditions by which a man moved to his wife's community.

The Ila of Zambia are an example of a mixed-agricultural society that came to reckon lineal belonging in ways that elevated the status of a father's lineage but did not transition to patrilineality. Early twentieth-century European missionaries often misinterpreted this point. From 1902 through 1904, the British missionaries Smith and Dale recorded important details about Ila lineage systems, but the presumptions they brought to their studies skewed their analyses. They declared, "The father rules in the family, though his power over it is conditioned by the presence of clan rules, among which is the rule giving the mother's brother greater power than his over the children." Here they are invoking assumptions about a Western, nuclear family ideal in which a father "ruled." But their own words belie this, highlighting that the matrilineage, which they attribute to the mother's brother, held actual authority over the children. The children belonged to the matrilineage via "clan rules."

These British missionaries continued to note that "A gulf separates a man from his children for although they are his and in case of divorce remain with him, yet they are reckoned as members not of his [the father's] but their mother's clan, and he has less power over them [the children] than their maternal uncles."[27] Again, in this passage, and indeed throughout the ethnology, the father's patrilineage, what they call family, is of secondary authority to a mother and her children's matrilineal line. The Ila organized in matriclans to which a wife and her children continue to belong. What Smith and Dale did

---

[27] Edwin William Smith and Andrew Murray Dale, *The Ila-Speaking Peoples of Northern Rhodesia* (London: Macmillan, 1920), 283–287.

not recognize is the clear heterarchical relationship among the paternal lineages and maternal clans. Their lapse reflects their own origins in a society steeped in male-centered hierarchy.[28]

The notion that history is linear, moving toward an evolved form that resembles Eurocentric norms, led other twentieth-century anthropologists to theorize, and some historians to fall into the same trap, that matrilineal societies inevitably evolve toward patrilineality over time. Yet recent history shows that even patrilineal Bantu communities can become matrilineal. And this shift could have been possible in earlier Bantu eras as well. Such an example is found among the originally patrilineal Ngoni, whose earlier homeland in the 1820s was located along the Indian Ocean coast of far southeastern Africa. About 195 years ago, due to economic pressures and political uprisings in the region, some patrilineal Ngoni fled northward. Their peregrinations as refugees took them into areas with matrilineal societies in eastern Zambia, Mozambique and even Tanzania. Ngoni, who descended from speakers of Nguni languages, arrived in eastern Africa with a formal organization into military units unlike anything the local peoples had seen before. Because of their turbulent history of fighting in southeastern Africa, the immigrants entered these matrilineal societies in a militarized fashion and attempted to impose patrilineal practices on conquered populations. Yet, as historian Cynthia Brantley explains, Ngoni were not successful in transforming the descent systems of the people they conquered. Rather, the Ngoni adapted and became matrilineal, too.[29]

In the early sixteenth century, a similar history unfolded in what is today Luapula Province of Zambia, where the patrilineal, Lunda, moved east with military support from the western DRC, invading the areas around the Luapula River in the eighteenth century to establish the Kazembe Kingdom. The patrilineal Lunda compelled matrilineal Sabi peoples to pay tribute to them in fish, agricultural, and other desired products. Even now, more than 250 years after the founding of the kingdom, only those people who belong to the Lunda ruling elite follow patrilineal descent. Not only have the Sabi inhabitants of the region maintained matrilineal descent, but even some of the ruling Lunda elite have abandoned patrilineal systems

---

[28] Smith and Dala, *Ila-Speaking*, 284.

[29] Cynthia Brantley, "Through Ngoni Eyes: Margaret Read's Matrilineal Interpretations from Nyasaland," *Critique of Anthropology* 17, no. 2 (June 1997): 147–169.

and embraced matrilineal social organizing. The Lunda case high-lights that political dominance, control of lucrative economies, and tributary relationships do not necessitate predominance of patrilineal organizing. Rather, it teaches that two types of social belonging can coexist within a heterarchy.

West-central Africa's Kongo Kingdom provides a different kind of example. There the *kanda*, the old matriclan basis of belonging and access to authority, faced a diminished role in the face of new developments in the sixteenth century. Early in the century, the new *Mani Kongo* Afonso I sought to build a politically more central-ized state. During its most economically and politically influential phase in the sixteenth and early seventeenth centuries, Kongo had extensive relations with Europe and especially the Portuguese, and Catholic Christianity became a prominent and important religion not just among the elites but to some extent in the countryside as well. Originally the hereditary chiefs of the major matrilineal clan chiefdoms, the *kanda*, formed the council of royal advisors known as the *mwissikongo*. From around 1535, as Afonso I began to appoint advisors from his own *kanda* to serve in government, the composi-tion of the *mwissikongo* changed.[30] Additionally, young men were able to use wealth accumulation from commercial activities to wrest some of the power from female and male elders and chiefs. In this context, the authority of both elders and chiefs and their matriclans weakened. By the later sixteenth century, important figures without *kanda* connections came to include Catholic churchmen and impor-tant merchants. Those without *kanda* connections looked instead to patrilineal relations.

Others who sought to use their patrilineal connections were the children of kinless wives.[31] Kinless wives were women who had become separated from their families during slave raids in the sixteenth century. Such women did not have a matriclan to protect them, to procure bride service, or to claim children. Thus, in the midst of a matrilineal society, a large section of influential people reckoned their descent and identity through the father's line.

As surrounding polities eclipsed the Kongo Kingdom in trade during the mid-sixteenth century, the Kongo economy returned to a

---

[30] Anne Hilton, "Family and Kinship South of the Zaire River from the Sixteenth to the Nineteenth Century," *Journal of African History* 24 (1983): 194.

[31] Hilton, "Family," 197.

focus on agriculture over other types of trade, and this development allowed the *kandas* to regain authority, as they controlled access to most land. In addition to changes in the economy, the influence of Christianity began to wane. As a result of these factors, *kanda* authority increased and eventually by the middle of the 1700s the *mwissikongo* again consisted solely of members who reckoned descent matrilinealy.[32] In this 250-year history, the authority of the Kongo matriclans diminished and then rose again, due to changes in economic conditions and religious values. These shifts illustrate both the historical flexibility of kinship and the enduring influence of matrilineal worldviews among Bantu speech communities.

In essence, societies that have a deep matrilineal history have generally continued to have either matrilineal systems or to develop a mix of lineage systems. Even where the balance of authority may have shifted toward men because of economic and political reorganization in more recent centuries, women have tended to maintain strong influence and authority in the social relations of the society. The authority of women and men has not been static regardless of era or form of social organizing. A kind of stratification could exist in matrilineal societies as illustrated in particular by the influence and power of mothers-in-law relative to their sons-in-law. As some communities shifted toward patrilineal organization, new configurations of stratification arose, often with elder men taking on greater power and authority vis-à-vis women and younger males, but still often with mothers-in-law maintaining a degree of authority over sons-in-law and women retaining authority over their daughters and the ceremonies that gave their daughters adult status.

Societies that organize matrilineally conceptualize and honor marriage and motherhood in quite different ways than do patrilineal societies. In patrilineal, patrilocal communities, the typical sanctifier of a marriage was the payment of bride wealth, a set of items transferred from the groom's family to the bride. This payment was meant to compensate for the transference of the woman's work and productivity to the husband's family and to acknowledge the social significance of the children she would bear as members of her husband's patriclan. Typically in Bantu societies that shifted to patriliny, there continued to be female initiation ceremonies, but

---

[32] John Thornton, "Elite Women in the Kingdom of the Kongo: Historical Perspectives on Women's Political Power," *Journal of African History* 47 (2004): 437–460.

no longer a first pregnancy ritual, as in earlier Bantu history. In the patrilineal worldview, marriage became a more important and significant transition. Also, since people in patrilineal societies determined inheritance and identity through the paternal line, they aimed to insure the paternity of children by controlling the sexuality of in-marrying women. In matrilineal societies, there was less need to control female sexuality because a child's identity and inheritance came through the mother's line.

In patrilineal societies with primarily crop-cultivating, as opposed to pastoral or commercial economies, members of a patriclan often managed to gain access to agricultural surpluses. Polygyny, a man's marriage to multiple women, facilitated the production of agricultural surplus for such men. Because more than one wife producing crops could increase the yield for the lineage and clan, this in turn gave men more opportunities for the accumulation of goods and wealth. This kind of amplified production was more complicated to achieve in matrilineal societies.

Though some might assume matriliny and patriliny to be mirror-opposite worldviews, the reality is more complicated. Several anthropologists have noted that divorce for a young woman in patrilineal societies was difficult, because her patrilineage would have to return the bride wealth equivalent. Yet, once she had given birth to several children, a woman could depart without recompense. In the twentieth century, some Agikuyu women of Kenya who were postmenopausal and divorced became well-established, economically independent people in their own right.[33] They could become influential and attain wealth and social status that, within a patrilineal system, gave them the authority otherwise reserved for males. One role such women could take on was the role of *female husbands*. Within Agikuyu patriclans, only fathers could start a lineage. As an adaptation to make the system work for their circumstances, an older, independent woman would pay a bride price for a younger woman and thus become a female husband. Her "wife" took on a male paramour in order to have children. Because the female husband had paid the bride price, all the children were members of the female husband's lineage. In this way, elder women of great wealth were able to start their own patrilineage within a patriclan, demonstrating that lineage systems were

---

[33] "Agikuyu" refers to people of Kenya who speak Gigikuyu languages. They are typically referred to in scholarship as "Gikuyu" or the Swahili term "Kikuyu."

flexible enough that people could reimagine and reconfigure both belonging and hierarchy.[34]

This ability to transcend the lineage ideology also applied to matrilineal societies. The matrilineal Yao provide an example of this. In matrilineal societies, there was no need for a "female husband" because all children of the mother already belonged to her matriclan, but under certain historical situations, men looked for ways to increase their authority within the matrilineage. In the nineteenth century, among the Yao of modern Mozambique, many men became traders in the interior of East Africa. These traders bypassed the powerful older women of the matriclans and their requirement of bride service for marriage. Wealthy men purchased and took as wives unfree, kinless women. The interior trade included the movement of people who were severed from their lineage for a variety of misfortunes. By the nineteenth century, these unfree and kinless individuals increasingly became entangled in commoditized forms of slavery. Again, to be unfree in this context meant one had no kinship ties. Within a matrilineal milieu, a Yao man could father children with a kinless wife without obligation to perform bride service for a matrilineage, thus creating a patrilineage within an otherwise matrilineal community.

Although people might affiliate at different moments with members of either their mother's or father's lineage, over the long term of history patrilineal and matrilineal Bantu societies tended to hold to distinctly different values, and these values often led to different trajectories in economic history. Matrilineal societies, for example, commonly distributed goods more widely among members of the matriclan than did patriclans. The distribution of food and other goods to more distant relatives formed a type of social safety net for difficult times. This matrilineal philosophy made sense for migrating peoples who sought to build their lives in new areas and most especially in agriculturally less productive lands. But even in societies with highly productive farming economies, the cooperative human relations engendered by matrilineal descent still often long maintained their appeal.[35]

---

[34] Claire C. Robertson, "Gender and Trade Relations in Central Kenya in the Late Nineteenth Century," *The International Journal of African Historical Studies* 30, no. 1 (1997): 45; Jean Cadigan, "Woman-to-Woman Marriage: Practices and Benefits in Sub-Saharan Africa," *Journal of Comparative Family Studies* 29, no. 1 (Spring 1998): 95.

[35] For example, the Yao and the Kongo, who became wealthy through trade, but in the long term remained matrilineal.

Therefore, matrilineal and patrilineal organizations could have different consequences, as argued here, for economic history and for women's lives. Patrilineal social institutions facilitated the accumulation of surplus within individual lineages, which controlled both the sexuality and labor of in-marrying wives. Polygyny, a man marrying multiple spouses—though the practice existed among Bantu matrilineal peoples—seems to have been more common in patrilineal societies. The fact that marriage in patrilineal societies involved bride wealth, the transfer of wealth to a potential wife's kin meant that the young wife's productive and reproductive capacities belonged to her husband's patriclan. But marriage in Bantu societies did not change a person's clan or lineage, and in troubled times a woman could turn to her lineage of birth for support. A young woman moving to her spouse's village would have few rights until she had children of her own. Yet when she returned to the village of her people, she would have full rights to status and in all the products of her birth family.[36]

MOVING UP: AGING, ELDERS, AND LIFE STAGES

The way belonging mattered varied across time and context. What was common in the Bantu historical tradition is that since early times, communities commemorated lineage members across their lives. They did this with ceremonies to mark life stages, with each stage imbuing the initiated person with a firm sense of belonging and reasserting the person's social responsibilities. In particular, they educated youth (discussed in chapter 3) through initiation processes that marked their transitions from childhood into adulthood and parenthood. In large part, ceremonies memorialized lineage members' levels of increased seniority and potential authority. Life stage is one more angle from which historians can examine conceptual and historical connections among lineages, belonging, authority, and the spiritual realm that Bantu speakers invoked and sustained.

Gerontocracy, Elderhood, and Seniority

The corpus of linguistic and comparative ethnographic evidence pertaining to life stages strongly suggests that early Bantu societies

---

[36] Karen Brodkin Sacks, *Sisters and Wives: The Past and Future of Sexual Equality* (Westport, Conn: Greenwood Press, 1979).

were heterarchical and gerontocratic. As lineage members aged, they held increasingly elevated status and authority. Though this precept is not unique to Bantu communities, what perhaps is distinctive is that they gave primacy—in recognizing power, influence, or authority—to age and knowledge and to networks and the collective more than they did to gender or individual wealth. "Heterarchy" is a useful term for describing these dynamics. In heterarchy, authority can reside simultaneously in multiple institutions. The group or people who wield authority can vary depending on the context. Thus, heterarchical systems are neither singularly hierarchical—although communities may include multiple hierarchies—nor are they hegemonic, with one person or group holding all power at all times. In some contexts, political leaders were authoritative, but there were circumstances where political leaders had no sway and only spiritual or medicinal practitioners could affect a situation, whether it was political, social, environmental, or cultural. Both women and men could serve as authorities in this kind of historical contexts, and anyone who achieved recognition as an elder would hold some level of social power and authority, even if they did not wield them in a specifically political, spiritual, or economic arena. The members of the early Bantu societies understood and recognized these crosscutting ideals about authority.

Across diverse Bantu-speaking communities, becoming an elder accorded increased seniority, honor, and authority. This meant that older women and men had status over younger women and men. Knowing one's place in the gerontocracy was a priority for community members. The significance of their relative seniority is commonly reflected in how Bantu-speaking peoples refer to their siblings, marking older and younger siblings with specific terms and modifiers. Seniority impacted relationships both within and outside the lineage.

As with other Bantu worldviews and social organizing, the concepts of age and aging were fluid. Precisely what constituted elderhood and youth varied across time and community. For instance, a person who married into or in some other way was adopted into a lineage would mark his or her seniority not necessarily by birth age, but by when he or she was accepted into the community. Additionally, one might also attain seniority status vis-à-vis younger members within the birth community for exceptional achievements. The varying ways in which seniority played out exemplify the complex nature of authority, social organization, and belonging in the early heterarchical Bantu societies.

Female Life Stages: Girls, Mothers, and Elders

Late nineteenth- and early to mid-twentieth-century ethnographic studies of Bantu communities commonly detail female initiation as a social institution through which female elders guided young members into adulthood. The linguistic evidence suggests that, at least as early as the Sangha-Kwa era, the later second phase of Bantu expansions, Bantu peoples had come to define the period from a young woman's menarche to the birth of her first child as a distinct life stage, using the widespread root word*-*yadi* for that stage.[37] Over time this root took on different nuances in different languages, but these meanings continued to be ones that gave primacy in the Bantu historical tradition to the birth of new lineage members. Even in languages where speakers replaced *-yadi* with new terms, nearly always the focus on the life stage leading to motherhood persisted in the culture. Bantu speakers may have changed their particular words and even specific details of practices, but female elders continued to lead the initiations using spiritual signs and symbols that were meant to reinforce belonging and ensure the successful birth of children and thus preservation of the lineage and clan.

A second old root word tied to a woman's move toward motherhood and reflective of continuing salience of these practices and this worldview is *-gole*. This root was probably originally a synonym for *-yadi*. It came into use around 1000 BCE (fourth phase) in the ancestral language, proto-Kaskazi, of the majority of the later Bantu languages of eastern Africa. The history of the term *-gole* exemplifies

---

[37] Christine Saidi, *Women's Authority and Society in Early East Central Africa* (Rochester, N.Y.: Rochester University Press, 2010), 115. Found in Eastern Savanna Bantu languages and also in some languages of the Njila, or Western Savanna branch spoken in Angola, western Zambia, and northern Namibia, *-yadi* is a term for a girl either undergoing initiation at puberty or to the stage of life between initiation and either childbirth or marriage. In the Nyanja-Cewa language and its nearest relative, Tumbuka, it specifically connotes the period of life from the time of the initiation at puberty up to the celebration of the first pregnancy. In Tumbuka it is also the word for "bride," as it is in the Njila language, Luvale. In at least two languages more distantly related to the Eastern Savanna Bantu branch, Kuba and the Njila language, Herero, it names a woman who has recently given birth, while in one Mashariki language, Chaga, it refers to a pregnant woman. In a few widely scattered individual languages it also came to mean simply "adult woman."

the ways that the early Bantu understandings of a young woman's life stages did not fade away but came to be elaborated in new ways in different communities.[38]

Among matrilineal Bantu-speaking peoples in central-east Tanzania, the root *-gole*, by the second half of the first millennium CE (fifth phase), had narrowed in application to the beginning stage of a woman's physical maturation, applying specifically to "a girl in the physical process of developing breasts."[39] The precision of this reference signifies that the transition to motherhood was considered so vital that each step toward this physical, and thus social, transformation of a young woman required recognition. In these societies *-gole* marked linguistically and ceremonially the life stage distinct and immediately prior to a young woman's becoming a *-yadi*. Not surprisingly, accompanying the social shift from matrilineal to patrilineal descent and the incipient emergence of more centralized polities in the African Great Lakes during the same era, *-gole* changed meaning in a different direction. The proto-North Nyanza speakers around 700 CE gave *-gole* the

---

[38] In the first half of the last millennium BCE, there were two separate terms for a girl, *kipinja* and *gole*. Earliest meaning of *gole* was woman or female and *kipinja* meant young girl. There was a new term that meant "maturing girl" and Kati languages made it more specific for "woman"; *-gole* was a proto-Kaskazi term. Gonzales, *Societies*, chap. 4; Schoenbrun, *A Green Place, A Good Place* (Portsmouth, N.H.: Heinemann, 1998), 160–165; Rhiannon Stephens, *A History of African Motherhood: The Case of Uganda, 700–1900* (Cambridge: Cambridge University Press, 2013), chap. 2.

[39] Proto-Kaskazi *-goli* "woman, female"; e.g., Rundi *ku-gora* "to do woman's work" (housekeeping); *umu-gore (aba-)* "woman, wife"; *uru-gori (in-)* "wreath, crown, heathen crown worn on head or stomach"; *in-goro* "house of king"; *uru-gori* "crown worn by dancers"; Runyakore/Rukiga*abagore* n. "bridal pair; young wives," *bagore* n. "mistress (of)"; Kondoa/Solwe *mgole (wa-)* "girl"; Nkwifiya *kigoli* "girl"; Vidunda *kigole* "girl"; Swahili *kigoli/kigori vigoli/vigori* "young girl before menstruation" (the presence of /l-r/ means Swahili likely borrowed the word from Ruvu Bantu language). The most nuanced example among Ruvu language descendants was reported by Rigby, who found that among Gogo speakers "*mugolece* is a more respectful term, often used for a first, or senior, wife, or for the wife of an elder when a younger man is speaking." In this sense it approximates the meanings Schoenbrun recovered in Great Lakes Bantu. Schoenbrun, *The Historical Reconstruction*, 83; Peter Rigby, *Cattle and Kinship among the Gogo: A Semi-pastoral Society of Central Tanzania* (Ithaca, N.Y.: Cornell University Press, 1999), 271–272.

meaning "bride with maternal potential."[40] In that region, the concepts of motherhood shifted from a multistaged process aimed at reproducing the matrilineage to a worldview in which a woman moved through her life stages within the context of wifehood. Although motherhood was treated as special and still honored in this historical context, the authority and roles that mothers had played in the public sphere as members of matrilineages greatly contracted in the North Nyanza world.

The Ruvu and North Nyanza Bantu examples illustrate how differently people can finely parse their social ideologies, in this case their conceptions of female life stages, and how social, political, and economic factors can engender a restructuring of their worldviews. Societies can share the same deep historical background and yet innovate new concepts, and reshape the application of older ideas, in diverse ways. These variant trajectories of change in social thought illustrate for us something of the complex of continuity and change that has built up through the centuries-long histories of the many, today widespread, Bantu-speaking communities.

In line with a worldview in which ancestral spirits, elders, and lineage leaders operated as important actors shaping social and political life, another old root word, *-bumba, provides evidence for a coexisting presence of sororal groups among the eastern Savanna Bantu of the late second millennium BCE (third phase). The original application of *-bumba was probably to a woman who had graduated out of the life stage of *-yadi, into the life stage of a woman who had born children. But very early, probably already three thousand years ago (fourth phase), Savanna-Bantu speakers began to apply this term as a collective for a particular grouping of closely related adult women within a matrilineage and living in the same village.[41] The *-bumba comprised adult sisters, half-sisters, and maternal female cousins, and their mothers, maternal aunts, and maternal grandmothers, if still living, who exercised authority over the initiation ceremonies that readied mwali (the noun form of *-yadi) for motherhood and oversaw marriage processes.[42] These councils exemplified both the inner

[40] Stephens, Motherhood, 186.

[41] Saidi, Women's Authority, 40–44; earlier dates come from C. Ehret, personal communication. See also An African Classical Age, chap. 2.

[42] Audrey Richards, "The Bemba of North-Eastern Rhodesia," in Elizabeth Colson and Max Gluckman (eds.), Seven Tribes of British Central Africa (Oxford: Oxford University Press, 1951), 12; Bruce Kapferer (1967), 75.

workings of matrilineal authority at the micro-level and the role of seniority within a heterarchy. Historian Saidi concludes that where *-bumba* existed as a feature of matrilineages, these sororal groups held authority over the ideas and the interconnected practices and mores embodied in female initiation. This authority in turn gave the female elders authority in deciding whom their daughters' could marry, in that way contributing toward strengthening and preserving the social centrality of the matrilineage and matrilineal relationships.

In East-Central and East Africa, anthropological work of Audrey Richards, Clement Doke, Hugo Hinfelaar, and The White Fathers reveals that during the nineteenth and twentieth centuries, Sabi sororal groups oversaw a girl's initiation particularly in preparation for transitioning into her status as a future mother. A prospective husband, seeking to forge a connection of belonging with a woman and her matrilineage, first had to contribute productively to the woman's sororal group. Anthropologists use the term "bride service" for his contribution toward the matrilineages.

This word often fails, however, to convey the full scope of what this practice meant historically. While the ethnographic lens emphasizes the concept of the bride in discussing marriage and bride service, it is important to recognize that in the Bantu historical tradition the union and attendant ceremonies orchestrated by the sororal councils and other groups of elders focused far more on building, extending, and preserving a given matrilineage—on actualizing the principle of belonging—than on a mere transaction or exchange that might be implied by the term "bride service." As an institution, bride service served as a sort of initiation for men, created durable bonds, and ensured that the marriage unfolded as a series of approved events. Through these activities the male partner demonstrates his commitment to the woman's matrilineage and his aptitude for becoming a responsible father. At the same time the matrilineage developed a stronger obligation to this potential lineage member.

Twentieth-century Sabi societies provide a glimpse at the ways elders, in this case sororal councils, held authority within matrilineal agricultural societies. For agricultural societies to thrive, people's productive and reproductive labor was imperative, and matrilineages controlled access to land. It was the purview and responsibility of matrilineage elders to ensure that labor from husbands and lineage children was sustainable in the *longue durée*. When one considers that in matrilineal societies a son's children belonged to a different matrilineage than his own, while a daughter's remained within her matrilineage, elder women could leverage a great deal of social and economic power if they had daughters. Control of labor and access to land meant that they could exert considerable control in the economies of exchange.

Within this social system, women achieved greater seniority and certain rights by completing a series of actions and responsibilities. Young women in Bantu societies likely aspired to the ideals of their particular era and society. In agricultural societies, gaining the privilege from her sororal group to thresh her own grain and have her own cooking fire to prepare food was an outward recognition of her having attained maturity and of her increased stature. Elders typically bestowed a younger woman such privileges and rights only after she successfully completed her initiation assignments and went through her ceremonies. In the spiritual realm the ancestors consecrated the initiations of a young woman of the matrilineages, while in the temporal realm her sororal group served as the guide, final arbitrator, and referee of the prospective mother's attainment of full adult status.

Likewise, a man aspiring to marry a young woman of a particular matrilineage had responsibilities to complete before he could be allowed to do so. When marriage was the goal, the young man moved to the village of the prospective partner. He had to provide labor for several years to the matrilineage of his future bride. In this way elder women within the sororal group could control the labor of daughters and aspiring sons-in-law and in the process contribute to building a sustainable matrilineage and reinforcing identity. The man as well needed to father children in order to demonstrate his ability to contribute reproductively to the matrilineage, and often only then would he be fully accepted.

It is important to note some important nuances about matrilineal reckoning in the Bantu historical tradition. Although matrilineages often had great economic and social power, these were *not* matriarchies in which women dominated men. As explained previously, these were societies in which seniority—not gender—along with other socially particular factors determined one's status. Belonging to a lineage was vital in these societies. Power and authority had multiple centers and were more commonly diffuse rather than concentrated.

An example of the dispersed nature of authority can be seen in East-Central Africa. Among Sabi-speakers, a man had to observe mother-in-law avoidance during his period of bride service. A significant aspect of the process was the conclusion of avoidance.

Ethnographic studies in the twentieth century of the Bemba and Lamba reflect that mothers-in-law and sororal groups performed *mako*, a ceremony that reduced avoidance rules, if and when they deemed the male partner had proven to be suitable for marriage to a young woman, through his character as well as his productive and reproductive abilities. The *mako* ceremony unfolded as a process. First there would be a lessening of the strongest prohibitions. After a period of time, the young man could openly greet and eat a meal with his mother-in-law.

The complexity of this power must also be understood in the context of the rules that applied once bride service ended. Once the lineage had accepted the male as a full member of the community, when his service was complete, his nuclear family unit was unrestricted on where they settled. The couple could move to a location of their choosing, including to the man's maternal village. Ethnographic evidence and court records of the twentieth century suggest that it was not uncommon for women to remain with their matrilineage. The process of marriage allowed elder women within the sororal group to control the labor of daughters and aspiring sons-in-law, but ultimately married women and men had to negotiate, together and with the lineage, their decisions and life choices.

The entitlement that sororal groups and mothers-in-law possessed was circumscribed in other ways as well. For example, among Chewa spakers of Malawi and Eastern Zambia, young men could be initiated into Nyau male secret society. Nyau members wore elaborate masks and danced at religious ceremonies. Once the young man placed the mask on his face, he was no longer human, but a spirit or ancestor. He could, in this context, lash out at his mother-in-law in particular and members of the sororal group more broadly. This limited opportunity for a young man to react against the matrilineages or a segment of it mitigated the tensions and perhaps curbed any potential tendency toward harshness on the part of the elder women. Nyau, it has been argued, counterbalanced any extreme authority of the sororal groups within matrifocal Chewa society. It exemplifies how a heterarchical access to power can work out in practice, with interacting and intersecting lines of authority tying society together. Though this particular example is specific to nineteenth- and twentieth-century Chewa, the wider linguistic and comparative ethnographic evidence suggests that patterns like these have a much older history among Bantu peoples.

Male Life Stages: Boys, Fathers, and Elders

Linguistic evidence also shows that since early times, Bantu lineage members have taken measures to socialize male children into responsible community contributors through puberty initiation ceremonies that included both physical and intellectual training. Throughout Bantu Africa there are ethnographic evidence and oral traditions that provide details of enduring male life stages. Similar to girls, lineage elders supervised the religio-ritual ceremonies that guided men toward prospective fatherhood, as well as the vital roles of uncle, father, husband, farmer, hunter, iron producer, and elder. Early Bantu speakers believed a young man's social standing was elevated by age, achievement, and fatherhood.

Probably by the time the first phase of Bantu history was under way in the mid-fourth millennium, the proto-Bantu used circumcision in the rituals of male initiation. Certain evidence for this practice carries back to the Nyong-Lomami period (early second phase)—a Bantu verb, *-tib-, specifically connoting male circumcision dates at least that early. An accompanying, equally old noun root, *-kula, meant "age cohort" or "age group (of young men)." The derivation of this word from the proto-Bantu verb *-kul- "to grow up" makes explicit ties of this ritual to advancement into adult status. Together these two old root words reveal not only that the early Bantu initiations of young men involved circumcision, but that the young men went through, not individual, but instead group initiations into young adulthood.

Research remains to be undertaken regarding the details of how these ceremonies were carried out in the first and second phases of Bantu history. Scholars know much more about these customs, however, from the second millennium BCE onward (third phase). In the early Savanna Bantu society and among the early Mashariki Bantu of three thousand years ago, male elders every few years took the young men who entered puberty in the intervening years to camps in the bush for an extended period of seclusion, usually extending over several weeks. During seclusion they led the young men through a series of rituals and taught the young men about the social and ritual responsibilities they owed their society. Reflecting the importance of these ceremonial and pedagogical observances, new terms relating to the seclusion period came into use. These include *-alik- "to enter circumcision and initiation rites," *-alam-* "to engage in circumcision-related observances," and *-nkunka* "circumcision observances."[43]

Since that time, people have transformed, in both subtle and more major ways, practices pertaining to circumcision and age sets and to male initiation. Mashariki-descended societies belonging to the Kusi subgroup, notably the Nguni and Sotho in southeastern Africa, who became patrilineal in descent and belonging, continued to use circumcision to initiate young men and continued to initiate those young men into age sets. In recent centuries these age groups often acted as military contingents and so have often been called "age regiments" in the historical literature.

In some areas, particularly in eastern Africa, encounters with non-Bantu peoples who also socialized their boys through similar life stage practices have reinforced these customs among Bantu populations.[44] Kaskazi-descended Luyia and other East Nyanza people of Kenya and northern Tanzania and the Upland Bantu peoples, such as Chaga of Kilimanjaro and Gikuyu of the Mt. Kenya region, are particularly notable examples in which a crucial influence in preserving circumcision was the close cultural interaction of Bantu with Southern Cushitic people who also circumcised.

In other areas circumcision dropped out of use, although other elements of the initiation ceremony might persist. Among Ruvu-descended people of central-east Tanzania, both historical outcomes took place. Some Ruvu peoples, notably Gogo who had strong interactions with Southern Cushites and Parakuyu Masai, both of whom practice circumcision, maintained circumcision as part of their male initiation observances and actually shifted over from matrilineal to patrilineal descent during the past five hundred years. Other Ruvu societies, however, remained matrilineal and also ceased to circumcise sometime in the past one thousand years. The male elders and post-child-bearing female lineage members oversaw the process. They separated the youths from their communities and brought them to temporary camp environments,

---

[43] Ehret, *Classical Age*, 156, 157, 315; J. J. Wolff, "Circumcision and Initiation in Western Kenya and Eastern Uganda: Historical Reconstructions and Ethnographic Evidence," *Anthropos* 78 (1983): 369–410; Jeff Marck, "Aspects of Male Circumcision in Sub-Equatorial African Culture History," *Health Transition Review*, supplement to vol. 7 (1997): 337–359.

[44] Ehret, *Classical Age*, 155–156.

where they would remain until their *mlao* "coming out" ceremony. They called the initiation in camps by the word *kumbi*. Cultural shifts led to the maintaining of the seclusion observances of male initiation but the dropping of circumcision among these particular Ruvu speakers.

At least 1,500 years ago, the ancestral Botatwe and Sabi-speaking peoples of east-central Africa dropped male circumcision. Male initiation ceremonies no longer are part of Sabi practices, and Botatwe peoples practice only a modest, individual observance for male initiation. Male circumcision has in fact disappeared among Bantu peoples inhabiting much of the eastern parts of the southern savanna belt, from Sabi and Botatwe in Zambia to Chewa of Malawi and Makua, Yao, and other peoples of northern Mozambique and southeastern Tanzania. How, when, and why male circumcision ceased to be practiced, across these regions, remains an intriguing history still to be explored. To be sure, the histories of Bantu communities from western to eastern to southern Africa reveal thought-provoking developments and complexities in how historical changes, gender configurations, and expectations have unfolded.

CONCLUSION

In the long span of Bantu history, Bantu speakers drew upon and developed these core concepts and practices over the *longue durée* of five millennia. Their varying institutions were not mutually exclusive entities; rather, they were interconnected through heterarchy and customary practices intended to teach and sustain social belonging. Bantu speakers in many different contexts and eras concurrently employed both deeply rooted and newly evolving strategies to address immediate situations as well as to plan for the future.

Deep common historical strands in belief, practice, and social relations in Bantu culture were often greatly reshaped by the forces of history. Although there has been no universally preferred lineage form that all speakers of Bantu languages followed through all historical eras, matrilineages, from the linguistic evidence, seem to have been the important organizing institutions in earlier phases of Bantu history, and they have often continued to have salience in new configurations in later history. Interesting questions emerge from considering the many matrilineal Bantu societies whose inherited customs and ways of belonging and of organizing their comprehension of the world today intersect with quite different new ideas presented through Islam, colonialism, Christianity, and the nationalism of African states. All of these influences promote organization around their own ideologies, and some of these newer historical factors actively oppose adherence to matrilineality, matriclans, and, in many cases, the belief in ancestral spirits. The persistence of older ideas underpinning cultural and social belonging may be a testament to the resilience of these forms of organization among Bantu-speaking peoples. For history and historians, these systems provide informative examples of the ways people have imagined social organization and social belonging outside the paradigms of hierarchical state formation.

A Kaonde Oral History

Oral narratives often communicate entanglements related to the complexity of power dynamics. An excerpt of a Kaonde oral history, provided here, offers an opportunity to analyze and interpret meaning from an individual account using concepts of heterarchy and belonging.

> In 1998 a the son of a Kaonde chief, Mr. Kajoba proudly recounted an oral history of his matrilineal peoples who reside in northeastern Zambia today. In the history, his female ancestors were central to the survival of the Kaonde people. Kajoba explained that, "in earlier times, before colonialism, the queen mother was the most important person during any battle." He continued, noting that "She did not lead the battle, but instead she was placed in a hollowed-out tree trunk filled with the traditional medicines like [those] used by our ancestors." The best warriors stood watch to ensure the security of queen mother as she sat in the hollowed trunk. It was believed by the Kaonde that as long as she remained safely in the medicine, they would win all their battles.[45] If she were forced to leave the tree trunk, they would face a loss, thus it was critical to stay rooted to ensure security.

While male members were cast as warriors and fought against challengers and enemies, the role of the queen mother was considered equally important. She, with her presence, created ritual, spiritual, and medicinal protection for the community. The physical guarding of her position in the medicated tree and the knowledge she possessed necessitated the soldiers. Therefore, both the male guards and elder women shared power and responsibility to defend the Kaonde community—physically and spiritually.

---

[45] Saidi interview with Mr. Kajoba, son of Kaonde chief, in Solwezi, Zambia, July 1998; for an alternate perspective, see also Kate A. F. Crehan, *The Fractured Community: Landscapes of Power and Gender in Rural Zambia* (Berkeley: University of California Press, 1997).

Table 2.1 Shifting Ancestor and Lineage Concepts in Linguistic Data

ROOT	MEANING	NOTES: ATTESTATIONS MAY VARY DUE TO REGULAR SOUND CHANGE AND MEANINGS CHANGE OVER TIME IN DESCENDANT LANGUAGES.	BANTU EXPANSION PHASE/ERA	SAMPLE MODERN LANGUAGES WHERE WORDS ATTESTED BASED ON GUTHRIE'S REGIONS AND ZONES[1]
*-dĩmù	Ancestor or Spirit	Later ancestor spirit *-zimu. Through regular sound change dI becomes zi in languages.	Phase One Expansions Proto-Bantu	Bisa, Duala, Gweno, Lwena, Lundu, Mongo, Rundi, Sukuma, Yao
*-jambe / *-yambe	God	*Nyambe, a common attestation for Creator God, likely derives from *-amb-, Niger-Congo root that meant 'to begin', dating back to at least as early as 5000 BCE.	Phase One Proto-Bantu 3500	Herero, Kikongo, Lunda, Ngumba, Nzebi
*-dog-	To Bewitch	Evil behavior of humans has widespread attestations and varies on meaning only slightly. For example, it covers meanings such as witchcraft, to bewitch, to cast a spell, and poison in different locations.	Phase One Proto-Bantu circa 3500 BCE	Bemba, Chokwe, Kikongo, Kikuyu, Manyanja, Rundi, Shambala, Tebeta, Venda, Yao
*-gàngà	Religio-Medicinal Healer, Medicine	Widespread attestations suggest its early origins.	Phase One Proto-Bantu circa 3500 BCE	Bulu, Chewa, Ganda, Kuba, Luyana, Makua, Mbongwe, Nilamba, Nyakyusa, Venda
*-cuka	Matrilineage	*-suka termite hills, matrilineage	Phase Two	Bushongo, Lega, Ngonde, Nyakyusa
*-lungu	Creator God (term derived from a verb for 'to become fitting, to become straight')	from *-dùnγ- reconstructed to Southern Kaskazi word for God meaning fitting, straight, right attested as *-lungu. Through regular sound change d becomes l.	Phase Three	Bemba, Kikongo, Kikuyu, Lumbu, Mbundu, Mpesa, Nsenga, Shambala, Xhosa, Yao
*-gàndá	Place of Settlement of Community	Root shifted to mean a settlement for a community.	Phase Two circa 3000 BCE	Ganda, Herero, Kikongo, Rundi, Sukuma, Zulu Tio, Teke

Root	Gloss	Description	Phase	Languages/Regions
*-gàndá	Matriclan	Early on matrilineages were primary unit of organization. About 2000 years ago the root referred to a hearth where women maintained family alters and cooked.	Phase Two ca 2500 BCE	Sangha-Kwa languages Gabon, Namibia, Great Lakes
-kòdò	Base of tree, roots	Not yet fully reconstructed, but widely attested Bantu root.	Proto-Bantu	Kauma, Kikongo, Manyanja, Songe, Yao, Zigua
-kòdò	Grandparent		Phase Three circa 500 BCE	Giryama, Manyanja, Unguja, Yaka
*-kólò	Matriclan	*-kólò from root *-kòdò tree trunk metaphor for matriclan generalized to 'clan' among Kaskazi	Phase Four	
*li-uba	Creator God (transfer for older word for 'sun' to new concept of God)	Kaskazi on Lake Nyanza replaced mulungu term when adopted 'sun' as a metaphor for God from neighboring ??? and applied older Bantu root for sun to signify this new conceptualization.	Phase Four circa First millennium BCE	Yao
*-ded-	To Nurture	This more geographically limited root meant 'to nurture' in Sabi and Botatwe languages. In time, it came to mean 'Creator God' attested as Leza. In Kusi languages such as Nyanja and Chewa, it came to mean one who sustains life. The root *-dedla is a causative form that meant 'to be nurtured' d- became l- while -dla becames -za in Savanna Bantu languages.	Phase Four Sabi circa 500 CE	Bemba, Ila, Nyanja, Chewa

¹ On regions and locations, see Malcolm Guthrie, Comparative Bantu volumes 3 and 4 (Farnborough: Gregg, 1970); for evolving views on *-dímu see Jan Vansina, How Societies Are Born (Charlottesville: University of Virginia Press, 2005), 48 as well as *-dímo Jan Vansina, Paths in the Rainforest (University of Wisconsin Press, 1990), 297 and David Lee Schoenbrun, The Historical Reconstruction of Great Lakes Bantu Cultural Vocabulary: Etymologies and Distributions (Köln: Rüdiger Köppe Verlag, 1997), 182–3 ; on *-gàndá and *-dìnŋ- see Christopher Ehret, An African Classical Age (Charlottesville: University of Virginia Press, 2001), 159, 166–7; on *li-uba see Christopher Ehret, Civilization of Africa (Charlottesville: University of Virginia Press, 2002), 185; on *-cuka see Jan Vansina, Paths in the Rainforest (University of Wisconsin Press, 1990), appendix 169 and Kairn Klieman, The Pygmies Were Our Compass (Portsmouth, NH: Heinemann, 2003), 69–71.

FURTHER READINGS

Declish, Francesca. "Gendered Narratives, History, and Identity: Two Centuries along the Juba River among the Zigula and Shanbara." *History in Africa* 22 (1995): 93–122.

Gonzales, Rhonda M. *Societies, Religion, and History: Central East Tanzanian's and the World They Created, 200 BCE–1800 CE.* New York: Columbia University Press, 2008.

Schoenbrun, David Lee. *A Green Place, A Good Place.* Portsmouth, N.H.: Heinemann, 1998.

Smythe, Kathleen R. *Africa's Past, Our Future.* Bloomington: Indiana University Press, 2015.

Stephens, Rhiannon. *A History of African Motherhood: The Case of Ugàndá, 700–1900.* Cambridge: Cambridge University Press. 2013.

Educating Generations

This chapter addresses the history of Bantu education, particularly the way historical memories, ideologies, and material knowledge were communicated and adapted from one generation to the next generation. The primary sources for reconstructing Bantu education include historical linguistic analysis, comparative ethnography, oral tradition, and archaeology.

In the Western historical tradition, there is a common expectation that education will occur in a school, a physical building with rooms that hold desks and chairs, where teachers will instruct their students. Parents encourage their children to attend and perform well in school, with the expectation that to do so will improve their professional prospects as young adults. Similarly, parents in Bantu speech communities historically wanted opportunities for success for their children. Young people learned skills ranging from practical to esoteric. Children in farming societies learned about weather and botany, which included an understanding of plant biology and chemistry. The young in pastoralist societies became experts on domesticated animals, their care, their reproductive cycles, and their diseases. Gathering and hunting peoples taught children from an early age to recognize a great variety of plants, fish, insects, and small animals, in addition to knowing where potential food was located, what time of year they were plentiful, and under what conditions they were edible.

Children also learned animal habitats and biology, as well as hunting methods. Those living near large bodies of water learned to fish, set fish traps, or basket fish in shallow water as well as how to maneuver watercraft. Across many of these societies, some also learned more specialized knowledge and skills.

This chapter has four sections. The first section, "Performance as Education," examines intellectual meanings of education in proto-Bantu speech communities from as early as 5,500 years ago. It introduces early education, its varying types and contexts. The second section, "Traditions and Transitions," emphasizes teaching youth about becoming responsible and productive community members. The third, "Advanced Learning," demonstrates that, for some Bantu people, specialized education continued into adulthood. Finally, communication in the "Bantu Historical Tradition," considers the histories of Bantu worldviews and modes of transmission. Collectively these sections provide critical insights into Bantu ontologies, theories of existence they held and passed on to new generations over five millennia.

PERFORMANCE AS EDUCATION

A variety of proto-Bantu word roots reveal ways in which societies shared knowledge with and educated the young. One example is the verb, *-gan-*, which meant both "to tell a story" and "to show." Both meanings can be traced to the proto-Bantu period of 5,500 years ago. A related, equally ancient proto-Bantu term, the noun form, *-gano*, meant "story." Around the second millennium BCE among early Bantu (third phase), it had taken on the additional meaning "wisdom."[1] The prevalence and application of *-gan-* and *-gano* suggest that deep in the past for the earliest Bantu speakers, telling stories, communicating through showing and performing, and transmitting wisdom were

---

[1] The root *-gan-*"to think" in Tetela, Gusii (northeast of Lake Nyanza), Sukuma, Gogo, Bobangi, Nyanja, and Yao *-gan* "to tell a tale" in Bulu, Bene (Cameroon), Chagga, Nyoro, Hima, Ganda, Kikuyu, Sukuma, Lunda; "to sing a tale" in Luba Katanga; *-gano-* "wisdom" in W. Kongo, Sanga, Tabwa, Ila, Nsenga, Manyika-Shona, Duala, Makua, Chokwe, and Luvale; *-gano* "tale" in Luba-Kasai, Burundi, Nyoro, Hima, Shambala, Swahili, Shona, Venda, Pedi, Nandi, Kikuyu, Sukuma, Kanyok, Ila, Ambo, Lunda, Yasa (S. Cameroon), Herero, Kamba-Kenya, Tete, Rwanda, see Guthrie, *Comparative Bantu Vol. 3*, CS 772, 773, 775, 776.

actions and ideologies intertwined in early Bantu worldviews. A distinct proto-Bantu verb with similar, dual associations is *-dag-, which meant "to teach" and/or "to show." This suggests that Bantu-speaking peoples from an early period saw teaching and showing as interconnected concepts and actions. Widely across Bantu-speaking societies, people apply the two word roots *-gan- and *-dag- not just to verbal instruction and storytelling but to learning stories, ideas, and ideals expressed in dance, music, and song.

Listening, speaking, absorbing ideas and practices, and performing actions collectively imbued one with wisdom and enhanced the sense of belonging. Testimony of comparative ethnography across Bantu regions indicates that, far back in history, the general pedagogical approach has been for students to actively participate in the learning process and for teachers, through hands-on activities, to ensure mastery of content. Teaching and learning were active processes. Oral histories, stories, myths, songs, riddles, and proverbs recounted at evening campfires or in other informal and formal situations served as communal forms of education. Audiences might be expected to respond at certain designated moments. Older members of the community would have the responsibility to correct or challenge aspects of the history, lyrics, or oral tradition that they believed the performer had ignored, forgotten, or recounted incorrectly.

Comparative ethnography and oral traditions from across Bantu-speaking Africa suggest that formal learning typically began once children were weaned, probably around two years of age. Their education likely involved both learning from their elders within the community as well as mastering skills needed for survival. They listened to elders reciting history, proverbs, and myths, and they observed and learned from song, music, and dance performers executed in communal spaces. On the practical level, they learned from carrying out their daily and seasonal chores how to become contributing participants in the work and productive activities of their societies. For example, in central African villages today, it is common to see young boys and girls, five or six years old, carrying a newborn baby on their back and skillfully rocking the infant to keep it from crying. Through these seemingly mundane tasks, the youth learned important nurturing and caregiving skills that served them in many capacities, including in their future, expected role of parent.

In recent times ethnographers and art historians have documented public performances as education throughout Bantu Africa. Whether in the public arena in the daytime or in the evening with the stars and a communal fire as the only light, or around the family hearth, children would be awed, frightened, and delighted as they absorbed knowledge from dance and ceremonial performances or from story sessions. The ground might even shake as instruments and rhythms intensified at the story's climax. Suddenly, masked dancers embodying spirits might appear all around, twirling and jumping. With people clapping and singing stories, lessons, and history were exhibited in dynamic ways. One was not merely hearing the facts but was immersed in the words, imagery, sounds, and smells of the history or myth recounted and performed.

For most occasions, dance and songs were performed in communal areas, and these performances were crucial in educating the next generation. Two proto-Bantu verbs and two nouns of the fourth millennium BCE connoted, respectively, singing and dancing: the verbs *-yímb- "to sing" and *-bín- "to dance," and the nouns *-yímbo "song" and *-bínà "dance." A fourth equally ancient proto-Bantu root word, *-goma, named the "drum." Three aspects of performance denoted by these words remained closely intertwined and accompanying elements of performance and education among Bantu peoples down through more than five thousand years and in all but a very few recent Bantu societies.

Although there were clearly individual terms used for each aspect of performance, often various Bantu peoples used these words to mean more than one element of performing. This long history of close intertwining of song and dance shows up sharply in the semantic histories of these old verbs and nouns. Separately, for example, in the Thagiicu languages of the Mount Kenya region, in an areal cluster of languages in Rwanda and southwestern Uganda, and in Sotho language of Lesotho, the verb *-bín- took on the dual meaning of both "sing" and "dance"; and in the Kuria language it lost its meaning "dance" and became simply the verb for "sing." Similarly, several far separated Bantu languages independently combined the meanings "to dance" and "to sing" in their versions of the old verb yímb- "to sing"—notably the Bube language of the Atlantic island of Bioko and the far distant Safwa language of southern Tanzania.[2] As for the proto-Bantu word *-goma "drum," contexts in which people use this term often link the drum, in conjunction with song, dance, and spoken word, to accessing

---

[2] On the root *-yímb- see Gutherie, *Comparative Bantu* Vol. 3 CS 942 and CS 2010.

spirit power for transformative purposes.[3] Among the Kongo people of Angola and the western Democratic Republic of Congo (DRC) as well as among kiSwahili and kiKongo speakers of East Africa's littoral, dancing and drums are *ngoma*. Among speakers, the trees from which the drums could be carved were called *ngoma-ngoma*.[4]

The linguistic and ethnographic evidence shows dance and music were not separate artistic endeavors for the earliest Bantu. Most Bantu peoples of more recent ages also combined body movement and auditory arts to express common cultural heritage and to convey knowledge through performance. Overlapping meanings of these word roots show that musical performances were pivotal in education even during the earliest eras of Bantu history. Bantu-speaking peoples have long employed music, dance, and singing as key components within communication and education. Between 1500 and 1900 CE, Bantu-speaking peoples, who were enslaved and transported in the era of Atlantic Slave Trade, brought aspects of these worldviews and practices to the Americas. For example, from East Africa to Angola the Bantu-derived term *samba* is applied to name dances central to female initiation. In Brazil, the same term, *samba*, is the name given to a group of dances people of African heritage perform.[5] Although movements and meanings may have changed, *samba* provides intriguing links between Bantu speakers' deep cultural history in Africa and those who brought such contributions to the Americas.

Whereas it is easy to understand how storytelling is somewhat similar to a history course lecture, viewing musical performance as a way to educate young people from an early age may seem less familiar. For the long term of Bantu history, performance was more than entertainment: both spectator and participant were engaged in an active, communal educational event. Dance and its many meanings, for obvious reasons, are not well reflected in archeological

---

[3] For *-goma-* distribution see Gutherie, *Comparative* 1970, cs. 140, 844, 845, 846; Peter Pels, "Kizungu Rhythms: Luguru Christianity as Ngoma," *Journal of Religion in Africa* 26 (1996); Ehret, *African Classical Age*, 324; John M. Janzen, "'Doing Ngoma': A Dominant Trope in African Religion and Healing," *Journal of Religion in Africa* 21, no. 4 (1991): 290–308.

[4] James Gordon Ellison, "Transforming Obligations, Performing Identity: Making the Nyakyusa in a Colonial Context," Ph.D. diss., University of Florida, 1999.

[5] Bruce Gilman, "The Politics of Samba," *Georgetown Journal of International Affairs* 2, no. 2 (Summer/Fall 2001): 67–72.

records for the last five thousand years. But the ethnographic and art historical studies of the role of musical performance among various Bantu-speaking people in more recent times shed light on the key roles of dance and performance in educating the young. The similarities in musical and dance performance found in such regionally distant Bantu societies as Punu from southern border areas of the Republic of the Congo near the Congo River, Sukuma of northwestern Tanzania, and Chewa of Malawi, in addition to the proto-Bantu terms, confirm that this was surely a main social component in the earliest Bantu speech communities.

Punu people provide an illustrative example of musical performance as a tool for both practical and cultural education. Since the 1960s anthropologists and ethnographers have documented *ikoku*, a popular Punu dance that oral traditions claim to be at least a hundred years old. *Ikoku* begins with two drummers playing a rhythm and a vocalist singing and clapping with the beat for a dance. Once the introduction was underway, others were drawn in to join the dance. Punu people have a belief that dancing brings communal joy and a sense of unity and belonging to everyone in the community, but those watching particular dances also learned important lessons. First, there are movements to symbolize fertility, the importance of children, and the honor associated with motherhood and parenthood in general. But probably the most instructive aspect of the *ikoku* dance was the movements that imitate pool fishing. During the dry season in Punu country, groups of women captured fish, which provided sources of protein, with their *fyke* nets. In the *ikoku* performances, the dancers pounded their feet quickly and heavily as if stomping the grass in the shallow pools, mimicking a technique the women use to force the small fish out of the grass and into the center of the pond for easier catching with baskets. From the *ikoku* the young children learned this way of expressing joy and of honoring the importance of reproduction. At the same time, young girls learn from the dance movements the techniques and rhythms they will need when they are old enough to join in fishing as part of a team.[6]

Ethno-musicologists have documented two kinds of dance performances with a different set of lessons for boys in the southeastern Great Lakes region among Sukuma. Oral traditions date these two dances to the early 1800s CE. The first, *bayeye*, was the dance

---

6 Canne Plancke, "On Dancing and Fishing: Joy and Celebration of Fertility among the Punu of Brazzaville," *Africa* 80, no. 4 (2010): 620–664.

of the snake hunters, and the second, *banuunguli*, was the dance of the porcupine hunters. Porcupines attacked the crops, and snakes harmed people; thus, it was the responsibility of hunters to remove these pests for the good of economic prosperity and public health. Dances taught techniques for hunting these pests. Drumbeats hypnotized creatures, which would then move to the rhythms. Sometimes *banuuguli* would dance with live snakes, let them bite them, and then apply special medicine to demonstrate their own power as healers. Watching these dances, young boys in the audience learned how to capture porcupines and snakes. Later, when Sukuma men were forced to become porters under colonial rule during the first half of the twentieth century, they performed these dances to maintain their identity and dignity as well as to bolster their courage as they carried items throughout the northeastern region from the Great Lakes to the coast for the Germans and British.[7]

A slightly different tradition, one of masked dances, was a key element in the central and southwestern regions of Bantu Africa. Men, almost universally, wore elaborate and colorful masks and costumes mainly made from wood and raffia. For example, among the matrilineal Chewa, the masked Nyau dancer performed during all-important religious events, such as at a funeral or at the graduation ceremony of girls from female initiation. Anthropologists and art historians have have written extensively on Nyau performances, from which we can make historical inferences.[8]

According to Chewa oral tradition, Nyau masked dance societies are at least five hundred years old. Nyau societies initiated men with rituals that almost exactly mimicked female initiation, and, strikingly reflective of this social debt, an initiate was called *mwale* (from the proto-Bantu root *-yadi*), the same term used for a young woman during female initiations. Nyau dancers often portrayed over sixty legendary and living characters during their dances. They did not depict all at any particular dance, but they always performed characters. With the mask, Nyau dancers were no longer considered human. Rather, they became the spirit the mask represented and could commit acts forbidden to humans. Often the masks were animals, ancestors,

---

[7]   Frank Gunderson, "'Dancing with Porcupines' to 'Twirling a Hoe': Musical Labor Transformed in Sukumaland, Tanzania," *Africa Today* 48, no. 4 (Winter 2001), 3–25.

[8]   Matthew Schoffeleers, "The Nyau Societies: Our Present Understanding," *The Society of Malawi Journal* 29, no. 1 (January 1976): 59–68.

and historical figures—both male and female. In the twentieth century, there were even a few masks that represented British colonial officials or that symbolized contemporary problems facing Chewa communities.

Elaborately costumed Nyau dancers used their movements to depict historical events and convey important values. Their knowledge transmission included performances about the relationship between humans and the animal world as well as humans and the spirit world. Another major educational impact of Nyau masked dancers concerns their instructions for young boys and girls on their roles in Chewa society. Nyau masked dancers conveyed that women were responsible for life through birth and growing crops, while men were responsible for death through hunting animals, slaughtering livestock, and dancing at funerals. From these elaborate masked dances, the young would learn key social values as well as lessons from the history of their communities.[9]

Each of these performances educated children on practical skills, but they also reinforced the worldviews of each society. Examples include the *ikoku* dance, which taught audiences both to express joy through movement and practical skills like shallow pool fishing. Male Sukuma dances served several educational purposes, such as demonstrating the method for ridding cultivated and inhabited areas of porcupines and snakes, while also speaking to deeper values of bravery and strength. And finally, Nyau masked dances depicted people and characters from earlier history. These narratives educated the young about appropriate relationships among humans, spirits, and animals, and confronted new problems and characters that might appear within the community.

Ethnographic evidence of recent history shows that in geographically diverse regions, performances—a synergy of singing, playing musical instruments, and bodily dancing—were used to educate the young. Words for these kinds of performance trace just how ancient these ways of educating and passing on culture were. These various source of evidence on the past suggest that Bantu-speaking children for several thousands of years watched musical and dance performances for entertainment but also gained knowledge of their community's mores, expectations, and history from these performances.

---

[9] Kenji Yoshida, "Masks and Secrecy among the Chewa," *African Arts* 26, no. 2 (April 1993): 34–45.

TRADITIONS AND TRANSITIONS

Once young people reached puberty, their education entered a new phase, taking on a private as well as public dimension. Youth went through a set of religious and educational transitioning observances that extended over a period of weeks, months, or years. Major elements of education were conducted at sacred sites in seclusion from the rest of the community to guard knowledge. In seclusion from the rest of their community. Everywhere among Bantu societies the comparative ethnographic records show these periods to have been times of intensive education, designed to shape young people into productive members of their respective societies. Elders taught life skills, logic, decorum, clan and lineage history, local history, child care, childbirth, parenting, and sex education to young people. The transitional education ceremonies for boys usually included circumcision, as discussed in chapter 2; those for girls rarely did.

The close of the seclusion period more often than not involved the entire community participating in public ceremonial graduations. Anthropologists have often referred to these life transitions as puberty rituals. They were indeed transitions to a new life stage, but less emphasized is that they were also educational, serving as affirmation of young people as part of a community.

Already in the proto-Bantu era of the fourth millennium BCE, young men apparently passed through group initiation observances, as shown in the existence of a proto-Bantu root word *-kúdà for the age group of young men initiated together.[10] But female initiation education among Bantu people was originally individual and carried out by the female elders of the girl's family, who would have supervised and overseen her period of seclusion and education in the values and customs of her society. The seclusion, education, and initiation of girls in small groups appears to have been a new development, coming into being possibly as early as the second millennium BCE among the Savanna Bantu. By the early first millennium BCE, group initiations of girls were certainly customary among the proto-Mashariki descendants of the Eastern Savanna Bantu. The clear marker of this history is a root word traceable to the proto-Mashariki, *-nyamkungui,

---

[10] Ehret, *An African Classical Age*, 155–157.

specifically denoting the female elder whose role was to oversee and govern those female group observances.[11]

A notable comparative ethnographic indicator that group initiations of young women actually go back to Savanna Bantu of the second millennium BCE is the use in recent centuries, among widely separated descendant societies of the Eastern Savanna stage of Bantu expansions, of a particular kind of teaching tool in female seclusion observances—namely, clay and wooden figurines. Ethnographers over the last hundred years have recorded the use of this kind of teaching tool in female initiation from peoples as far flung as Chokwe speakers in southwestern Africa, Nguni of southern Africa, Bemba of Zambia in central Africa, and Ruvu peoples of eastern Tanzania. Outsiders have often referred to these figurines as "dolls," but they were not at all for play. They were mnemonic devices for intensive learning in a usually relatively short but information-packed period of social and cultural education, which introduced a young person during initiation to history, religion, worldviews, biology, practical skills, and behaviors considered essential for the transition to parenthood or adulthood.[12]

A number of Bantu societies perform a second female initiation that could be months or even years later than the seclusion at puberty. The second ceremony was celebrated during a woman's first pregnancy. The existence of two stages in the female initiation into full adulthood is typical among Sabi Bantu communities of east-central Africa and in this region dates back at least 1,700 years during the fourth phase of expansion.[13] Among these peoples the second initiation ceremony at the first pregnancy marked the close of the *-yadi life stage discussed previously. The ancientness of the root *-yadi in Bantu languages—and the fact that it probably originally named the life stage between a woman's first menstruation and her first

---

[11] The term is preserved separately in the geographically widely separated Ruvu and Nyasa subgroups, one a Kaskazi subgroup and the other Kusi, of Mashariki, with fully regular sound correspondences. It is a noun derivative of a much older Bantu root *-kunk- or *-kung-, for undertaking rites of passage, also found outside the Eastern Savanna Bantu branch in languages of the Njila (Western Savanna) branch. Ehret, *An African Classical Age*, chap 5.

[12] Gonzales *Societies*, chap. 4; Karl Hechter-Schultz "Fertility Dolls: Cults of the Nguni and Other Tribes of the Southern Bantu, *Anthropos*, Bd. 61, H3.6 (1966): 516–528.

[13] Saidi, *Women's Authority*, 101–103.

child—and the practice of this second initiation may hark back much earlier than historians can yet fully demonstrate.

Ethnographic studies from the last hundred years in geographically diverse regions of Bantu Africa are useful for making sense of how these intensive educational and social institutions worked. Three examples from different regions of Bantu-speaking Africa provide insight into historical commonalities and transitions in educational practice. One comes from Central Africa, Bemba female initiation, *icisungu*, which several scholars have studied. A second comes from the patrilineal Chaga of East Africa, who included both male and female initiation schools. The third is in southwestern Africa, where matrilineal Chokwe have both male and female initiation ceremonies.

In Bemba female initiation ceremonies, a girl at puberty was secluded for a period and was taught about her lineage history, her clan's history, and how to be a productive member of the society, a mother, and a spouse.[14] The first act of female initiation or *icisungu* commenced when a village headperson called upon the ancestral spirits to bless the ceremony. *Nachimbusa*, the *icisungu* instructor, gave ceremonial baskets to women, starting with the eldest first.

The second set of activities involved seclusion and a long period of multifaceted education of young women. Attending women sang songs and recited poems, and they taught using clay and wooden figurines as well as paintings, all called *mbusa*. According to Richards, a ceramic *mbusa* called *cilume ca ciboa* had the shape of a man with a large head, a sex organ, and no arms. In the early twentieth century, young women were taught that this figure represented a man who stays in the house all day finding fault with his wife, yet does no work himself—a type of husband initiates were instructed to avoid.[15] Another *mbusa* consisted of large models of unfired clay, which were often decorated with seeds and other items.

Mbusa also consisted of drawings on inside walls and floors of the seclusion house. Women who supervised *chisungu* painted geometric designs with their fingers. Each design had a special meaning, and the occurrence of many of the designs, both in decorations that local women potters gave their pots in past centuries but also in the far

---

[14] "Mbusa: Sacred Emblems of the Bemba," 1982, Jean J. Corbeil papers, MotoMoto Museum, Mbala, Zambia

[15] Richards, *Chisungu*, 211.

older Batwa rock art, shows these rituals incorporated and preserved imagery and ideas present among peoples of the region far back into the past.

On the last night of the ceremonies, initiates were required to jump across large hoops made of unfired clay covered with grain seeds and tree branches. Performing this act symbolically transformed a girl into a mother. Then the community considered her properly spiritually educated and thus ready to enter into the life stage of motherhood.

In East Africa, patrilineal Chaga, living on the slopes of Mt. Kilimanjaro in Tanzania, practiced male initiation ceremonies involving circumcision into the late twentieth century. Young men were initiated in public and in groups that were referred to as age sets. As discussed in chapter 2, these age sets crossed familial bonds and counterbalanced family, clan, and territorial alliances. The age set created bonds among nonrelatives. Men remained in the age set for life. They performed service for the chief as an age set and could not marry until the chief approved.

On the other hand, Chaga communities initiated young women individually or in small groups. Older Chaga women in recent times claimed that this secret initiation imparted to women special knowledge and produced solidarity among initiates. These rites provided a counterbalance to the solidarity engendered among men's age sets. Women passed through physical tests meant to educate. For example, young women caught tadpoles, and then the instructors told them to place the tadpoles on their stomachs so as to teach them what the first movements of a fetus would feel like. Elder Chaga women instructed the young women in great detail about how to become pregnant and how to prevent pregnancy, and about labor and childbirth, often explaining that childbirth would take the courage of a warrior.

Such practices had deep roots, but people reinterpreted them moving forward in time. A tool elders used during women's initiation in the early twentieth century was *mrego*, a stick about a yard in length and carved with patterns. An initiation instructor had the knowledge to decipher the carvings on the *mrego*. Each indention and carved design on the *mrego* represented an important person or event initiates were expected to remember. Chiefs and male elders employed *mrego* with other patterns to teach history to the entire community.[16]

---

[16] O. F. Raum. "Female Initiation among the Chaga," *American Anthropologist* 41, no. 4 (October–December, 1939): 558, 560.

Like Sabi peoples in east-central Africa, Chaga performed a second ceremony of life transition for a woman at the time of her first pregnancy. Details of the rites were different, and Chaga observances were, if anything, more elaborate than those of Sabi communities. But the presence and formal recognition of this life-stage transition in recent history in such far separated regions coupled with linguistic evidence supports the conclusion that the origin of these observances goes back at least to Savanna-Bantu of the second millennium BCE.

In addition, different from those of Sabi speakers, Chaga observances of the second life transition, to impending motherhood, involved an additional period of education. After a Chaga woman married and successfully became pregnant for the first time, three pregnancy feasts were held. During the first feast, elders separately educated potential mothers and fathers about the safe development of a fetus, and their duties as parents. The second feast was a celebration full of dances, songs, and food, all to invoke ancestors to endow health upon a young mother and growing fetus. During the last months of pregnancy, Chaga lineages held a third celebration called the "Great Wedding." The fact that the final pregnancy celebration was referred to as "Great Wedding" suggests that the first pregnancy and birth of a child into the lineage were, as also among Sabi peoples, more significant than the marriage ceremony.

Far away to the west, Chokwe people of northeastern Angola and the far southern DRC, provide another notable case study in how a recent historical Bantu society might both preserve ancient features of Bantu female and male initiation and develop new variations in those customs. Tributaries of the powerful Lunda Empire in the seventeenth and eighteenth centuries, Chokwe chiefdoms by the middle nineteenth century had acquired guns, and men in these chiefdoms engaged in elephant-hunting expeditions all across the regions around the upper and middle Kasai River. With their guns, and prospering as suppliers of ivory to the then-burgeoning trade westward to the Atlantic, Chokwe forces broke away from Lunda control and began to expand their territories deep into the western parts of the Lunda heartland itself.

Chokwe populations were matrilineal and had complex initiation schools for both boys and girls. They referred to female initiates as *mwadi*, a reflex of the previously described proto-Bantu root *-yadi* for this period of life. *Nyamwadi* designated a female initiate's mother, whereas *Nyatundanji* named a male initiate's mother. Both of these titles had a prefix (*-nya*), derived from the Bantu root for "mother."

Tellingly, Chokwe speakers referred to both male and female initiation as preparation for parenthood, underscoring and carrying on the far older Bantu emphasis on the importance of securing a lineage's next generation. In recent times female initiation observances, called *ukule*, from the ancient Bantu verb *-kud- "to grow up," could last for as long as four months. Male initiation, *mukanda*, extended over a variable period, from a few months up to a year. Chokwe often referred to *mukanda* as "male womb," reflecting their view that, over the long transition period, a major consequence of these ceremonies was the lessening of a mother and son's connection.

When a group of young Chokwe men were determined to have reached puberty, elders trained them collectively in seclusion. The first step was for them to be circumcised—a practice going back to the proto-Bantu—and during this first stage mothers had to follow dietary and sexual restrictions. At the time of the circumcision procedure itself, community women encircled the initiates' mothers. They sang loudly and danced rapidly so that mothers did not hear their sons' screams. *Mukanda's* educational aspects involved learning their clan history, social expectations and responsibilities of men, and biology, including sex education, as well as esoteric male knowledge.

As part of the initiation observances, Chokwe men learned how to make masks and perform dances, which represented approximately one hundred *likishi* spirits.[17] The word *likishi* derives from an early Bantu root word *-kitI*, whose reflexes across western savanna regions of Africa and in the diaspora reference a range of meanings that include ancestral and territorial spirits, as well as medicinal charms and wood-carved figures and masks that embodied such spirits.[18] It was understood that masked performers were transformed during their

---

[17]   Note that the in the published ethnographic record the noun root–*kishi* is uniformly *makishi* when plural; however, in its singular form it is written as either *likishi/akishi*.

[18]   Guthrie, *Comparative Bantu Vol. 3*, CS 1072, 1073; Wyatt MacGaffey and John M. Janzen, "Nkisi Figures of the Bakongo," *African Arts* 7, no. 3 (1974): 87–89; Wyatt MacGaffey, "Fetishism Revisited: Kongo 'Nkisi' in Sociological Perspective," *Africa: Journal of the International African Institute* 47, no. 2 (1977): 172–184, http://www.jstor.org/stable/1158736; Dunja Hersak, "There Are Many Kongo Worlds: Particularities of Magico-Religious Beliefs among the Vili and Yombe of Congo-Brazzaville," *Africa: Journal of the International African Institute* 71, no. 4 (2001): 614–640, http://www.jstor.org/stable/1161582.

dance, becoming a particular *likishi*. During *mukanda* graduation and public ceremonies, *nyakandanji* led important dances, while their sons displayed their new understanding of masquerade and danced for the first time for the community. Success of the *mukanda* depended upon how well both mothers and sons danced, yet the graduation ceremony symbolized the breaking of close bonds between a woman and her son.

In *ukule* young women learned practical lessons on subjects such as sex, pregnancy and its prevention, as well as childbirth and child rearing. Unlike male initiates, female initiates did not make or wear masks. When a girl first menstruated, she was secluded from the village, and a woman elder was chosen to serve as her sponsor. The elder commenced *ukule* during a chosen evening, wearing a cloth over her face, and dancing while twirling blazing sticks. Her performance was visually intense, meant to scare off men and children. It was a warning that a young woman's *ukule* was beginning, and that they should stay clear of the initiate. This *makishi* dance, was a communication between the ancestors and the initiate. Ancestors facilitated her transition to *mwadi*—from *-yadi*—the life stage of a young woman who was not yet a mother. During the several months of her *ukule,* she learned all she needed to know to become a mother. At the conclusion of *ukule*, she was painted in symbolic colors of red, black, and white. Then she, along with her sponsor and community members, performed lively dance all night long.[19]

Despite variations in details in different societies, many common threads of continuity leading far back to the beginning phases of Bantu history in how people conceived coming of age, education, marriage, parenthood, belonging, seniority, and authority. Graduation for young people among Bantu speakers in large parts of Africa involved intense education, gender segregation, and a period of isolation from their families and the larger community. During transition ceremonies, they learned about the history of their community, how to perform various important tasks, and how to support and maintain healthy sexuality and personal relationships. In addition to practical skills, there were also critical ethereal elements initiates learned, such as how to connect to the realm of spirits and ancestors. It was this very knowledge that ultimately gave them access to authority, status, and power over the course of a lifetime.

---

[19] Elisabeth L. Cameron, "Women = Masks: Initiation Arts in North-Western Province, Zambia," *African Arts* 31, no. 2 (Spring 1998): 51.

ADVANCED LEARNING

In addition to education attained through coming-of-age ceremonies, some people participated in advanced technical education. Apprenticeship to become a technical professional was usually open to anyone who showed promise, but in some societies there were restrictions on who could be admitted, based on clan, lineage, or other such requirements. A unique aspect of advanced education in Bantu-speaking societies was that instructors typically outnumbered students, which the exact opposite of most Western institutions of higher learning.

Readers are encouraged to think about the range of possibilities in the *longue durée* of history for different types of more specialized or higher education fields available across Bantu societies. People became involved in technological training, which included pottery production, iron smelting and blacksmithing, and wood carving, as well as pharmacy and medical healing, to name a few commonly discussed professions. Others became religious specialists or musicians. In a number of societies in the rainforest and neighboring high-rainfall savanna, some people trained to become specialists in raffia cloth (see Figure 3.1) weaving and others in barkcloth production. Both of these were textiles that had been produced for thousands of years by Bantu societies, for local use and for trade, and raffia cloth in particular became a highly valued trade good in the Atlantic era (1500–1900) all through the equatorial rainforest region and southward into what is today the country of Angola. It also became an important currency around the lower Congo region, essential in trading endeavors.

Technologies such as iron and ceramic production, wood carving, raffia weaving, and barkcloth production typically required those interested in becoming specialists to secure an apprenticeship. Once people became skilled in the production of technology, they became recognized artisans and continued production in association with those already trained. Whereas in some societies, an individual with aptitude could apprentice for a particular skill, in other cases certain rituals or signal events were required before a person could be chosen to apprentice. For example, among Bemba and other central African peoples, an individual first dreamed of an ancestor who was a potter and in her dreams learned how to pot. Only then was an individual selected to work with older more mature potters.[20] Similarly, almost universally across Bantu speech communities, those who became

---

[20] Saidi, *Women's Authority*, 147.

FIGURE 3.1   A Kuba raffia cloth from Katanga Province, Democratic Republic of the Congo, has several designs, which communicate Kuba beliefs. Men weave the base, and women embroider designs onto the face of the cloth. Raffia was often used as currency in various precolonial Central African societies. Photo by Anne Manmiller. From private collection of C. Saidi.

medicinal healers almost always were selected because of their demonstrated ability to learn extensive pharmacopeia and necessary ritual skills. Often healers experienced a transcendent episode calling them to profession. The key role that these skilled workers performed in Bantu societies will also be an important topic of the next chapter.

Scholars have referred to one form of higher education as "secret societies," yet the phrase "secret societies" has often been interpreted as occult-like with negative value judgments attached to it. [21] Instead, the term used here is "associations." These associations can be conceptualized as institutions of higher education as members gained specialized and guarded knowledge. Association members had knowledge that often increased their social status because very few people had access to information, and yet in moments of crisis this intelligence was often necessary to solve particular challenges or social problems. Eventually members became teachers of their specialties. Their expertise often provided guidance in the areas of spirituality,

---

[21]   Mary H. Nooter, "Secrecy: African Art That Conceals and Reveals," *African Arts* 26, no. 1 (January 1993): 54–69; John Thornton, *Africa and Africans in the Making of the Atlantic World, 1400–1800*, 2nd ed. (Cambridge: Cambridge University Press, 1998), 220.

history, economics, and politics. Their knowledge united them and cultivated a sense of loyalty and action. Association members gained a hospitable community, status, and protection. This was especially helpful when away from home. Membership in these association facilitated entrée into established networks. These associations had key secret and mystical elements, but they were also exclusive organizations of status and mutual aid societies somewhat comparable to Masons, Knights of Columbus, or university honor socities of the Western world.

In Bantu Africa these types of associations developed near major trading points along the Congo River, possibly as early as a thousand years ago (fifth phase). Such ideas then moved southward toward the central and eastern modern-day DRC.[22] Three examples of such associations include Luba's *Bumbudye*, Lake Mweru's *Ubutwa*, and Lega's *Bwami*. By about 1600, *Bumbudye* served as intellectual checks-and-balances on power of the Luba Empire's political elite. They legitimized Luba chiefs by giving their consent and ceremonial blessing. *Bumbudye* helped to counterbalance despotic behavior at the center. *Bumbudye* local leaders influenced Luba's central government, because they controlled important ritual sanctions. As the Luba Empire expanded, *Bumbudye* helped to integrate smaller Bantu speech communities into the Luba world by allowing local leaders to remain leaders if they went through *Bumbudye* training. And it functioned as a means to integrate new people into the Empire.

Early twentieth-century European missionaries, explorers, and colonial occupiers noted *Bumbudye*. According to them, Luba people had calculated that their associations were four hundred years old. Recently art historians have studied *Bumbudye*, a multilevel organization which one joined and could advance to higher levels. The only prerequisite to the first level of membership was adulthood. Both women and men could achieve a high level within the association, as long as they had proven intelligent enough and resources to pay for the privilege of this higher education. Geography, history, literature, and religious ideas were part of the lower level curriculum. Intricate maps found on walls in small houses located in outlying rural areas depicted the entire Luba Empire, which was about 200 square miles with all the major lakes and rivers, the symbols for each of the chiefs in every

---

[22] Christopher Ehret, *Civilizations of Africa: A History to 1800* (Charlottesville: University of Virginia Press, 2016), 418–419.

region. It also illustrated the homes of *Bumbudye* leaders, which were used as *Bumbudye* schools.[23]

Through the process of joining the organization and after the first level, the initiate gained a new identity and began a path of spiritual awakening and intellectual challenges. The second level involved the development of the initiate's knowledge. The *kamanji*, an important elder, led the initiate down a path in the forested areas. Along the path there would be figures representing Luba history, spirits, and *Bumbudye* hierarchy. The third level, *lukala* or the house of symbols, required both financial assets and intellectual ability. Members communicated using a sign language known only to them. They had to study knowledge encoded in wall murals of abstract and figurative signs depicted on interior walls houses. Initiates also had to find one's spirit pair and the initiate became this spirit at all *Bumbudye* celebrations. The final level was when the person rose to highest authority. He or she learned to read and interpret the *lukasa*, a mnemonic device. It was made of hand-size pieces of wood with beads and shells that formed designs that helped initiates in retaining their knowledge.

Ubutwa, which means the state of being sharp, appears to be an ancient form of higher education that developed in the Luapula river region, before there was a Bantu presence there. According to oral accounts, *Ubutwa* maintained Batwa and Sabi histories and traditions. Their responsibilities included taking care of the sick and burying deceased members. They recount that the original members of *Ubutwa* were Batwa, as the word root suggests. Ultimately membership transcended kinship, family, clan, and ethnic boundaries. Unlike *Bumbudye*, *Ubutwa* was not tied to political leadership. Instead, it seems that Batwa populations used it as a means to integrate newcomers. Based on linguistic and archaeological evidence, about 1,500 years ago, Sabi Bantu speakers moved into the area. Indeed, oral traditions reflect that Batwa used *Ubutwa* activities and structures to integrate Sabi into the regional community. In the 1500s, another Bantu group, Lunda, began ruling the region through centralized leadership. Yet *Ubutwa* members, in an effort to protect

---

[23] John D. Studstill, "Education in a Luba Secret Society," *Anthropology & Education Quarterly* 10, no. 2 (Summer 1979): 67–79; Mary Nooter Roberts and Allen F. Roberts, eds. *Memory—Luba Art and the Making of History* (New York: Museum for African Art, 1996).

historical integrity of the association, precluded these new leaders from joining.[24]

Ubutwa were comprised of initiates, confirmed members, and senior officers. Those becoming members took an oath of loyalty to never reveal *Ubutwa* knowledge, and all members were required to learn the *Ubutwa* language.[25] To reach higher levels of the association, a person had both to know ancient history of the area and to demonstrate spiritual power. Leaders in each autonomous lodge were *nangulu*, mother of the spirits, or *shingulu*, father of the spirits. The *na-* and *shi- ngulu* served as protectors of members from malevolent spirits.

In the northeastern Congo forest just west of Lake Kivu, Lega developed *Bwami* associations by the nineteenth century. Ethnographers have noted seven levels of *Bwami* for men and four for women.[26] New initiates had to memorize and recite more than three hundred proverbs and their symbolic representations carved in wood that communicated a belief system and instructed *Bwami* members on proper conduct. Lega used *Bwami* to maintain their culture, social order, and unified Lega identity. This resource served them well in social and political turmoil of the late nineteenth and early twentieth centuries.

Throughout Bantu-speaking Africa, specialists formed associations such as *Bumbudye*, *Ubutwa*, and *Bwami* to teach specialized knowledge and pass on information they possessed. Although some were connected to political power, others were used to integrate diverse populations and to maintain moral standards. Each association required learning specialized knowledge that was used in maintaining, upholding, and guiding their societies.

---

[24] The longer term impact and implications of the balance of power orchestrated between centralized states and associations can be seen, for example, in the work of Markus Rediker, *The Slave Ship* (New York: Penguin Books, 2007), 95–97.

[25] Mwelwa C. Musambachime, "The Ubutwa Society in Eastern Shaba [Katanga] and North East Zambia to 1920." *International Journal of African History Institute* 27, no. 1 (1994): 77–99.

[26] Evan M. Zuesse, "Action as the Way of Transcendence: The Religious Significance of the Bwami Cult of the Lega," *Journal of Religion in Africa* 9 (1978): 62–72.

COMMUNICATION IN THE BANTU HISTORICAL TRADITION

Although most Bantu languages were not represented in written form until the nineteenth and twentieth centuries, their oral cultures preserved great bodies of old knowledge. From proto-Bantu times onward, the ability to express oneself orally and recount history orally and visually must have been a highly valued skill across Bantu-speaking Africa. Bantu speech communities that had close contact with Muslims and Islamic intellectual traditions often adopted the practice of literacy, yet writing down the past, even then, did not hold primacy over orality as the means of transmitting cultural and social traditions.

The transition from oral, kinesthetic, and visual to written knowledge to store information outside the human person is a process still unfolding across Bantu speech communities today. In earlier centuries, visual imagery often represented broad concepts. Bantu speakers did not develop a written communication method where a particular character denoted a particular word, syllable, or sound. Rather, visual representations were often schematic or nonpictorial. Images and designs held connotations not always obvious to outsiders. Although most adults within a given society, after initiation school, could interpret the meanings of symbols, some people became experts trained in more esoteric definitions and implications of cultural transmitted down through time. Education at all levels emphasized the ability to remember oral traditions, oral literature, and myriad visual symbols.

Most Bantu communities lived close to or traded with other communities and, because of recurrent episodes of Bantu expansions into new regions, where neighboring communities were not always Bantu speakers. Over the long run of Bantu history, people in a Bantu societies often would have been bilingual or multilingual and have been fluent speakers of two or more Bantu languages, along with being fluent in a first language and a cultural tradition that was non-Bantu in origin. The need to be fluent in two or more languages, coupled with high respect for oral history and visual literature, required a good memory. Bantu speakers very often employed mnemonic devices to aid themselves in bringing alive their lessons and to aid their audiences in learning and retaining cultural and historical knowledge but also more profound thoughts that they sought to impart. Wide geographic distribution of such tactics points to the use of mnemonic devices as early elements within Bantu thought and practice, probably dating as far back to the third phase of expansion, if not earlier.

In Central African initiation, schematic art painted on stationary walls along with portable clay items served this purpose. Chaga communities in eastern Africa, as described earlier, used the *mrego*, a transportable wooden carved stick, to teach history during female initiation ceremonies. Another example of how people speaking Bantu languages used mnemonic items can be seen among Luba of Central Africa. Artists, art historians, and art collectors of Europe and the United States know Luban artistic traditions well. What is less known is that each of their carvings and iron art pieces includes symbols used to remember and pass down knowledge about important people and events of the past.

Even more important for speakers Luba populations was the *lukasa*, a memory board that they relied on for more complex interpretations and communications of memory. *Lukasa*—fashioned out of rough-hewn wood and decorated with pins, beads, and incised ideograms—was the size of a large paddle that could be held with one hand. Whereas some ideograms and beads held universal meaning among Luban adults, others required mediation by experts to interpret them.[27] Interpretation of the *lukasa* was crucial at certain public events and played an integral part in private *bumbudye* higher education. The expert who interpreted the *lukasa* communicated historical events and social mores, but within the context of his or her understanding of the audience and local issues and views. The interpreter among Luba had to possess special knowledge and effectively impart it to audiences.

A number of communities used ropes as mnemonics for communicating history. A notable example is the Shona kingdom of Mutapa, which dominated the northern half of modern-day Zimbabwe from the middle fifteenth century to the late seventeenth century and lingered on as an independent, although less important state in the eighteenth and nineteenth centuries. In that kingdom a court historian tied one knot at the beginning of the reign of each new ruler. In 1929 there were thirty-five knots on the royal rope, representing all the rulers of the kingdom over the previous 480 years.[28]

---

27   Roberts and Roberts *Memory—Luba*, 41.

28   Dirk Huylebrouck, "Mathematics in (Central) Africa Before Colonialization," *Anthropologica et Præhistorica* 117 (2006): 149.

Chokwe communities employed a different kind of device, the *sona*. These were graphs and diagrams that captured geometric theory, which students learned to use during initiation schools. The initiates were instructed in the calculations, signs, and computations needed to determine which candidate would be chosen as the new leader upon the death of the chief.[29] These diagrams were taught to all adults so that everyone understood the process for selecting a new ruler. Using various types of calculations, *sona* also showed the relative position of all born into a community as well as those who had become ancestors.

Another method of communication was through music. People performed music and played musical instruments not just as entertainment but to evoke specific ideas, emotions, and events, and to communicate with both the living and the ancestors. Some instruments were used to help trigger memories of history and served to support the transmission of oral tradition. Others were used to relate news and current events.

While musicians played drums throughout most of Bantu history and the primary accompaniment for almost all musical performances, Bantu peoples in west-central Africa far back into the past have famously used drums, "talking drums," to transmit important information to people within hearing distance. In the recent history of Uganda, people in the countryside often relied on the drumbeats to tell them important news, such as calling people for public meetings or communal work projects, announcing a serious problem or the death of an important person, or broadcasting the beginning of a hunting expedition. In villages children learned at an early age to decode different voices and messages of drums. The rhythm, speed, intensity, and type of drum used were differently for each event announced. Often there was even a different drummer for each type of drum.[30] In large communal performances, the use of different drum rhythms could indicate which clan was to dance.

Another very widespread instrument for communication was the flange-welded double bell used widely across the whole Congo Basin during the period between around 500 and 1000 CE, spreading

---

[29] Huylebrouck, Mathematics, 144.

[30] Aaron Mushengyezi, "Rethinking Indigenous Media: Rituals, 'Talking' Drums and Orality as Forms of Public Communication in Uganda," *Journal of African Cultural Studies* 16, no. 1 (June 2003): 107–117.

still farther south as far as the city of Great Zimbabwe by the twelfth and thirteenth centuries. Blacksmiths in Africa already developed bell marks as a major advance in iron welding probably a bit before 500 CE. Equally important historically was the ritual and political significance of the double bell. In the early period of its spread, the double bell was consistently an implement of chiefs and kings. Each of the two conjoined bells had a different pitch. Bantu languages all were two-tone languages, with each syllable in a word having either a high tone or a low tone. So, for example, any stock phrase praising a chief or king would have its own different sequence of tones. If the ringer of the bell rang out a particular sequence of tones, everyone in the community would immediately recognize which phrase the bell was mimicking.

Still a different, although related, instrument of this kind was the carved wooden double bell found in the lower Congo River region. KiKongo speakers called the wooden bells *kunda*, a noun that derives from the verb *-kunda*, which means "to pay homage or to supplicate."[31] For people of Kongo, its two bells represent the mediation between the worlds of the living and the dead. Each bell represented one of these worlds, but to accentuate their unity, the *kunda* was carved out of a single piece of solid wood.

Further south the "thumb piano," or *mbira*, became part of Shona epistemology. It was more than music; *mbira* was used to communicate with the spirit realm. Among Shona religious observers, the *mbira* was a way people prayed to God and the world of the spirits. They believed that the *mbira* was a bridge between the living and the ancestors, spirits and God. Shona claimed that a highly skilled musician was able to draw spirits down toward the earth.[32] Individuals who served as spirit mediums needed the spirit's presence to be possessed. In addition, the *mbira* music encouraged people in the community to continue dancing for long periods of time, an action that they believed kept the spirits physically close.

As recently as the late twentieth century in southeastern Africa, people used musical instruments and music in retelling oral histories of Zulu and Swazi people forcibly removed from their lands between

---

[31] Wyatt MacGaffey, "Ethnographic Notes on Kongo Musical Instruments," *African Arts* 35, no. 2 (Summer 2002): 17.

[32] Paul Berliner, "Music and Spirit Possession at a Shona Bira," *African Music* 5, no. 4 (1975/1976): 130–139.

1948 to 1970 by the apartheid-era government of South Africa. This intense period of change threatened preservation of cultural and social institutions. Previously, women in this area played the mouth bow, *unqangala*, making music when they had to walk long distances. Over twenty years ago, anthropologists met with older women from this area and brought various types of *unqangala*.[33] Once the women started playing the instruments, the music inspired memories of their past traditions and history. For some women it had been forty years since they played the instrument or heard the music, but once they started playing the *unqangala*, the music unleashed a flood of memories for them.

CONCLUSION

Children in Bantu-speaking societies over the last five and a half millennia have engaged in a variety of educational activities, from informal to intensive, which commenced early in life and developed and changed as their abilities to watch, understand, and contribute to events of their community grew. Although specific forms and practices varied across time and region, once an individual was a teenager, she or he underwent rigorous and specific courses to prepare intellectually, economically, morally, emotionally, and spiritually for the next stage of life, parenthood. The social norm, parenthood, became an aspiration of all community members. Parenthood did not exclude men or women from the public sphere. Some chose to study a trade as a hunter, iron smelter, potter, or raffia cloth weaver or embroiderer (see Figure 3.1), while others desired to become medical practitioners, herbalists, or spiritual leaders. In societies of the eastern interior Congo Basin, a further sort of education took shape over the past one thousand years, with the rise of voluntary associations, also called "secret" societies because of esoteric knowledge they imparted to their members, as their members graduated to successively higher ranks in those societies.

Bantu-speaking people developed a variety of effective means and methods for transmitting knowledge, education, and spiritual knowledge across generations and into new regions, as Bantu expansions proceeded

---

[33] Angela Impey, "Sound, Memory, Dis/placement: Exploring Sounds, Song and Performance as Oral History in South African Borderlands," *Oral History* 36, no. 1 (2008): 33–44.

over the centuries. Visual imagery and oral performance were particularly important in communicating complex ideas. Mnemonic devices served to enhance teaching and help students to consolidate and retain what they learned. Rock art, wood carvings, ceramic pieces, knots in strings, geometric patterns in raffia cloth (see Figure 3.1), carved sticks, and memory boards were among the means each Bantu community had of preserving the myriad symbols and meanings. In addition to visual forms of communication, Bantu-speaking peoples also used music and dance to communicate knowledge and to inculcate their cultures' understandings of earthly and spirit worlds.

FURTHER READINGS

Frank, Barbara E. "Field Research and Making Objects Speak." *African Arts* 40 (Spring 2007): 13–17.

Huylebrouck, Dirk. "Mathematics in (Central) Africa Before Colonization." *Anthropologica et Præhistorica* 117 (2006): 135–162.

Kreamer, Christine Mullen, Sarah Adams; National Museum of African Art. *Inscribing Meaning: Writing and Graphic Systems in African Art.* Washington, DC: Smithsonian National Museum of African Art, 2007.

Roberts, Mary Nooter, Allen F. Roberts, S. Terry Childs; Museum for African Art. *Luba Art and the Making of History.* New York: Museum for African Art, 1996.

Saidi, Christine. *Women's Authority and Society in Early East Central Africa.* Rochester, N.Y.: Rochester University Press, 2010.

Creating Technology and Art

An important area of historical inquiry includes the processes involved in the invention of scientific technologies, production of material culture, and the conceptualization of art in societies. Though the artifacts people leave behind cannot tell scholars the languages their manufacturers spoke, modern-day languages can be analyzed to recover information about the products past societies used and valued. From Cameroon to Zambia, there are Bantu-speaking peoples who equate a potter and the act of potting with the Creator and the act of human creation. This conceptual and linguistic analogy provides philosophical insight into the intertwined nature of art, science, and worldview in Bantu history and daily life. Early Bantu populations continually reimagined their artistic and technological traditions and incorporated and adapted other peoples' useful and appealing ideas.

"Technology and art" refers to the broad spectrum of tools and techniques that people typically have invented and applied in making daily life more efficient and tasks easier or more productive. This chapter turns attention to some of the significant and transformative technological achievements among Bantu societies over the *longue durée*, with particular emphasis given to the most recent two thousand years. It examines the role of science and art in the development of economies, aesthetics, desired materials, useful tools, and items needed in day-to-day life.

FOOD PRODUCTION

Although for many people today getting a meal may involve calling for a pizza or nuking dinner in a microwave, over the long term of history, people have collected, grown, harvested, and raised their own food and then prepared the foods for consumption and storage. From these resources they prepared meals. Until the industrial age, people throughout the world spent a large portion of their time and energy on procurement and provisions. Historically, communities looked for and found ways of producing food efficiently and abundantly with varying degrees of success. This section will explore the innovative spirit of ancient and modern Bantu communities in regards to dietary technology and the science and art of food production.

In previous chapters, examples of Bantu innovation and borrowing across many realms of life have been highlighted as transformations that Bantu instigated as they expanded into new areas. At the same time, it has also been important to recognize continuities in practice that overlaid new lifeways. Food production in the form of agriculture, fishing, hunting, and the raising of goats and guinea fowl trace back well before 3500 BCE when proto-Bantu society took shape. But in later times the techniques Bantu used in food production were adapted to distinct environments, and other times they used their technologies to change their new environments to meet farming needs. At least five thousand years ago, early Bantu descended communities were living in the southern parts of modern-day Cameroon. There they exploited the resources of several notable ecological niches. As early as that time they had a complex of linguistic words for distinct types of lands. This implies they likely had a use-based appreciation of their environments. For example, they distinguished rainforest environments, which they called *-titu, from patches of intercalary savanna within the forests, which they referred to as *-subi. The root *-subi named the type of land that would have been ideal for planting their staple crops. And they also distinguished a secondary forest type called *-saka, which for them named an area of forest that was growing on previously cultivated land, from yet-to-be-domesticated land *-kanga, a distinction that suggests Bantu viewed *-kanga as land that had the potential for food acquisition and production. By that time, too, they also farmed and processed at least two varieties of yams, *-kua and *-pama, as well as cowpeas, *-kúndè, and groundnuts, *-júgù.

As Bantu speakers moved into forested territories, yam farming required that they change the landscape. The practice of forest clearing became an essential first step before planting yam cuttings in the ground. Archeologists have found the tools suggestive of forest clearing and yam planting in this area, and also farther south in the western equatorial rainforest. Recovered artifacts include polished stone axes, which would have been the essential implements for the work of cutting back the trees where yam cuttings needed to be planted. What is more, this kind of ax probably was used as a planting tool as well. These would have been helpful in areas with highly lateritic soils found in many parts of the equatorial rainforest where the direct beating down of the rain turns the soil into a rock-hard surface. In rainforest areas, one way early Bantu farmers protected the land from leeching rains and soil hardening was with the techniques of leaving cut-up vegetation covering the soil after clearing fields. Then, rather than dig up the ground for planting, which would have disturbed the soil nutrients that were on the topsoil, women farmers used a blade to slice into the soil, then inserted a yam cutting into the slit, and pushed the ground back together around the cutting. This effort protected the soil from erosion and ensured successful harvests. The etymology of the proto-Bantu word, *-soka*, which named an ax, is revealing of this history. The word derives from an earlier verb *-sok-* that meant "to poke" and not, as one might expect, from a verb for chopping. This linguistic evidence is a strong indication that, while people may have used the ax to cut down trees, early Bantu farmers likely used the same blade for poking or slicing a hole in the soil to insert the yam plant cutting.[1]

Over the centuries, Bantu speakers migrated further across the forest zone. As well as taking advantage of areas of savanna interspersed in the forest, they settled along rivers, which, because of the break in the tree canopy at the river's edge, provided greater sunlight for their crops and, of course, gave them access to good fishing resources. By around 3000 BCE (second phase) their expanding areas of settlement brought them more and more into contact and trade relations with Batwa people of those regions. Batwa found a market among Bantu communities for the honey and wax they gathered in the forest, as well as for hides they made from the animals they hunted. Over the long run, Batwa began to supplement their gathered and hunted foods with foods they secured through trade with Bantu farmers. As discussed previously, this meeting of Batwa and Bantu

---

[1] Ehret, *Classical*, 112–113.

communities was the impetus for enduring trade relationships that expanded the variety of foods available to each community, but it also set them up for an intertwined history more generally.

In areas near larger bodies of water, Bantu men built small wooden canoes and boats to use in the Sanaga and Nyong Rivers, and they fished using fishhooks they fashioned from shell and bone. Modern Bantu languages' persistent use of proto-Bantu roots such as *-lobo, for "fishhook," and the verb *-lob, "to fish with hook and line," is evidence that ancient people fished with these technologies. The comparative ethnographic evidence from across the Bantu regions confirms that women would have been fishers as well, using fishing baskets to catch fish in shallow water. In the previous chapter, as the reader learned, fishing in the shallows of streams was crucial to providing protein during the dry season for the Punu community of southern Gabon. An ancient feature of this kind of fishing, still widely preserved in Bantu-speaking regions in recent times, was for women to wade in groups through the water while singing songs addressed to the water spirits while rhythmically moving in unison so as to better direct small fish into their baskets as well as to protect themselves against crocodiles.[2]

For the first two thousand years of their expansions, Bantu communities would have largely intermingled with people of Bantu backgrounds or of Batwa origins. But in the last five hundred years of the second millennium BCE (third phase), as the ongoing expansions reached the southern and eastern fringes of the equatorial rainforest zones, Bantu-speaking communities entered into a period of adaptation within new environmental frontiers that raised challenges and opportunities. From about 1000 BCE (fourth phase) Bantu-speaking people reaching the Great Lakes region met up with Nilo-Saharan-speaking people whose deep ancestry traces back to the areas along the middle stretches of the Nile River. In contrast to Bantu tuber cutting agriculture, Nilo-Saharan production centered on seed agriculture and the keeping of cattle. Contacts with Nilo-Saharans opened up an opportunity for Bantu people to add these new farming practices to their retinue. With their old and newly adopted farming abilities, Bantu had the flexibility to settle new communities in many diverse niches. Some took to large grassland savannas that were dotted with trees, and others settled alongside or close to riverbanks.

---

[2] Plancke, "On Dancing," 639–640.

Still others migrated to higher altitudes, making homes in the cool climates of the highlands and mountainous regions of the Western and East African rifts. In contrast, some Bantu continued migrating in a southerly direction clear to the drier savanna regions of southern Africa, while other populations moved easterly reaching as far as the Indian Ocean. By 300 CE, Bantu-speaking people had established communities across the landscape of sub-Saharan Africa.

It is to Kaskazi Bantu-speaking people, whose descendants settled along the East African coast about two thousand years ago that we turn our attention. With their inherited farming science and technological history that by then included seed farming, and tuber planting, fishing, and animal husbandry, those Bantu people came into connection with migrants, known today as the ancestral Malagasy, who traveled to the East African coastlines from Indonesia's Borneo islands.[3] Their interactions ushered in an exchange of ideas and people that over the course of the subsequent two-thousand-year period added significant new foods to their local diets as well as seafaring technologies that in many instances ended up influencing African societies far beyond the East African coasts and hinterlands.

Relying on the Indian Ocean monsoon wind regimens and their ancient, but efficient outrigger canoe crafts, Indonesians travelled sea-lanes from Borneo to East Africa. Moving southward from along the Kenyan and Tanzanian coasts, they introduced Asian crops. These included taro, sugarcane, yams, chickens, and cooking bananas, which thrived in temperate environments along the East African coast, as well as in the Great Lakes and the Congo Basin, regions with similar humid climates like those of the Indonesian tropics. In time, Bantu and settled Indonesians farming these newly introduced crops began to move them from coastal zones inland. Using well-developed trade networks across inland communities, the products had natural pathways of diffusion. These conduits became a means for the movement of these crops and their farming technologies. Of these new crops, cooking bananas, followed by chickens and Asian tuber crops, were the most influential transformations in the provisioning history of sub-Saharan Africa.[4] Notably, Indonesian populations also

---

[3] Nicole Boivin et al., "East Africa and Madagascar in the Indian Ocean World," *Journal of World Prehistory* 26 (2013): 213–281.

[4] Sidney Mintz, *Sweetness and Power: The Place of Sugar in Modern History* (New York: Viking Penguin Books, 1986).

adopted Bantu techniques and technologies of raising cattle, sheep, and goats indigenous to and domesticated in Africa. This is shown by Indonesian immigrants' adoption of the words for each of these animals from the early Bantu communities of that region. By the end of the fourth century CE, many ancestral Malagasy people had spread farther south, to the island of Madagascar.[5] Their Austronesian language became the early form of spoken modern-day Malagasy.[6]

The Asian yam and chicken were new food sources, but they likely were not completely unfamiliar to East African Bantu, as they long had similar products in their diets. Domesticated guinea fowl, which for millennia had been a source of meat and eggs, paved the way for their adoption of domesticated fowl new to them, the chicken, introduced to the East African coast by the ancestral Malagasy in the early first millennium CE. Bantu speakers in eastern Africa came to call Asian chickens by versions of the word *-kuku, derived from the Malagasy word akuku. Mapping the spread of this word across sub-Saharan Africa demonstrates that the domesticated chicken moved from eastern Africa to Bantu peoples in southern Africa and westward across the equatorial rainforest to peoples inhabiting land as far west as the Atlantic Ocean.[7] Bantu peoples adapted their technology for and knowledge of indigenous African yams to propagate East Asian yams. As will be discussed in the next section, it was people's adoption of the cooking banana that produced a new year-round, high-calorie food source that would have a revolutionary impact not only on farming but also on society more generally.

BANANAS

An additional example of the influences Bantu speakers had over the *longue durée* in innovation and cosmopolitan outlook is exemplified in their incorporation of the Asian cooking bananas as a staple starch analogous to a potato. This also became a sphere where they

---

[5] Charles E. M. Pearce and Francis M. Pearce, *Oceanic Migration: Paths, Sequence, Timing and Range of Prehistoric Migration in the Pacific and Indian Oceans* (Netherlands: Springer, 2010), 67.

[6] Nicole Boivin et al., "East Africa and Madagascar in the Indian Ocean World," *Journal of World Prehistory* 26 (2013): 213–281.

[7] Ehret, *Classical*, 279.

elaborated new agricultural technologies for banana and new arenas for cultural and political activities in eastern Africa. Bantu communities in the East African coastland shared their knowledge of banana cultivation and technology with inland neighbors. In time, Bantu-speaking farmers further westward adopted the technologies and through these processes, bananas diffused through western Africa. This crop later became important among Bantu and non-Bantu in tropical western Africa, where it was eaten as a side dish.[8]

By 400 CE (fourth phase), Bantu farmers expanded banana cultivation inland across eastern and central Africa all the way to the Great Lakes region, where it became a preferred food source. Bananas provided dense calories that when combined with animal protein or legumes contributed to a balanced diet.[9] This crop produced large surpluses of food, and farmers made effective practice of intercropping within banana groves. Intercropping is a technique of pairing complementary crops together, usually one deep rooted and one shallow rooted, in gardens, groves, and farm plots to maximize yields, space use, and biodiversity while also increasing needed soil nutrients such as nitrogen. The banana crop also created comfortable shaded areas that served as new social spaces for community gatherings. In several regions, notably in the Great Lakes region, around the mountain areas of modern-day northeastern Tanzania, and in the highlands of southwestern Tanzania, this crop contributed to a dramatically changed ecological and economic landscape. Importantly, banana farming was less labor intensive than the raising of most other crops, freeing up farmers to work at other productive activities.

Bantu communities took advantage of banana outputs to remake and transform their production modes and capacities. Today in Africa, there are more than a hundred hybrid banana varieties, whereas in

---

[8] Katharina Neumann and Elisabeth Hildebrand, "Early Bananas in Africa: The State of the Art," *Ethnobotany Research & Applications* 7 (2009): 353–362; Mbida Minzie et. al., "The Initial History of Bananas in Africa: A Reply to Vansina," *Azania* 40 (2005): 128–135; Mbida Minzie et al., "Evidence for Banana Cultivation and Animal Husbandry During the First Millennium BC in the Forest of Southern Cameroon," *Journal of Archaeological Science* 27, no. 2 (2000): 151–162; Gerda Rossel, "Taxonomic-Linguistic Study of Plantain in Africa" (Leiden: Research School CNWS), 1998.

[9] Thomas Spear, *Mountain Farmers: Moral Economies of Land and Agricultural Development in Arusha and Meru* (Berkeley: University of California Press, 1997), 124.

Asia, where bananas were first domesticated, there are about a dozen. Not only were they an important food source in Bantu Africa, but also cooking bananas became a major crop in Central America and, in the past few centuries, in the Caribbean, where they were transported via the Atlantic trade of the fifteenth through the nineteenth centuries. For enslaved Africans in the Americas, bananas continued to be a preferred food. Despite the traumatic ruptures of dislocation, enslaved Africans (both Bantu and West Atlantic speakers), as well as those who established maroon societies, where possible, maintained cultural continuity by recreating banana groves in the Americas.[10]

Indeed, in parts of eastern and central Africa bananas became a type of wonder food. Scholars have contended that this high-producing food crop, brought by Indonesian immigrants to East Africa two thousand years ago and adapted by Bantu speakers, had both economic and demographic consequences.[11] In highland areas of East Africa, this crop produced an abundance of food that enabled more people to live on less land. With higher caloric intake, people were healthier and population densities increased. By the tenth century CE (fifth phase) in the highlands around Mount Kenya, Thagiicu ancestors relied on a diverse group of crops in addition to bananas. On the higher rainfall middle slopes of Mt. Kenya and the Nyandarua Range, they cultivated both African and Asian yam species along with other introduced Southeast Asian crops, such as arrowroot and, eventually, taro and sugarcane. Lower down on the slopes they raised sorghum and pearl millet, drought-resistant ancient African crops. To the south of Mt. Kenya, around the middle slopes of Mt. Kilimanjaro late in the first millennium CE, ancestors of modern-day Chaga took up intensive banana cultivation and developed a large number of new banana varieties, as well as raised finger millet and yams. This diversity of ecological niches and crop production fostered the rise of large regional markets and networks of trade across these regions.

Far to the west in the Congo Basin, the arrival of bananas in the first millennium CE enhanced the opportunities for Bantu communities to participate in the growing trade along the Congo River and

---

[10] Judith Carney, *In the Shadow of Slavery: Africa's Botanical Legacy in the Atlantic World*, 1st ed. (Berkeley: University of California Press, 2011), 94–99.

[11] Schoenbrun, "Cattle Herds and Banana Gardens: The Historical Geography of the Western Great Lakes Region, ca. AD 800–1500," *African Archaeological Review* 11, no. 1 (1993): 39–72; Ehret, *Civilizations*, 182–183, 272–279.

its tributaries. As historians Jan Vansina and Kairn Klieman have argued, the lesser labor demands of banana cultivation freed up time for people to engage in the production of goods, such as raffia cloth, pottery, and metal products, specifically intended for the expanding trade relations in the succeeding centuries.[12]

By 700 CE (fifth phase), many people living around the Great Lakes of eastern Africa had added banana cultivation to their farming of other crops—yams, sorghum, and pearl and finger millet. By 1000 CE, many areas between Lake Nyanza and the Western Rift region, once thick with trees, had become open grassland savannas. Farmers had removed extensive forested habitat and reshaped the landscape. They shrank the areas that had been suitable to the tsetse fly, the insect that carries "sleeping sickness," a disease that is harmful to humans and deadly to cattle. The tsetse fly needs shade to survive, and so they thrive in bush and woodland areas. As long as such areas remain wooded, the main sources of food had to come from cultivation. But once people cleared such lands, they could raise cattle in the resulting savanna grasslands, where tsetse could not survive. The effect of deforestation for these Lake Bantu communities in this era was that it opened land up for successful livestock raising economies. At the same time, agriculturalists continued to develop specialized production centered on agricultural cultivation in a variety of new environments.

Well before the eighth century BCE (fourth phase), Kusi-speaking communities had migrated south into southern Africa's savanna zones. The arrival of Kusi Bantu speakers by possibly as early as the second century BCE set off a long-term history of cultural and economic interchange with Khoesan populations who had been living in and predominantly practicing gathering and hunting for at least 10,000 years. The interactions of Khoesan and Bantu are evidenced in linguistic, technological, and political exchanges. The most apparent sign of borrowing is the way in which Bantu languages like isiZulu and isiXhosa borrowed words and certain click consonants from Khoesan languages. The less obvious exchanges can be found in the subsistence economies of each of these language groups. The Khoekhoe—one subgroup of Khoesan peoples—had recently taken up an economy distinct from those of the rest of Khoesan, communities having created an economy in the second half of the first millennium BCE that combined sheep and cattle raising with supplementary

---

[12] Jan Vansina, *Paths*, 61–65; Klieman, *Pygmies*, 96–97.

hunting and gathering. Into this context, Kusi brought to southern Africa the science of farming sorghum and pearl millet as well
as ironworking technology. These communities had complementary
economies and were able to exchange on this basis, but in time they
influenced one another's economies.

Much like examples explored in earlier chapters, in which
cross-cultural interaction between Bantu and non-Bantu generated
synergies, the encounters of Kusi agriculturalists with a new set of
communities led them to conceive and initiate a variety of economic
and political changes unique to southern Africa. Kusi speakers
initially centered their food production on grain cultivation, but their
engagement with Khoesan neighbors, who gathered and hunted large
savanna game, and with KhoeKhoe, who raised cattle, made for a
robust circuit of exchange relations. Bantu manufactured goods, such
as pottery and iron goods, were traded for wild game products from
the gathering-hunting Khoesan communities and for cattle from-
Khoekhoe herding peoples. As Kusi peoples, especially those to the
south of the Limpopo River, grew wealthy in cattle, livestock became
a preferred form of wealth, and the ownership of cattle in particular
accorded the emerging class of cattle owner-raisers prestigious social
standing. Luxury goods like beads Khoesan communities crafted
from ostrich shells, as well as leopard skins and ivory from elephant
tusks, became prestige goods that in time elites exploited as part of
their regalia and for tribute and taxation.

Over the course of the first millennium CE, Bantu and Khoekhoe often married across cultural lines. The long-term absorption of
more and more Khoekhoe groups into the ancestral societies of today's Bantu-descended Sotho and Nguni societies of South Africa
led to major social and cultural change as well, with these societies
shifting over from the earlier Bantu pattern of matrilineal descent to
Khoekhoe patrilineal patterns. The new Kusi communities that arose
out of this age of cross-cultural encounter developed mixed economies, in which women probably continued to provide the majority of
the dictary calories through farming, while men likely garnered near
exclusive control of cattle production in this part of southern Africa.

With this new mixture of cultivation and herding, the Sotho
and Nguni moved into the dryer savanna areas where their populations continued to grow. Archaeology evinces that chiefs who
became wealthy in cattle probably used their wealth to attract clients
that enabled them to build some of the first mini-states in southern
Africa between around 500 and 900 CE. In the later first millennium

CE, Bantu peoples, such as the ancestral Shona, then living in what is today the Limpopo province of South Africa, along with Sotho of the High Veld and Nguni of KwaZulu-Natal, developed similar political ideologies that rooted political authority in cattle ownership. The older Bantu institutions of lineage and clan chiefs gave way to a new scale of polities in which chiefs, and eventually kings, belonged to royal clans, while the majority of people in their polities belonged to commoner clans.[13] The empire of Great Zimbabwe from the thirteenth to fifteenth centuries and the Zulu kingdom during the nineteenth century provide striking examples of the adaptability of this kind of ideology even to the creation and maintenance of quite large states.

Bantu creatively used new environments, developing new and modifying older technologies to create viable agricultural strategies. Some Bantu even settled in territory covered with the brightly colored but parched copper-rich soils of east-central Africa. Beginning around 600 CE, Sabi Bantu moved from moister areas further west in the southern Congo Basin into east-central Africa. They moved into regions Mashariki Bantu had previously settled and adopted their agricultural techniques. But significantly they applied their old *citemene* techniques, involving cutting down and then burning vegetation to enhance soil fertility, in a more systematic fashion than before.

Botatwe, whose ancestors emigrated from humid Katanga regions in the north, moved into arid southern Zambia. Sabi, Botatwe farmers employed *citemene* technology by the eighth century CE. Though the precise techniques of Botatwe *citemene* differed from those of the Sabi, both groups turned marginal soils into more fertile earth by tilling into the soil the ash that came from burning the vegetation to clear fields. Farmers could yield larger grain harvests and support larger populations as a result of the boost they created in soil nutrients. From Kaskazi and Kusi communities who had preceded them in southern Zambia, the Botatwe adopted cattle raising to supplement their seed farming practices.

Botatwe history provides a clear example of Bantu-Bantu cross-cultural interaction. Linguistic evidence consisting of cattle loanwords as well as archaeological evidence relating to pottery styles and decorations indicates that Bantu peoples of the Kusi subgroup inhabited the

---

[13] Christopher Ehret, "Transformations in Southern African History: Proposal for a Sweeping Overview of Change and Development, 6000 BC to the Present," *Ufahamu* 25, no. 2 (1997): 54–80.

region both prior to and during the period when Botatwe first began arriving in southern Zambia. In the ways that Bantu had so often integrated with gatherer-hunter populations, in this case Botatwe intermixed with and incorporated members of Kusi communities beginning around the eighth century CE. In central Africa, innovations came not from non-Bantu but rather through Bantu borrowing technologies and ideas from distant Bantu-descended relatives.

CERAMICS AND IRON

The invention of science-based ceramic and iron technologies in sub-Saharan Africa provide avenues for understanding the complexities and layers of developments and the roles of sociocultural meanings and relations to the carrying out of their production. The timeline between these two inventions are vastly different. Distant Niger-Congo linguistic ancestors of the Bantu independently invented ceramic technology some time before 9400 BCE, while the independent African invention of iron smelting emerged several millennia later, with the earliest African ironworking so far known dating to around 1800 BCE in today's Central African Republic (CAR). Pottery making was thus an ancient inherited technology of the proto-Bantu. Ironworking, in contrast, first spread from the CAR region to Bantu-speaking peoples in the Africa Great Lakes around 1000 BCE, when the Bantu expansions were first reaching the western edge of those areas. The *longue durée* legacies of these inventions are innumerable and impossible to capture fully, but what is broadly clear is that Bantu people continued to develop and expand those technologies and to evolve new social relations and economic approaches to technology. Furthermore, their technological history led to new political endeavors and spiritual observances and resulted in environmental transformations as well.

In addition to archaeological findings, linguistic evidence also tells us a good deal about the ancient history of pottery among Bantu speakers. The very earliest Bantu verb that has been reconstructed "to fashion a pot" was *-mat-*. About 4,500 years ago (second phase), another verb, *-bumb-*, was innovated and began to replace *-mat-*. While the older verb, *-mat-*, continued to be used in reference to other kinds of activities involving clay, in particular the plastering of the house, the root *-bumb-* took on a variety of uses in social imagery during the third phase, notably as a verb for the Creator God's action of creating humans. Additionally, several reconstructed noun roots for different kinds of pots widely used today in Bantu languages dating to the proto-Bantu era show that the early Bantu made a variety of ceramic containers (see Figure 4.1). These include *-bìgá, which referred to a "water (or liquid holding) pot," and *-(j)ùngú, a "cooking pot".[14]

In the Bantu historical tradition, the complexity of technological processes involved in successful potting and iron production required both application of material science and spiritual tenets and adherence. To make a pot, the woman technician had to first find appropriate clay. Clay could be acquired from a variety of sources such as termite hills, deep clay shafts on the savanna, lakebeds, and riverbanks. She then had to create the right mixture of sand, gravel, herbs, and ground old ceramic potsherds to form the temper essential for binding the clay and helping it to fire evenly without cracking. Women shaped their pots by hand, since they did not tend to use coiling or pottery wheels. While the clay was still moist, potters imprinted designs that had an understood cultural meaning. They then dried their creations for a

FIGURE 4.1 A Luangwa ceramic pot made in Mbala, Zambia reflects a pottery style many matrilineal peoples made in East Central Africa over the last thousand years. in 1998. Photo by Anne Manmiller, from private collection of C. Saidi.

---

[14] Gonzales, *Societies*, chap. 3, paragraphs 68–71.

few days, after which they fired them. The firing technology required extensive experience and a high degree of skill to get the temperatures, timing, and size of the fire just right. Bantu potters in general did not create kilns to fire their pots—instead, they increased their durability on open fires, rotating the pot with long sticks.

Previous chapters discussed the ritual and educational role that ceramic items played in the lives of Bantu people. It is equally important to understand that this was women's technology. Women were the primary bearers of the technological knowledge of potting, crop cultivation, and the cooking of foods. Although men were sometimes able to take over commercial potting in recent centuries, right through the twentieth century women produced nearly 90 percent of all pottery in Africa.[15] Ceramic wares were essential to storage as well as the carrying out of agriculture and culinary techniques. And they were also culturally and religiously meaningful.

Although people produced ceramics for utility, they were also attentive to creating aesthetically pleasing and precisely engineered ceramics. The best known ceramic arts of early eras among the Bantu are the seven fired terracotta "Lydenburg" heads that ancestors of Shona- and Sala-speaking Bantu produced by the sixth century CE in what is today the Mpumalanga Province of South Africa. The artists molded these ceramic heads with coiled bands of raised clay to represent facial features and incised the surfaces with elaborate decorations that suggest a level of wealth and opulence. Since Bantu peoples widely used ceramic items for spiritual purposes, the likely explanation is that the Lydenburg heads had some kind of ritual meaning also.

A pervasive bias in the Western tradition is to divorce complex, scientific technology from spiritual ideologies. But the Bantu in their historical traditions saw science and spirituality as symbiotic. The widespread Bantu metaphor encapsulated in the use of the same verb for fashioning for the Creator fashioning humanity displays such an understanding. This understanding led in at least two different regions to Bantu societies creating new terms for the Creator from this verb. Centuries ago Asu people of the Pare Mountains in today's northeastern Tanzania coined their own new word for God, *Mumbi*. This word adds the Asu noun prefix *m-* and noun suffix *-i* to their

---

[15] Dale Walde and Noreen D. Willow (eds.), *The Archaeology of Gender: Proceedings of the Twenty Second Annual Conference of the Archaeological Association of the University of Calgary* (Calgary, AB, Canada: University of Calgary Press, 1991), 436.

version *-umb- of the old verb *-bumb-. Perhaps more arresting because of its social as well as religious allusions is a term *Nakabumba*,
innovated probably as much as 1,500 years ago among early Sabi
speakers of east-central Africa. Its core element *-bumb- "to make
a pot or to mold clay" derives from an old Bantu verb root. The *na-*
is a widespread Bantu prefix in east-central Africa that emphasizes
female qualities or a position in society held by a woman. The *ka-* in
this case is a prefix that signifies a position of honor and respect. This
name views the Creator as metaphorically an honored female potter.
Nakabumba created humanity in the same way a woman makes a
pot.[16]

Bantu people in different regions coined the new appellations
Mumbi and *Nakabumba* during the past two thousand years. But as
the oral traditions of Babessi Bantu of Cameroon show, equating the
process of creation to the molding of a pot is a much older aspect of
the Bantu worldview. For Babessi communities when the Creator is
molding a human we cannot know what is on the inside until he or
she is fully formed. For the same reason Babessi potters did not want
strangers to see how they closed the bottom of their pots.[17] Babessi are
geographically far from the east-central African Sabi speakers and
from East African Asu people, and their languages belong to separate
deep branches of Bantu, which diverged from each other as much as
five thousand years ago. These shared ideas that they preserve in their
languages and cultures reveal a set of views of the Creator and creation
that must go back to the earliest phases of Bantu history and worldview.

Like the Creator, Bantu potters viewed their work as joining the
realms of the ethereal and the temporal to produce something both
utilitarian and sacred. Potters did not just master the technological
skills; they also observed spiritual obligations in applying those skills.
Even today, from Bantu Bafia communities in the grasslands of modern
Cameroon to those in east-central Africa, potters engage in a suite of
religious observances during the process of pottery production. In
modern Zambia, for example, clay sources are viewed as sacred places
that only senior potters, who are mothers or grandmothers, are permitted to have access to. And it is in those very locations that they produce
a first ceremonial pot from that clay source. The first pot a potter makes

---

[16] Saidi, *Women's Authority*, 131.

[17] Sylvia Forni, "Containers of Life: Pottery and Social Relations in the
Grassfields," *African Arts* 4, no. 1 (Spring 2007): 44.

represents an act of gratitude, an offering given to the Creator. Among other spiritual adherences, potters understood menstruating women to be in a temporary state of power. In that state they should not fashion pots, nor should a woman engage in sexual relationships at least one day prior to making a pot, because to do so meant that, when fired, the pots would crack. Neither menstruation nor sexuality should be interpreted as mere taboos or superstitions. In Bantu understandings, energies or forces tied to human capacities to reproduce, including the menstrual cycle and sexual expression, could disrupt production.

In contrast to ceramic production, which was a female-directed technology, iron production was a male-centered scientific process. By 2,500 years ago, Bantu speakers in the Great Lakes region had integrated iron production into their technological knowledge and applied these skills to the making of new kinds of farm implement, notably iron hoes and axes, and new kinds of weapons. Already by 500 BCE this technology had begun to spread far westward and also southward to the rest of Bantu-speaking Africa. The technological process for transforming ore into metal involved heating it to high temperatures (approximately 1200°C) in an atmosphere that is at least 75 percent carbon monoxide. The carbon monoxide separated the oxygen in the iron ore fragments, reducing the iron oxide to iron metal. Inside the smelter, commonly called a furnace, a charcoal fire burned, but to get the temperature high enough, smelters either employed young men and boys to work bellows to blow oxygen into the furnaces; or, in the natural draft method, they placed tubes with plugs leading into the bottom inside of the furnace and manipulated the plugs to allow in the proper amount of oxygen to raise the temperature high enough to create iron metal. Sometimes the iron producers could make the temperature so high that they transformed iron ore into carbon steel many centuries before it was done in European factories.[18]

---

[18] For more information on iron smelts in Niger Congo and Bantu regions Africa, see *The Blooms of Banjeli: Technology and Gender in African Ironmaking*, directed by Carlyn Saltman with Candice Goucher and Eugenia Herbert (Watertown, Mass: Documentary Educational Resources, 1986); *The Tree of Iron*, directed by Peter O'Neill and Frank Muhly, Jr. with Peter Schmidt (Watertown, Mass: Documentary Educational Resources, 1988). See also Eugenia W. Herbert, *Iron, Gender, and Power: Rituals of Transformation in African Societies* (Bloomington: Indiana University Press, 1994), 224; Peter R. Schmidt, ed., *The Culture and Technology of African Iron Production*, 1st ed. (Gainesville: University Press of Florida, 1996).

Across Bantu-speaking Africa, iron producers constructed a variety of furnaces. They sometimes included gynecomorphic physical and spiritual features. According to anthropologist Eugenia Herbert, in iron-producing Bantu-speaking societies, women commonly gathered the ore, and in some societies, such as the Fipa and Haya of Tanzania, women contributed to making the furnace itself.[19] The furnace was more than just a place to smelt iron; its production of iron was figuratively analogized to a woman giving birth. Different societies conveyed this conception in varied ways of decorating the furnace. In some regions furnace builders molded symbolic breasts on the external surface of a smelter; others positioned the furnace to mimic the position of a woman giving birth. In still other societies the smelters ritually addressed the furnace using words and songs reserved for a woman during child labor.

A diverse group of Bantu speakers from Zambia, Malawi, Zimbabwe, Mozambique, and Tanzania through the DRC to Angola, built gynecomorphic-smelting furnaces. The distribution of this of furnace type correlates with a particular set of words for smelting and smithing. Together these features trace one of the major routes of the spread of ironworking west from the Western Rift region of East Africa, in this case westward across the southern savanna belt to the Atlantic Ocean in Angola.

That men controlled production and working of iron is uncontested to date. However, the rituals, traditions, and cultural mores associated with iron production, on the other hand, likely drew inspiration from the far earlier beliefs and science used in women's potting processes and traditions. In their respective industries, men and women observed necessary restrictions to protect the smelt from the power of sexual activity and menstruation that could easily draw away energy and hinder successful iron production. The older association of women as the extractors from the ground of the material, clay, used in their work of potting sometimes carried over, as already noted, in another respect: women often were the extractors of the iron ore from the ground and, in some cases, played a part in providing the clay for building the furnace.

Iron in the early and middle first millennium BCE in eastern Africa was initially a relatively rare material, probably more valued for personal adornment than tool making. Two early root words for

---

[19] Herbert, *Iron*, 25–31.

iron illustrate this conclusion. One root, *-uma,* became the general word for iron among the northern, Kaskazi communities of Mashariki speakers in the early first millennium BCE. This word had been the noun for one's "belongings" in general in early Bantu and had taken on the narrower meaning "valuable belonging" during the third phase of Bantu expansions in the second millennium BCE. In the same era or possibly late in the first millennium BCE, some of the southern, Kusi communities of the Mashariki applied to iron a different root, *tImbi,* which had originally denoted "beads."

By 500 BCE, however, iron had become a familiar and widely desired material, first in the Great Lakes region and then more and more widely across the whole of Bantu Africa during the next five hundred years. Ironsmiths produced tools that aided people's work and had long-term impacts on the landscape. The spread of words for a new tool, the iron hoe, show that blacksmiths in and around the Great Lakes region of East Africa most probably invented this item by the middle of the first millennium BCE. From that region the iron hoe then spread south and west to the rest of the Bantu peoples.[20] With this tool, women farmers' enhanced their capacities for digging savanna soils and preparing fields. Another useful product, the iron ax, allowed men not only to cut down green trees—something that stone axes did almost as well—but also for both men and women to chop up dry wood and to more effectively clear forested land and gather wood for building and for fires. The adoption of these useful tools shifted social dynamics and production relations as well, in particular because women no longer made their own farming tools but depended on a male-controlled technology, ironworking, for hoes and axes.

The spread of Bantu peoples transmitted iron smelting and iron smithing ideas and practices as far west as the equatorial and southern Atlantic coasts by the third century BCE and as far south as southern Africa almost as early (fourth phase). The addition of iron smelting and ironworking technology added a major product to Bantu-Batwa commodity trade in the equatorial forest regions, and the spread of this technology across eastern and southern Africa set off an era of growing long-distance transport of goods for trade in those regions.

---

[20] Christopher Ehret, "The Establishment of Iron-Working in Eastern, Central, and Southern Africa: Linguistic Inferences on Technological History," *Sprache und Geschichte in Afrika* 16/17 (2001): 125–175.

HOMESTEADS, ARCHITECTURE, AND ENGINEERING TECHNOLOGIES

Building materials, technologies, and aesthetics provide us with rich details about people's resources, interactions, and knowledge. Today, numerous communities of Bantu people display great variety in the way they build and utilize their personal homes and public structures. Still, there are often similarities discernable across large regions that have very deep historical roots. In this section the history of key words, the work of archaeologists, art historians, and ethnographic records, as well as written documents, make it clear that Bantu people, although retaining older ideas, innovated and adapted housing styles across the expansions.

The wide variety of house styles and housing materials reflect not just Bantu innovativeness in adapting to the environments around them or the materials available but also their flexibility in adopting house-building technologies and styles from their neighbors. In the proto-Bantu era people built rectangular homes with gabled roofs made of woven palm thatch (first phase). Their engineering techniques took the environment into consideration. Building roofs in this way prevented heavy rains from pooling and putting pressure on their structures. Around three thousand years ago, the first Mashariki Bantu who moved into the African Great Lakes area still likely built this type of rectangular house with gabled roofs, which continues into the present. Only when they began to move into new environments where it made sense to change their structures did they begin to implement alternative techniques and architecture.

By 500 BCE, if not earlier, many Bantu-descended communities had shifted over to building round houses with conical roofs, a style they learned from Nilo-Saharan-speaking neighbors in the Great Lakes region. In concert with this architectural changeover, Mashariki Bantu added a new word for 'house' *-umba, which is used today wherever this kind of house is built. They began as well to thatch their roofs with grasses, as evidenced by their creation of a verb for "to thatch," *-bimb, which before this era was a general verb in Bantu languages meaning "to cover up."

Not all of the early Mashariki communities gave up the older rectangular, gable-roofed house plan with woven palm roofs. The descendants of one set of Mashariki communities, the Northeast-Coastal Bantu, who settled in the first millennium CE in areas along the Indian Ocean between the Tana and Rufiji Rivers, have maintained this house style down to the present. Another grouping of early Mashariki communities, who moved into the north and north-central areas of modern-day Tanzania in the early first millennium CE, also built rectangular houses. But, differently from the northeast-coastal Bantu, they adopted from their southern Cushitic neighbors in those areas a distinct style of rectangular house, with a flat thatched roof plastered over with a thick layer of clay. The diversity of housing found today among Bantu peoples is not surprising, considering that the Bantu moved into a diversity of new regions, encountering new environments and borrowing what they liked from new neighbors. For centuries these various kinds of houses with thatched or woven roofs remained the predominant styles among the everyday people of the countryside.

In the later first millennium CE, one group of northeast coastal Bantu, known as Swahili, engaged in transoceanic commercial enterprises that brought new levels of wealth accumulation that influenced political economies, religion, and life ways. Along the East African coast, partially as an outcome of international trade in the Indian Ocean, Swahili communities established city-states and began to practice Islam formally as part of this transformation around 700 CE. Today, along the East African Coast, archaeologists have identified the ruins of at least seventy-five city-states, whose wealth depended both on successful food production for their own use and on the Indian Ocean trade. Many of the commercial towns and cities of that time, such as Lamu and Mombasa, remain thriving commercial and urban centers today.

Swahili people built their distinctively styled houses and mosques from coral that skilled divers cut and shaped under water while it was still pliable. They then brought it up to shore to dry into lasting porous building materials ideal for insulating people from the hot, humid environment of the East African coast. Extensive mangrove forests surrounded Swahili settlements. Swahili building engineers used mangrove trunks as roof beams and supporting beams for the coral houses. Their thick, insulated walls maintain cool indoor temperatures. Builders sealed them with a white limestone plaster to protect from the deterioration that tropical heat and moisture could easily cause.

Swahili artisans and craft specialists also modified Bantu decorative traditions in a unique aesthetic fashion that is widely recognized as distinctly Swahili. Bantu-speaking peoples as far back as the proto-Bantu era had been noted woodcarvers, who specialized in the creation of human forms, animals, and spirits from wood. Muslims

Swahili carvers directed their talents toward creating ornate wooden doors and furniture with flowers and abstract designs that people widely appreciated for their valued aesthetic. It became customary for Swahili merchant classes to live in increasingly intricately decorated homes. And, in the case of the wealthiest families, their houses were equipped with indoor plumbing technology by the fourteenth century. Though noted for their coral, wood, and plumbing technologies, Swahili houses carried on, although in more complex form, the rectangular floor plan of the northeast-coastal Bantu ancestors, but to it they added a new kind of flat roof adopted from the Middle East by way of their Indian Ocean trading contacts.

While wealthy merchants and other elites lived in opulent homes, the average Swahili person in coastal towns continued to live in traditional rectangular, gable-roofed dwellings. Moroccan geographer Ibn Battuta, who traveled throughout the Islamic world from West Africa to China in the early 1300s, described Kilwa, a Swahili city-state responsible for trading southern African gold to the Indian Ocean world, as one of the most impressive cities he had ever seen.[21]

South of the Zambezi River and inland from the coast laid the territories of the Zimbabwe Empire. The rulers of this state controlled the southern African gold trade, which passed from the city of Great Zimbabwe via the seaport of Sofala to the Swahili city of Kilwa between 1200 and the early 1400s CE. Shona engineers developed new techniques for cutting stone to build the massive monuments of Great Zimbabwe. Set in a valley surrounded by hills with a landscape of giant boulders, it comprised the residence of the Empire's ruler. The masons began the century-long construction process in the later 1200s. Over the next century and a half, the subordinate chiefs of the empire built their own smaller cities of stone, also known as *zimbabwes*. In all, there were more than two hundred of these smaller provincial and local capital sites.

The largest structure at Great Zimbabwe itself, the Great Enclosure, is an ellipsis constructed of millions of shaped granite stones fit into place without mortar and topped with large carved stone birds. Based on ethno-archaeological analysis, the great stone birds held spiritual significance for the Shona people. The enclosure

[21] Ibn Battuta, "The East Africa Journey," in Said Hamdun and Noël King, eds., *Ibn Battuta in Black Africa* (Princeton, N.J.: Markus Wiener Publishers, 2003), 22.

construction, which has remained partially intact for over seven hundred years, is approximately 820 feet long, 36 feet tall, and 17 feet thick in certain places. The structures of Great Zimbabwe were built of the same kind of granite that surrounded the structures and looked as though they were part of the landscape. It serves as an example along with Swahili coral and mangrove construction of the ways architects and engineers in these various regions incorporated local environmental elements and new technological processes into their design and construction.

Archaeologists estimate that as many as 18,000 people could have lived within the valley and structures surrounding the Great Enclosure. From the remains of this city, archaeologists have unearthed glass beads and porcelain from China and Persia along with gold coins, testifying to the vast extent of long-distance trade connecting East Africa's coast, southeastern Africa's hinterland, and the wider world abutting the Indian Ocean.

In addition to the structure of homes, household furnishings provide insight into the history of day-to-day life and the spread of admired ideas and practices. Early Bantu speakers used locally available fibers to weave mats for sleeping. In eastern Africa, Mashariki Bantu interacted with existing southern Cushitic populations, and in the late first millennium BCE or early first millennium CE, many Bantu communities adopted a new kind of furniture, a style of raised beds innovated by those Southern Cushites. From the East African Bantu speakers, the use of this kind of bed then spread much farther west in the first millennium CE to Bantu-speaking peoples of the southern savanna belt.

Another type of furniture new to Bantu who moved into eastern Africa in the first millennium BCE were three-legged stools carved out of single blocks of wood. Stool carving fit in well with the old woodworking tradition of the Bantu, but the design of such stools came from the Nilo-Saharan peoples encountered by the Bantu in the Great Lakes region. From the Great Lakes region the practice of making these stools diffused from the Great Lakes Bantu westward to Bantu peoples of the rainforest and the southern savannas.[22]

Many Africans employ headrests, sculpted by carvers out of a single block of wood, as sleep aids. A person ready to slumber placed the headrest under one ear and along the side of the chin to support the

---

[22] Ehret, *Classical*, 119.

whole head. In this position on the headrest, one's nerves are slightly numbed by the pressure, which users report produces a pleasant tranquilizing effect that leads to deep sleep. Bantu-speaking peoples arriving in the Great Lakes region by the early first millennium BCE likely first witnessed headrests in use among their Nilo-Saharan-speaking neighbors. Headrests provide additional evidence of the cross-cultural influences and interactions in which Africans engaged. Earliest finds are in Ancient Egypt and Nubia, where Nilo-Saharan peoples of the Middle Nile Basin first carved elegant simple wooden headrests, while Bantu communities applied their honed woodcarving skills and added schematic and figurative designs on carved headrests. Sometimes they included on them animal or even ancestor representations. By 500 CE, wooden headrests were in use among Bantu peoples from the Great Lakes to the southern savannas and west to the equatorial rainforests.

CLOTHING AND BODY ART

Art historians have argued that the first canvas for art in the world was the human body. In line with this, we know Bantu-speaking peoples in Central Africa created detailed body art.[23] Bantu people also crafted designed clothing and jewelry from locally available materials. Cattle- and goat-keeping Bantu people used animal skins for clothing; people in the forested and woodland areas made plush bark cloth; and those in areas with raffia palms wove clothing and other products woven from raffia fibers, decorating their weaving with striking geometric forms. The weavers also sewed beads and shells into the garments to decorate them in appealing ways.

Many Bantu people created body art appealing to the aesthetic of the time and place but also to mark sociocultural events, such as passing through rites of transition, or the lineage connections of a person, and for healing. The body aesthetic was culturally determined and could be permanent, semipermanent, or temporary. Body painting was an aspect of important ceremonies in many parts of Bantu-speaking Africa. White clay is present in many parts of the Bantu-speaking world (discussed in chapter 3). Painting with white clay connotes a transformative state, such as the passage from one

---

[23] Enid Schildkrout, "Inscribing the Body," *Annual Review of Anthropology* 33 (2004): 319.

life stage to another. Other body paint was used during dances and masquerade celebrations. Muslim Bantu women living along the East African coast decorated their bodies with henna, a tradition adapted from Indian Ocean trade partners. Especially at weddings, women drew elegant designs and then colored them in with varying types of henna.

Henna washes off, whereas raised marks and scarred designs on the skin, referred to in the scholarship as scarification, were a permanent form of body art among many Bantu in Central Africa. This aesthetic of layering of beauty marks and the process of body modification was a means of creating personal, generational, and community identity. Whereas most east and southern African Bantu do not today practice scarification, the custom is spread over a wide geographic span of Bantu populations. For example, in the DRC, among the practitioners of this kind of art include peoples such as Yombe, Bakutu, and Topoke of the western DRC; and Yasayama, Luba, and Tabwa of the eastern DRC; Safwa of Tanzania; and Shona of Zimbabwe. Body artists used sharp blades to make fine incisions into which he or she infused soot and the juice of a fruit that turned shiny black in the incisions to create a design of small scars on the skin. Luba called this form of scarification *ntapo*, a term descriptive as well of the decorative arts on gourds, pots, mats, baskets, walls of houses, and any royal regalia. Young women would begin this body art after going through initiation. Each woman would choose culturally specific designs, which she added to throughout her lifetime as she became a mother and grandmother. Luba viewed these operations as enhancing a woman's status and beauty. The adult woman who had no scars might be ridiculed. In more recent times she might be called a "man," "banana tree," or "slimy mushroom."[24] In their crafted statues of women, Luba and Tabwa artists include ornate body art that is very visible, capturing the importance of this practice in celebrating motherhood (see figure 4.2).

Whereas body art was both a technology and art form that Bantu communities widely practiced, so was the processing of different materials for clothing. Clothing designers treated and processed the skins of various animals in ways that made them soft enough for comfortable clothing. The making of bark cloth was one of the

---

[24] Mary Nooter Roberts, "Luba Art," in Mary Nooter Roberts, Allen F. Roberts, and Terry S. Childs *Memory: Luba Art and the Making of History*, exhibition catalog for the Center for African Art, New York (Munich: Prestel, 1996), 98–112.

oldest technologies that ancient Niger-Congo people, Bantu ancestors, invented more than eight thousand years ago. Proto-Bantu,
having inherited this knowledge, were producing bark cloth as early
as five thousand years ago, as the comparative cultural evidence and
the existence of a proto-Bantu term *-kando* indicates.[25] They produced *-kando* cloth by peeling the inner bark off particular *Ficus*

FIGURE 4.2   A Tabwa wood statue of a
pregnant woman from Katanga Province,
Democratic Republic of the Congo. Such statues
communicate the honored position of mothers
among these matrilineal people. Elaborate
hairdo and scarifications express that one is a
mother in the region. Her shortened legs symbolize the squatting position of women during
childbirth. Carver unknown. Photo by Anne
Manmiller. From private collection of C. Saidi.

---

[25] Vansina, *Paths*, 293.

trees, then chemically treating the peeled-off bark, and finally pound-ing it. They then dyed pieces of the processed cloth that they sewed together to make designs. Unfortunately, in tropical climates, bark cloth, like other organic material, deteriorates in the long term and thus archaeologists so far have found only a very few remnants of the most ancient cloth in graves dating back to about 500 CE. Written records of the past five hundred years tell us that individuals coveted bark cloth, which made it an in-demand commodity in regional, tran-sregional, and global markets. As far back as the fifteenth century, for-eign visitors remarked in written accounts that bark cloth had reached the status of currency in some societies. In more recent centuries, bark cloth has shown up as iconic wall hangings and throw pillows in both colonial-era decorating and in present-day high-end interior design.

Another type of cloth that Bantu weavers produced since prob-ably proto-Bantu times was raffia cloth, a soft, silky, yet durable material. Portuguese and Dutch travelers in the 1600s remarked on the beauty of the raffia cloth worn by the elite of the Tio and Laongo Kingdoms of the areas just north of the Lower Congo River. They de-scribed the cloth as resembling velvet or silk.[26] Weavers, usually male, wove raffia cloth from the undermembranes of palm tree fronds, a supple material that could be easily dyed. Raffia cloth had complex designs embroidered upon it. In the Kuba kingdom of the seven-teenth century, located inland along the Kasai and Sankuru Rivers, men grew the raffia palm and wove the cloth. Women embellished the raffia with embroidered geometric designs and transformed the cloth into various items, including ceremonial skirts, tribute cloths, head-dresses, and basketry.[27]

Among Bantu of the equatorial rainforest and western parts of the southern savanna, raffia cloth served as both a textile and a currency, and it was essential to ceremonial attire (see Figure 3.1). In the Kingdom of the Kongo raffia cloth replaced currency around 1575 CE when the Portuguese took control of the main source for the local currency, cowrie shells.[28] Documents of the time reveal that

---

[26] Suzanne Preston Blier, "Imaging Otherness in Ivory: African Portrayals of the Portuguese ca. 1492," *The Art Bulletin* 75, no. 3 (September 1993): 376.

[27] Monni Adams, "Kuba Embroidered Cloth," *African Arts* 12 (November 1978): 20.

[28] Phyllis M. Martin, "Power, Cloth and Currency on the Loango Coast," *African Economic History* no. 15 (1986): 4.

raffia could serve as payment of legal fees and fines in the centralized kingdoms of the region. People of the Kongo Kingdom also used raffia cloth to pay bride wealth and tribute to central rulers.

By the mid-1600s, the significance of raffia cloth as a currency came under challenge in southwestern Bantu Africa. This shift occurred as imported cotton cloth from Asia and Europe become fashionable and desired. Though cotton was almost exclusively reserved for those with political power, it became widely valued. Unlike raffia, which local craftspeople controlled and produced, cotton became an inexpensive import that brought with it some long-term economic imbalances. Raffia was still used for ceremonies, yet wearing imported cotton cloth became a sign of status for the elites. This economic shift had long-term deleterious repercussions for the profitability of local technology and local manufacturing.

CARVING SPIRITS: WOOD WORK

As the discussion of headrests and doors in the section on "Homesteads, Architecture, and Engineering Technologies" indicates, Bantu-speaking people excelled at producing goods that were both utilitarian and artistic. Carvers in Bantu-speaking regions stretching from the Atlantic coast to East Africa were renowned for their artistic wood creations. Wood technology had both useful applications and cultural implications. Woodcarving technologies have been foundational in the development of transportation by boat, in the carving of masks and other objects for religious observances, in the making of musical instruments, and in building materials, textile production, cooking implements, medicinal practices, and agricultural tools as far back as we can trace Bantu history. Symbolic carvings on behalf of ancestors, produced in a stylized fashion, were historically important because they were seen as containing spiritual energy that brought positive effects into the lives of the living. Because it was believed that the ancestors could impact the fate of the living, carvings of ancestors were extremely important, and carvers often produced sculptures of important persons after their deaths. Kongo people of modern Angola and the DRC created ancestor portraits they called *tumba*. These wooden human likenesses expressed sadness and symbolized a person looking inward to his or her role as a spirit. Kuba people during the heyday of their kingdom produced *ndop*, stylized carvings of leaders who were still alive, and people kept them in the houses of expecting mothers until after childbirth. When a ruler died, Kuba people believed that the spirit continued to reside in the *ndop*. Future rulers had to display this symbol at official ceremonies, so that the ancestor ruler could ensure success of the living.[29]

ROCK ART PRODUCTION

Although men were historically the primary producers of wood-carved arts, Bantu women were the makers of a particular genre of rock art associated with female initiation. In east-central Africa, this art used geometric figures and symbols to represent both concrete items and abstract ideas. Bantu artists who produced rock art for female initiation also integrated a variety of imagery adopted from Batwa artists. Differently from Batwa, who used various color pigments, Mashariki Bantu women usually relied strictly on white clay, because that was the ritual color and ritual material of spiritual matters far back in history among Bantu-speaking peoples. But in parts of Central Africa, Bantu-speaking women combined elements of the two artistic traditions, integrating both the colors and many of the signs and symbols Batwa used into their artistry. In female initiation ceremonies the initiate was covered in the white clay, but the rock or wall art the older women drew for these ceremonies included designs in red and black, applying and integrating the technology for making these pigments Batwa had earlier developed.

CONCLUSION

From agriculture to ceramics, metals, and rock art, Bantu peoples invented and transformed scientific technologies, techniques, and approaches for dealing with the variety of environments into which they moved. They also variously adopted, readapted, and influenced practices of peoples whom they encountered in various regions and times. The examples in this chapter illustrate, both through arts, beliefs, and productive technology, how in Bantu worldviews these were interconnected endeavors. Speakers of Bantu languages

---

[29] Monni Adams, "Eighteenth Century Kuba King Figures," *African Arts* 21, no. 3 (May 1988): 34–35.

developed great variation and yet maintained a strong Bantu historical tradition, in which individuals acknowledged spiritual forces of Creator, ancestors, territorial spirits, and reproductive energy. These are changes and continuities for which scholars find evidence in linguistic, ethnographic, and archaeological records across many generations and regions. From creating ornate woodworks to making detailed bark cloth, the historical developments among Bantu peoples provide evidence of both the commonalities of their historical background and the variety of ways that they ushered in change and transformed within the differing worlds into which they expanded.

African Arts, Museums, and Picasso

Art from Bantu societies has long been held in collections from London to Bangkok and Honolulu to Cape Town. But what is less known is that Bantu artists significantly influenced the works of Spanish artist Pablo Picasso, possibly the most famous artist of the twentieth century. As early as 1907, Picasso is known to have said, while looking at African arts that included Bantu masks, "I grasped why I was a painter. All alone in that Museum, surrounded by masks."[30] In 2006, the South African government together with the French government, where Picasso long made his home, sponsored an exhibition entitled "Picasso and Africa." The exhibit showcased sixty Picasso paintings side by side with the African art that inspired his work. While Picasso, who was clear about the African art that inspired him, is revered as a master artist, professional curators persist in classifying African art as "primitive or tribal." Why might that be? Readers are encouraged to take some time to investigate collections of African art at museums. It is useful to look for details and themes within both ancient and modern African art. An outstanding place for this kind of visit is the Smithsonian's National Museum of African Art on the Mall in Washington, DC. Perhaps you will recognize possible African influences that you can tie to the work of Western artists that you have long appreciated.

---

[30] Patricia Leighten, "The White Peril and L'Art negre: Picasso, Primitivism, and Anti-colonialism," *The Art Bulletin* 72, no. 4 (December 1990): 625.

FURTHER READINGS

Adams, Monni. "Kuba Embroidered Cloth." *African Arts* 12, no. 1 (Nov. 1978): 24–39, 106–107.

Dewey, William. *Sleeping Beauties, Fowler Museum of Cultural History.* Los Angeles: University of California, 1993.

Ehret, Christopher. *An African Classical Age: Eastern and Southern Africa in World History, 1000 BCE to AD 400.* Charlottesville: University of Virginia Press, 1998.

Forni, Silvia. "Containers of Life: Pottery and Social Relations in the Grassfields (Cameroon)." *African Arts* 40, no. 1 (Spring, 2007): 42–53.

Herbert, Eugenia. *Iron, Gender and Power: Rituals of Transformation in African Societies.* Bloomington: Indiana University Press, 1993.

Roberts, Mary Nooter. "The King Is a Woman Shaping Power in Luba Royal Arts." *African Arts* 46, no. 3 (Autumn 2013): 68–81.

Simon, Kavuna, and Wyatt MacGaffey. "Northern Kongo Ancestor Figures." *African Arts* 28, no. 2 (Spring 1995): 48–53, 91.

Negotiating Hospitality

Whereas previous chapters detailed some prominent ancient Bantu events and processes as well as historical inventions, divergences, and variations that different Bantu speech communities pursued over time, this final chapter focuses on hospitality. One major question scholars have raised is how Bantu communities so successfully spread their cultures and languages over such a large geographic area without resorting to widespread violence. Although Bantu certainly experienced setbacks, hospitality is an evidence-based theory that provides a framework to explain Bantu linguistic and cultural resilience over the *longue durée*. Many Bantu speech communities conceptualized hospitality both as an important relationship-building strategy and as a moral imperative. They employed hospitality as strategy when they settled into new areas where they often encountered firstcomers. This focus brings together a number of historical trends and events important in previous chapters. Hospitality has persistently been central to concepts of relationship building in their underlying worldview. The aim of this chapter is to demonstrate how histories in different eras might offer important lessons on strategies Bantu speech communities employed to socialize individuals, to incorporate outsiders, and to defend against violence, poverty, community breakdown, political deterioration, and other social challenges.

GREETING AND WELCOMING GUESTS

Hospitality can be defined as an approach to welcoming guests, whether insiders or outsiders. Euphrase Kezilahabi, a renowned Tanzanian novelist, notes that "greetings among Kerebe define kinship and good neighborliness. They also delineate character and draw lines of relationships. Greetings are a manifestation of humanness and respect for other people, known and unknown. 'To visit' and 'to greet' are conceptualized in one word, *kubwacha*. A visit (greeting) shows how much a relative values a relationship and suggests the way in which he or she wants it to continue. It is the highest manifestation of love and solidarity amidst the struggle for survival."[1] Kezelihabi contends the Kerebe case is representative of the approach many Bantu-speaking communities have engaged toward kin and neighbors. Although history reflects that the past is not absent of conflict and contestation, the larger point Kezilahabi makes is valid. So common among many Bantu speakers, requisite greetings can be identified as part of a hospitality paradigm. Historically, ancient Bantu speech communities imagined and put into effect a set of practices that privileged relationship building, reflected in the importance of welcoming and evidenced in a host of actions people performed.

Hospitality certainly begins when people welcome individuals with greetings, but it goes well beyond that initial moment of encounter to include provisioning food, accommodation, shelter, companionship, insights, advice, conversation, protection, an atmosphere of generous inclusion, and honoring firstcomers and ancestral spirits. Historically, communities in Bantu-speaking Africa employed hospitality to extend generosity to outsiders but also deployed this value system as a tool of social control over both insiders and outsiders. Expectations of hospitality became a means to guard against antisocial behaviors like greed, exclusion, pursuit of individual interest over community needs, wishing ill will on other members of the community, and even excessive power seeking. Standards of what constituted acts of hospitality and sufficient quantity and quality of munificence varied across communities, yet this value was commonly central in moral economies and social expectations within so many Bantu speech communities. Hospitality is a lens through which one

---

[1] Euphrase Kezilahabi, "A Phenomenological Interpretation of Kerebe Greetings," *Journal of African Cultural Studies* 14, no. 2 (2001): 181–193.

can understand worldviews and practices of Bantu speakers over the *longue durée*. Principles of hospitality seem to connect to and between the various dimensions of Bantu people's lives discussed in previous chapters. Some examples include relationships between ancestors and the living, borrowing and sharing of scientific technologies, value placed on incorporating new and old members to create and recreate a sense of belonging, honor given to firstcomers on land, social practices like initiations, and the heterarchical approaches in many spheres of life that emphasized lateral relationship building. The deep roots of hospitality are not fully understood, yet if one considers the 5,500 years covered in this text, and the animating roles Bantu migrants—pioneers on frontiers—played in different phases of this history, the enduring value placed on greetings and hospitality over many generations and social landscapes makes a great deal of sense.

The collective body of evidence suggests that pervasive and persistent principles associated with hospitality trace back as far as 3,500 BCE (phase one). Certainly over time communities uniquely elaborated and shifted these practices in different manners. Strangers (unknown) and guests (known) were, in many cases, referred to with the same root *-génI*.[2] However, there is evidence that communities individually elaborated the idea and practice over time. Indeed, early on, Niger-Congo descendants who moved south and east toward the equatorial forest, and who would become "Bantu" entered into interactions with "strangers," mostly of one deep historical background, Batwa people. But Bantu communities who pressed eastward in the first millennium BCE (fourth phase) and the first millennium CE (fifth phase) came into regular contact with a wide range of greatly differing cultures and communities. These encounters likely necessitated strategies that would allow Bantu to move into and through areas inhabited or in use by others. Elaboration of hospitality as a prominent social value would have been a tactic to mediate social relations among firstcomers and newcomers. The term "firstcomer" has several meanings in this history of Bantu expansions. It references the first people known to have put a territory into economic or social use. It also means a group that preceded other groups, being firstcomers relative to later arrived newcomers. Newcomers would be those who migrated to a territory already in use by another human population. Hospitality was a means

---

[2]   Malcolm Guthrie, *Comparative Bantu* Vol. 3, CS 805; Catherine Cymone Fourshey, "Stranger Come Heal Thy Host," *African Historical Review* 44, no. 2 (2012): 18–54.

of incorporating either newcomers or firstcomers. It was a means by which distinct populations would become blended, either forming a new hybrid or becoming coexisting communities, which although they influenced each other, remained culturally separate.

We can talk about social relations of Bantu agricultural newcomers with firstcomers like Batwa gatherer-hunters (Central Africa), Cushitic pastoralists (East Africa), and Sudanian agropastoralists (East Africa) in several ways. Because Bantu speakers were essentially Niger-Congo populations who moved out of western Africa into central, eastern, and southern Africa, at each stage of this history Bantu were in the beginning newcomers. Later, as their settlements became established and widely dispersed in the last millennium BCE and the first millennium CE, many Bantu communities came to hold the perceived status of firstcomers in relation to later immigrants. Conflict and territorial tensions were certainly present in these relations. In such contexts mutualism or reciprocity often came into play, as insiders and outsiders accommodated to each other and developed relationships of mutual benefit. Communities applied social norms centered on hospitality that governed standards of propriety and respectability among insiders and served as means to keep outsiders at a social distance without alienating them completely. Hospitality afforded a space of opportunity and a buffer of safety for hosts and guests to become acquainted with the strengths of each other.

HOSPITALITY IN MATERIAL CULTURE, PROVERBS, AND GREETINGS

Proverbs and other historical data suggest that hospitality is important in many parts of Africa. Frequent modern-day depictions of Congo, Angola, Rwanda, Burundi, Mozambique, and Kenya as conflict zones and Botswana, Tanzania, South Africa, Zimbabwe, Zambia, and Uganda as disease ridden or poverty saturated obscure the positive role that hospitality still plays in undergirding social and economic relations and in allowing some degree of prosperity to exist. Certainly exclusion, oppression, and conflict were and are realities in some circumstances, but the prevailing approach to strangers and outsiders has been to bring them into the folds of Bantu communities through various strategies that build up all kinds of networks—personal, social, economic, political, and cultural.

In the nineteenth century, Kuba who lived in the area of what is now the Democratic Republic of the Congo (DRC) demonstrated hospitality to guests by offering palm wine served in elaborately carved wooden cups. Beautifully hand-crafted vessels were valued material tools from which honored guests imbibed. More important, these functional utensils and contents-symbolized hospitality and relationships, and they helped to establish status and refinement. As such, the cups and the palm wine forged social bonds that had many political and economic impacts. Nineteenth-century Kuba cups are one clue into the history of hospitality among some Bantu in more recent times and the role that drink played in respectably conveying social values. Indeed, one's personal reputation rested a great deal upon how hospitable one showed oneself to be when encountering guests. Providing nourishment and generous displays of cuisine to express one's hospitability was very important as were the extending of proper and elaborate greetings and verbal exchanges.

Among Kerebe, a Bantu people further east in the Lake Nyanza region of northwestern Tanzania, there is a saying for "thank you" that reflects the centrality of verbal hospitality in this society. They say *Wakola kuzima*, meaning "You have done well"; or *Wasemazya*, meaning "You have caused good things to happen." The response to this is *wasemezya kusima*, meaning "Thank you also for causing good things with your thanks." Reciprocity is implied in these verbal exchanges. *Wasemezya* expresses a relationship of causality. The one who greets validates and makes valuable the human existence of the other; visitors respond using the word in a different sentence context, *Wasemezya kwizatubwacha*, meaning "You have done well to come and greet us." Ontologically one's existence hinges on interaction with others through greetings that acknowledge one's being. It is believed that one who imparts munificence to rescue others creates societal benefits.

In southern Tanzania, a Fipa greeting for newcomers is *Tuteesi Ta!*, with the emphatic meaning "Welcome, we are established!" It implies both a welcome that includes the newcomer in "we" but also reinforces the established foothold of the greeter.[3] Among Waswahili, Bantu people of East Africa's Indian Ocean coast, the greeting *Karibu* bids outsiders to come closer as a manner of welcoming visitors with generosity. The outpouring of Swahili hospitality was

---

[3] Roy Willis, *A State in the Making* (Bloomington: Indiana University Press, 1981), xvii.

legendary among travelers to East Africa. Like Kerebe speakers, Kiswahili speakers have a proverb—"*Mgeni njoo, mwenyeji apone*"—communicating that the stranger or guest or outsider brings prosperity and benefits. The translation is "Stranger come, so the host can heal and prosper." The saying is rich in meaning about the value of outsiders to a community. Greetings hold great importance in each of these communities, expressions of hospitality are integral to the greeting practices, and these practices provide us with historical and cultural context on social values.

Fipa people also use a number of proverbs that reflect the profit they see outsiders contributing to their communities. A telling proverb notes, "Young man, don't harm the black snake, you don't know it won't produce an abundance of edible black fish." The lesson imbedded in the proverb is that individuals should not inflict harm upon strangers merely out of fear of their differences. Kindness toward strangers and refraining from inflicting harm on them are two key values one is socialized to embrace through this and other such proverbs. Going through the full breadth of all proverbs related to hospitality that exist in the range of Bantu languages is not possible. But examples from many societies abound, and they convey how widespread and deeply valued hospitality has been in Bantu communities across sub-Saharan Africa.[4]

INSUFFICIENT HOSPITALITY: ORAL TRADITIONS OF MIGRATION

These values also imbue many well-known oral traditions, which highlight hospitality as an important social and political tool. One tradition from the seventeenth-century Fipa provides insight on issues of hospitality at the social and political levels. Chief Milansi's wife, Natalakalika, was to guard his stool, a symbol of political power, while he was hunting; Milansi told Natalakalika that while he was away no one should have access to it.

After his departure, three stranger *Twaci* women arrived. The chief's wife welcomed them, providing each guest with a stool to sit on. But one of them refused to accept the seat she was offered. She wanted the chief's stool. Natalalika hesitated but then gave her the stool because she was a guest.

---

[4]   Roy Willis, *There Was a Certain Man, Spoken Art of the Fipa* (Oxford: Clarendon Press, 1978), 112.

When Chief Milansi returned, he found his stool seized and, thus, his power challenged. Because he was unclean and unshaven, when the *Twaci* women asked where his rule extended to, he could hardly lift his arm to demonstrate where his authority extended, for he feared exposing his unshaven armpits. So he made a modest circle to demonstrate the area protected by his rule. In response, one of the women pointed widely across the landscape to proclaim the rest of the land under Twaci authority. Distraught Chief Milansi sought guidance from a Fipa elder, Wayesi, who replied, "You will be subject to them but they will protect you. Let there be no quarrelling." Fipaland from then on had two royal capitals, Itwelele under Milansi with ritual power and the rest under *Twaci* stranger women who held political authority and were charged with the responsibility of protecting Milansi. Each Twaci woman proceeded to marry men from within Fipaland.[5]

The *Twaci* women and interactions they had with the Chief and Natalalika symbolize the overriding importance of hospitality to Fipa. In tension with values of hospitality was the fact that the stool held a more ancient historical and social significance (see Figure 5.1). Clearly this story justifies a change of dynasty. What this history also shows is that values of hospitality allowed firstcomers to rationalize their accommodation to the new political authority while at the same time asserting their ritual and social agency within the new political order. So while this oral tradition reveals enduring ideas about social organization, relationships, gender, cleanliness, and matrilineages, it also reveals innovative ideas on the spatial, social, and political incorporation of distinct people.

The strength of social and economic relationships in a world laden with mobility meant that belonging had to be imagined in ways not reliant solely on one's kin group or place of birth, an idea that scholars of citizenship refer to as belonging based on "blood or soil." Though communities were small in the early phases of the formation and solidification of Bantu expansions and identities, they grew in time partly because they became sedentary agriculturalists but also partly because they successfully incorporated outsiders. In east, central, southern, and west-central Africa, Bantu societies used hospitality, cross-cultural alliances, exclusive societies, and generation-based organizations to bolster social connections and social and political institutions. As noted earlier, proverbs and oral traditions from

---

[5] Willis, *State*, 20–23.

Figure 5.1   Anthropomorphic three-legged stool. Nyamwezi people, Tanzania. Wood, 134 x 34 x 41 cm. Photo: Hervé Lewandowski. Location: Musee du Quai Branly, Paris, France. Photo Credit: © RMN-Grand Palais/ Art Resource, NY Image Reference: ART488114. Image size: 4096 X 5318 px.

Bantu-speaking regions of sub-Saharan Africa reflect that hospitality toward strangers and outsiders was to varying degrees an important value to speakers of Bantu languages. In this large part of Africa, people held an idea that strangers potentially would enhance knowledge or contribute to societal development in important ways. This view appears commonly in the oral histories. Fipa traditions, notably, suggest that women often played focal roles in the forging of political institutions and alliances.

HETERARCHIES OF HOSPITALITY AND SOCIAL BONDS

Tracing historical shifts in words used to identify lineal affiliation and collective belonging provides a way to access changing features of Bantu political history. Reconstructing names of leadership roles given to people who held authority positions, as well as names used to designate collective units, also opens up a way to glean dynamics of political heterarchy across time. One enduring, titled position *mukumu* dates back to the proto-Bantu period (phase one) when emerging Bantu communities organized themselves in decentralized small, village-based systems. In those times *mukumu*, defined for the period as lineage priest-chief, exercised political and spiritual authority for the matrilineage. Though influential within civil society, *mukumu* did not hold absolute political authority. In the Bantu historical tradition of heterarchy, the corpus of elders and heads of associations held authority that moderated the power of the *mukumu*. *Mukumu* could be either female or male, and most probably lineage elders, recognized and respected spiritual intermediaries who were revered for their possession of specialized knowledge that accorded them access to the ethereal realm of ancestors. Through the *mukumu*, living lineage members received guidance on how best to sustain their lineages. This might mean, for example, adjudicating local conflict resolution or solving environmental challenges that threatened their food sources. Their small-scale, local ritual authority guaranteed that they had a say in the politics of their close-knit early Bantu communities.

In varied historical contexts, these originally small-scale communities reimagined their values politically, culturally, economically, and intellectually to meet their contemporary needs. As Bantu-speaking people expanded into new environments and settled within a range of climate zones, and as the size and diversity of Bantu communities grew, the role of the *mukumu* changed in several regions into a more fully political office. *Mukumu* remains a widespread word in far-flung Bantu languages today, sometimes still connoting a clan ritual chief, as among Gogo of central Tanzania, but in other instances, it names the ruler of a chiefdom or small kingdom often connected to ideas of wealth or honor.[6] In time, the need or opportunity for additional leadership roles and collective groups emerged in some contexts.

---

[6] Vansina, *Paths*, 274.

During the last millennium BCE (phase four), as Bantu people settled into the Lakes regions of eastern Africa, new contexts that included intermingling with people of non-Bantu origins transpired. Within their increasingly diverse context, some eastern Savanna Bantu communities began to reconceptualize leadership and belonging. This occurred to an even greater extent as their descendant communities began spreading their settlements in a southerly direction, into savanna ecologies west of Lake Tanganyika. In these environments matrilineages grew in size and new matrilineages migrated away from established communities. Some Savanna Bantu communities forged an ideology suited to a larger scale of political and social relations across a wider geography. They innovated the concept of a unit larger than a matrilineage. They came to identify themselves as being related to a widespread network of distinct matrilineages that formed a matriclan. The effect was that their matrilineages shared an identity and sense of affiliation through the matriclan. Evidence supporting this is found in their development of a type of political, ritual position within the matriclan. This new role was called *mwami*, which derives from the verb root *-yam- meaning "to call out." The *mwami* took on varied configurations from central to east Africa and was responsible for bringing together the larger community, delivering guidance, and announcing decisions.[7] This new kind of leadership was specifically relevant at the clan level. It added a dimension to authority in addition to the *mukumu*, who headed a local lineage system, which in different regions and periods was very often matrilineal.

The role of clan *mwami* need not replace the lineage priest chief. Because of an understood heterarchical ideology, the position could coexist with standing authority figures. For those who adopted the idea of a leader whose role it was to maintain connectivity of a matriclan, people had to accept a slightly more distant type of leader, a political spiritual guide covering a geographically widespread region. In this way, spiritual lineage-based leadership was localized and personal.

Turning to an example of elaboration in political unit in the second millennium CE, in the region of modern-day central Tanzania, Bantu-descended Ruvu people innovated a term, *ikungugo, to name a grouping of related matriclans (*-kolo). This development reveals that Ruvu descendants saw a need to acknowledge a kin group even larger than the long-acknowledged matriclan. The term *ikungugo

---

7 Ehret, *Classical*, 146–147; Schoenbrun, *Green Place*, 103–105; Vansina, *Paths*, 183–186.

derives from a proto-Bantu verb *-kung-, meaning "to tie together," in the sense of gathering things together. This metaphor is explicit in the crafting of a collective unit in which their matrilineages, that comprised matriclans, now comprised the far-flung *ikungugo. This historical shift in scale of political affiliation meant that people were enfolded within three layers of belonging—lineage, clan, and *ikungugo. That this developed among Sagala, Kagulu, Vidunda, and Gogo speakers in an expansive region heavily involved with culturally distinct peoples of Sudanic and Cushitic backgrounds may suggest that this was a local strategy used to incorporate outsiders into their communities. It does appear that in Bantu tradition, an *ikungugo elder held spiritual and political influence. In Vidunda oral accounts, an *ikungugo female or male elder led religious-based ceremonies in honor of their founding ancestor. In 1883, J. T. Last, a geographer in the region, noted the efficiency of Sagala *ikungugo unit subdivisions to have leaders represent their collective interests. [8]

In the growing diversity people encountered, no doubt identity became more complex in how people saw themselves. Political leadership over a multilineage or multiclan polity required a leader whose authority was recognized as extending to broader social and regional challenges and prospects, and yet, too, it was important in that they, in the Bantu tradition, held both spiritual and political authority.

CLOSE ENCOUNTERS: INTERACTIONS WITH NON-BANTU

Major cross-cultural encounters of the first two phases of Bantu expansions, extending back to the middle fourth millennium BCE, involved Batwa and Bantu peoples. In recent centuries, particularly in the eras of Atlantic trade and colonial rule, Batwa gatherer-hunters were often relegated to a serf-like status by neighboring Bantu farming communities. But in earlier times their relationships seem to have varied. The term "Batwa" reflects a Bantu root *-túá translated as "neighboring people" (Ba- is a plural prefix for person in many Bantu languages). The meanings Bantu communities applied to the root *-túá across western, central, and eastern Africa in different eras points to Batwa and Bantu relationship dynamics. Across history, the root *-túá ranged in meaning from "pygmy," "bush dweller," "neighboring

---

[8] Gonzales, *Societies*, chap. 3, fn 58.

ethnic group," "despised group," and "chief."[9] These meanings from a person of little social status to one of high social standing reflect the diverse history among these groups. Furthermore, oral traditions and local practices that honor Batwa, as firstcomers and sources of knowledge, reveal the historical complexity of Batwa–Bantu relations. Though written accounts suggesting Bantu marginalized Batwa in the Atlantic and colonial eras are oft cited, historian Klieman notes that Bantu of the forest regions long accepted the authority of Batwa as purveyors of critical knowledge. Bantu recognized their own position as newcomers, in contrast to Batwa precedence and generosity for sharing territory and knowledge. Batwa were, historically speaking, culturally, linguistically, and economically distinct from their hosts.[10] Bantu bolstered their interdependence with Batwa communities through metaphors, historical memory, and real ties of hospitality. Over the millennia, because of mutually beneficial trade and the economic interdependence different subenvironments within—Bantu agricultural communities on riverside lands and savanna patches within the forest, and Batwa on equatorial forest itself—these relationships were reinforced and recreated. These relationship resulted in multiethnic communities that, whether Batwa or Bantu, have come to speak Bantu languages.[11] Though Bantu relied heavily on Batwa to thrive in forest regions, their own culture and language became dominant in Batwa communities.

One example of this mutualism today is the complex relationship that Baka and Bangando have developed in the Congo River Basin in southeastern Cameroon—just east of the heartland of early emergent Bantu communities 5,500 years ago. Anthropologists and historians have often fallen back on essentialist ideas of Batwa of central Africa as "Pygmies," primordial short people roaming, hunting, and gathering in forests. At the same time, literature of these regions has often purveyed equally essentialist views about people speaking Bantu languages, as invaders who settled a location, cultivated crops, produced culture, and marginalized Batwa. Baka and Bangando have not been immune

---

[9] *Comparative Bantu*, Vol. 4, CS 1804, 1805, and p. 467.

[10] Klieman, *Pygmies*, 67–70.

[11] Stephanie Rupp, "Multiangular Identities among Congo River Basin Forest Peoples," in Barry S. Hewlett ed., *Hunter Gatherers of the Congo Basin: Cultures, Histories, and Biology of the Pygmies* (New Brunswick, N.J.: Transaction Publishers, 2014), 277–298; Kleiman, *Pygmies*, 19–20.

to these problematic tropes—Baka being oft described as "traditional" nonsedentary, non-Bantu gatherer-hunters who resist all change, and Bangando as dominant, settled Bantu agriculturists. In reality, they resided in villages together, intermarried, and practiced a variety of professions that were not ethnically restricted. They created cross-ethnic alliances and communities. Similar Bantu-Batwa relationships likely have played out in the history of such diverse social and political worlds as those of the Kuba Kingdom of the seventeenth to nineteenth centuries in the southern DRC; the Bolia Kingdom of the twelfth to twentieth centuries in the west-central DRC; Fipa chiefdoms of the eighteenth to twentieth centuries; and among Sabi peoples of the Lake Bangweulu region of western Zambia since the tenth century.

In eastern Africa, interactions between people speaking Nilo-Saharan, Bantu, and Afrasian languages hinged on solidarities that crossed ethnic, linguistic, kin, and economic boundaries. Bantu speakers, when they settled in northern East Africa in the first millennium BCE, blended West African planting traditions of tubers and legumes and small stock raising with the raising of African savanna grain crops. As Bantu communities spread into southern Africa toward the end of the first millennium BCE and beginning of the first millennium CE, they continued their emphasis on grain cultivation. There they entered into many centuries of ongoing encounter with Khoesan gatherer-hunters and with Khoekhoe cattle raisers, as is evidenced in cultural and linguistic borrowing. With Khoekhoe they entered into enduring cross-cultural relations and intermarriages. Over the long-term they incorporated large numbers of Khoekhoe into their societies. As a result, they incorporated new forms of cattle raising into their economic practice. Through these cultural influences from Khoekhoe, southern African Bantu speech communities became notably distinct economically, socially, and linguistically from other Bantu.

Rarely are contacts among Africans seen as examples of cross-cultural exchange. However, Bantu Africa presents an opportunity to disrupt the emphasis that has been placed on cross-cultural interaction as deriving solely from European and Asian encounters with Africans. In fact, the very elements that commonly describe cross-cultural interaction—encounter, exchange, and hybridities—are recurring themes in Nilo-Saharan, Afrasian, Khoesan, Batwa, and Bantu histories. Their communities encountered each other again and again. In fact, Bantu speakers and those of other linguistic and cultural backgrounds with whom they interacted drew on promising ideas learned from their neighbors, producing a number of outcomes. Bantu speakers' adherence to values rooted in hospitality was an important factor in their successful integration with non-Bantu speakers over the course of five millennia. Importantly, there is a lesson to be gained from Bantu histories regarding population expansions. It need not depend on conquest. Although Bantu speakers came to inhabit large parts of sub-Saharan Africa, it does not appear that they violently dominated people of other cultural and linguistic backgrounds. Instead, they employed hospitality and elaborated this strategy as they moved into new lands already inhabited by others. Their worldview shaped how they integrated with, borrowed from, and adapted to perceived advantageous economic, political, religious and social ideas of other communities.

Although these historical processes should not to be assumed idyllic and free of contest and dispute, at the same time the value and utility of hospitality would have provided flexibility in managing interactions and relationships. Evidence from recent centuries shows how widely Bantu peoples valued hospitality as a process critical to community sustainability. Through kinship and friendship people forged spaces of belonging that accommodated insiders and outsiders. We can no longer uncover specific ways that hospitality played out in historical periods far back in the past. Such details are beyond the reach of oral tradition, and there are no written records for the period. But linguistic and archaeological data evince a long history of hospitality as a means of dealing with peoples of different cultures and economies. Ancestors of Ovimbundu, Huambo, Luena, and other Savanna Bantu peoples of the region between the Atlantic Ocean and further inland to the Zambezi River, for example, incorporated Khwe, Kwadi, and Batwa gatherers and mixed hunter-pastoralists, blending their ideas of pastoralism and gathering into their ways of agricultural subsistence to create diversified agripastoral systems.

Likewise in eastern Africa, three distinct traditions—Bantu, Nilotic, and Cushitic—came together. Ancestral Luyia, Gusii, Gikuyu, and other Bantu speech communities interacted and joined with Kalenjin and Tato Southern Nilotes, as well as Tale Southern Cushites. These populations learned useful technologies and approaches to subsistence and to surplus production from each other. Similar to their earlier forest encounters with Batwa, Bantu, who in later times gained access to cattle and cattle-raising knowledge from Nilo-Saharan and Cushitic speech communities in savanna lands, likely employed refined tactics of hospitality and generosity. The patron–client relationship, seen so commonly since the sixteenth century in centralized and often patriarchal and patrilineal cattle-owning Bantu communities of the Great Lakes region, might in fact be interpreted as a form of hospitality. However, it was one that reinforced hierarchies of political and social status, which stood in contrast to more diffuse power and lateral forms of status that commonly characterized decentralized communities.

Hospitality was an early Bantu ideal. Its practical strategic value aided their pursuits of a productive way of life and society building as they encountered firstcomer populations resulting from multiple population movements. Cross-cultural exchanges likely facilitated and enriched various endeavors and had enduring influences on their histories.

HONORING ANCESTORS: RELIGIOUS OBSERVANCE AS HOSPITALITY

Bantu political and social belonging rested on epistemologies that bound deceased generations to the living. This was reinforced by philosophies and practices of hospitality. Altars and shrines commemorating the deceased came in a variety of forms. Related ritual observances at these venues not only connected the living with their ancestors or with territorial spirits but also involved acts meant to convey generosity and cordiality from living generations toward the spirits. Offerings of food and drink to ancestral and territorial spirits mirrored the hospitality provided to living guests in the form of food, care, and protection.

Intersections of religious and political ideology and practice are evident in shrine histories from ancient to more contemporary times in widely separated areas where Bantu communities lived. For example, in the Great Lakes region of east Africa, by the early first millennium CE priestesses and priests led spirit possession groups called *mbándwa*. *Mbándwa* priests and priestesses healed those who had been possessed (*kubándwa*) with illness by a spirit. The work of these religious communities and practitioners was to remove affliction, and they performed their *kubándwa* healing rites at particular shrines.[12] Right into the twentieth century spirit shrines and oaths administered under the aegis of shrine guardians bolstered support in the countryside for the Maji Maji rebellion in colonized southern Tanganyika, 1904–1907. From the late twentieth century come examples of Matopo Hills shrines of Njila, Dula, and Dzilo. These shrines had

---

[12] Schoenbrun, *Green Place*, 266–269.

been politically important oracular sites, utilized by kings of Torwa and Rozwi Kingdoms of Zimbabwe in the fifteenth to nineteenth centuries, but they gained heightened salience during the political struggles for Zimbabwe independence during the 1970s and 1980s.

Cultural blending that took place over and over again across west-central, central, southern, and eastern Africa, as Bantu-speaking communities expanded into new areas, shows that Bantu speakers accepted their interdependence with the communities they encountered. Bantu who did migrate relied on finding one kind of accommodation or another from societies already operating in the territory, whether as gatherers, hunters, pastoralists, or cultivators. The existence of an ancient common Bantu root *-túá for those already living in a region expresses the importance they gave to firstcomers and to making necessary ritual and other accommodations to those people. Bantu people understood firstcomer communities as necessary to deal with because those people knew the spirits of land and how to deal with them. Until a Bantu community had established itself for several generations in an area and its elders had died and been buried there, the only ancestor spirits—the *-dImu, protectors and connectors of people to land— would have been those of firstcomers.

Many Bantu communities not only came to recognize firstcomers they encountered as holding ancestral ownership over land but also as important religious agents. As discussed in chapters 2 and 3, so often in Bantu communities, politics, religion, and knowledge were mutually reinforcing. Though not impossible to disentangle, they make far more sense when looked at collectively.

ACROSS THE SEAS: NON-AFRICAN FOREIGNERS

Notably, there are examples of coastal Bantu populations welcoming foreigners from across the seas.[13] The Kongo Kingdom provides

---

[13] Examples can also be found in European and Arab travel documents. Travelers encountered Swahili and pre-Swahili Bantu as far back as the 900s. Al-Masudi seems to have reported on the southern Swahili while Ibn Battuta encountered the northernmost Swahili and discusses the ways in which they hosted foreign traders. For early documents on East Africa's Swahili populations, see G.S.P. Freeman-Grenville, *The East African Coast: Select Documents from the First Century to the Early Nineteenth Century* (Oxford: Oxford University Press, 1962), 14–31.

one particularly intriguing example in the fifteenth and sixteenth centuries in the early decades of Atlantic trade. The Kongo Kingdom employed ample hospitality as a diplomatic tool in forging economic relations first with Portuguese and then other western European states and trading firms. Clearly Portuguese, Dutch, French, and other Europeans who arrived at Loango Island and coastal ports of the Kongo Kingdom were quite different culturally, and yet they were treated with generosity just as foreigners from the African continent had been historically. Kongo rulers, in particular, saw value that they could receive from building up this new network and allowing these outsiders a space and role in the social fabric. Kongolese élites adopted and adapted Catholic ideology, beliefs, and practices as benefits they could gain from these outsiders.

To put it simply, among Bantu peoples, politics were rooted in both practical and religious ideas. Religion and ethics informed political and social relationships. As early as the eleventh century CE, an old Bantu root -gàn- meaning "to narrate/tell stories" was in play in the Malebo Pool region of Central Africa. By the time the Kongo Kingdom coalesced into a centralized state, the leader's title was *nkáni* (derived from the root -gàn-) The *nkáni* was charged with using creative power of speech to maintain peace among various distantly related and loosely affiliated social clusters. In essence these leaders needed to be skilled in diplomatic speech, which was another manifestation of hospitality toward outsiders. Additionally, *nkáni* were mediators to ancestral spirits. In yet another demonstration of the role of heterarchical authority in the domestic sphere, religious leaders known as *kitomi*, intercessors between territorial spirits and community well-being, supported and balanced *nkáni*, power.[14] Although local religious ideas continued to play out among both commoner and élite populations, rulers also incorporated Catholic ideology represented in regalia, symbols, and rhetoric that bolstered their power and authority both in their own society and in the eyes of their foreign guests and trade partners.

Four hundred years after the Catholic Portuguese encounter with western central Africa, European travelers and Christian missionaries in eastern central Africa in the later nineteenth and early twentieth centuries, such as J. Frederic Elton, Joseph Thompson, and Edward Coode Hore, bemoaned "excessive" hospitality of the region as an impediment to their expeditions and goals. Thompson stated

---

[14] Ehret, *Civilizations*, 262, 352; Vansina, *Paths*, 146–148.

that despite European perceptions of Africans as constantly battling each other and outsiders "[a]lmost everywhere I was received with genuine hospitality and friendship."[15]

RESPECTABILITY AND ANTISOCIAL ACTS: HOSPITABLE AND INHOSPITABLE CATEGORIES

Hospitality as a vital social and political value and approach to the world is evident in sets of old Bantu words and practices that explicitly express notions of hospitability and its antithesis. Bantu roots such as "generosity" *-gàb-, "to honor" -dèm-, and "to receive" *-támb-underscore the ancient and enduring presence of these values.[16] Importantly, the absence of qualities associated with hospitality is also reflected in equally old ideas. This is captured in words used to describe antisocial people, including "evil/badness" *-bí, "witchcraft" *-dòg-, "stinginess" *-yIm-, and "shame" *-cónI-. People possessing these malevolent characteristics were thought to cause unrest, illness, and conflict. Examples epitomize elements of the Bantu worldview regarding etiology of good and evil discussed in chapter 2.

Nineteenth- and twentieth-century recorded proverbs provide another source of rich cultural evidence that validates expectation of hospitality practices. One example of a regional proverb common around southern Lake Tanganyika, at the crossroads of eastern and

---

[15] Joseph Thomson, *To the Central African Lakes and Back, East Central Africa Expedition 1878–80* 2nd ed., vol. I (London, Frank Cass and Co, LTD, 1968), vii–viii. Fourshey, "Stranger Come Heal Thy Host," 18–54.

[16] Guthrie *Comparative Bantu*, Vol. 3, 201, CS 755–757; see also, *Comparative Bantu*, Vol. 4 " "gift" and "give/give away" Vol. 2, 23; Guthrie *Comparative Bantu*, Vol. 3, 146, CS 527 and 530; see also "heavy" Vol. 2, 23; Guthrie *Comparative Bantu*, Vol. 4, 89, CS 1656 "to receive." In the Savanna Bantu period *-tamb- deriving from the root "to offer" has widespread distribution; see also CS 1655 and 1656; proto-Forest-Savanna Bantu -tamb- "to offer"; proto-Mashariki: -támb- or -támbik- "offer, sacrifice (by slaughtering or killing) in order to heal sick"; Shambaa *tambiko, ma-* "sacrifice," *kutambika* "to sacrifice"; proto-Ruvu -tambik- "ritual veneration for healing or prosperity"; e.g., Bemba -tambika (tambike) v.t. "to offer, hand out to"; -tambikisha "to call from afar"; Runyankore/Rukiga abatâmbi n. "healers"; eitambiro n. "place of offering." Nurse and Hinnebusch, *Swahili and Sabaki*, 608; Schoenbrun, *Historical Reconstruction*, 239–240.

west central Africa, is "'*We have no food at all*' caused the man to go until nightfall."[17] The proverb implies disdain for people who might cause peril to a traveller for refusing to accommodate, feed, or welcome a guest regardless of how little the host could give. Forcing a guest to continue journeying beyond dusk, into the night, and all of its accompanying dangers defied the value system. The proverb thus teaches that it is a social expectation and duty to host and provide food for all guests. A community that set a normative standard of providing hospitality ensured long-term security and short-term benefits for all. The moral economy was predicated on a sense of circulation: acts of generous hospitality would be reciprocated.

Outsiders potentially brought new and different perspectives, technologies, and social approaches. New knowledge and practices could lead to innovations that invigorated and restored the host. In this worldview, a host had a vested interest in the well-being of strangers and guests. The stranger/guest was to be welcomed as a source for mediating vulnerable circumstances. Cleary political strategies varied across time and space as Bantu speech communities expanded through the continent. Rather than merely devolving into tense competition and perennial conflict, Bantu communities saw good sense in incorporating outsiders. Community leaders recognized assets and securities that hospitality could garner. Effective leaders encouraged community members to practice and perform hospitality, generosity, and beneficence in all possible forms. Hospitality was a value reflective of one's reputation, honor, moral character, and good will. Inhospitable individuals could be ousted from leadership positions or shunned as social misfits or evildoers.

CONCLUSION

Despite notable commonalities among Bantu-descended cultures and languages that derive from a common ancient Bantu history, there is remarkable sociocultural diversity among populations. This diversity partly derives from innovation within communities over time. But it also is very much the result of new environments and encounters with new groups of people speaking entirely different languages,

---

[17] We quote the original full proverb, "We have no food at all" caused the man to go until nightfall, which has a quotation within the phrase. For ease of reading, the people's statement "We have no food at all" is italicized.

creating different cultural lives, and practicing entirely novel economies. Between 1000 and 500 BCE, people speaking Bantu languages
moved out of equatorial rainforests and began to populate woodlands, savannas, and highland niches in central, eastern, and southern Africa. As they moved into new territories and encountered new
groups of people, they maintained many of their linguistic, cultural,
and economic approaches. Yet they also often adopted technologies
from people they encountered and as a result sometimes revolution-
ized their agricultural practices, scientific technologies, and abstract
ideologies. Equipped with a combination of oft times advantageous
economic, social, and cultural knowledge, tools, and practices, they
settled into a wide range of environments and landscapes. These
historical processes often resulted in incorporation of outsiders into
the community. Although Bantu–non-Bantu interaction produced
new hybrid cultural elements, it also resulted in cultural erasure.
Throughout much of sub-Saharan Africa, Bantu-derived cultures and
languages predominate.

The period 400 BCE to 1000 CE (fourth and fifth phases) was
especially a time of political and demographic consolidation. After
1000 CE, some Bantu-speaking societies embarked on new directions of political change that led to the emergence of large and politically centralized states, such as Great Zimbabwe in the southeast,
the Kitara Kingdom in the African Great Lakes region, the Upemba
Kingdom of the upper Lualaba River region of the Congo Basin, the
Feti Kingdom of the upper Kunene River in Angola, and the Tyo and
Kongo Kingdoms, respectively, north and south of the lower Congo
River. Those societies created forms of political organization and authority that had not existed among Bantu or other groups south of
the equator in earlier periods. Still, the vast majority of Bantu people
maintained more decentralized political institutions for another eight
hundred years.

In the long period between 1000 and 1800 CE, Bantu peoples
increasingly interacted with people beyond the continent's borders.
In eastern Africa the great growth of trade via the Swahili city-states
from around 800 CE onward, in fact, expanded an involvement of
east African peoples with the Indian Ocean trade networks that had
begun even earlier in the last century or two BCE. Between 1000 and
1800 CE, goods reached east African Bantu peoples from as far away
as Southeast Asia and China. In west and west central Africa, global
contacts began in the late fifteenth century through the then-emerging

Atlantic trade routes. Eventually these routes reached East Asia and, from 1492 onward, the Western Hemisphere.

The political approach of the Bantu to provide a place of honor for those they encountered is a noteworthy alternative to the many narratives of conquest common in history. Hospitality was a key role in successful Bantu expansions over such vast territory. The configuration of centralized state building rested on enduring Bantu practices of hospitality. In the process of centralization, effective leaders worked to capitalize on the value strangers and immigrants contributed. They understood that the more people they had influence over, the more actual authority they potentially wielded. In turn, leaders who excelled in performing hospitality bolster their reputation, thus legitimizing their standing. This facilitated the allegiance of new members. Hospitality continued to be a salient social and political value and indispensable practice in various forms. The corpus of evidence compellingly demonstrates hospitality is a deep-rooted value that has remained relevant in varied forms for the *longue durée* of Bantu history. However, it is a fragile value; thus, it only survived when and where people renewed and continually nurtured it.

Hospitality, Hostility, and Refugees

In 1982, in a speech titled "A Guest Always Brings Cheer," former Tanzanian President Julius Kambarage Nyerere discussed the importance of hospitality in postcolonial nation-state building, demonstrating the enduring value this practice has in very new contexts. Nyerere cleverly drew on historic values and transformed hospitality from a localized, particular Bantu speech community's ethics into a national ideal.[18] This example echoes the historical connections and tensions among hospitality, society building, stability, violence, and politics (see pages xxi and xxiii Map 1 and 2).

A decade after Nyerere's speech, genocide, a devastating instance of hostility, unfolded in neighboring Rwanda. This genocide was part of a longer historical series of episodes. The violence of the colonial state, first German, then Belgian, created huge socioeconomic divides and rigid class lines, which erupted in the 1950s–1960s in violence in Burundi and Rwanda primarily against the majority Hutu, who were constructed to be ethnically

---

[18] Julius Kambarage Nyerere speech in brochure Compiled by Tanzania Tourist Corporation (TTC) Public Relations, *Karibu Tanzania* (Dar es Salaam, Tanzania Tourist Corporation, 1983), 2.

inferior and a potential danger to the rule of the dominant Tutsi class. Drawing on Western paradigms of ethnicity and "tribe," Tutsi and Hutu acts of violence and genocide went against the principles of hospitality manifested in patron–client relationships that existed among agriculturalists, pastoralists, and gatherer-hunters in Rwanda and Burundi in earlier centuries.[19]

Likewise in processes that led up to and became the 1994 Rwandan Genocide, Hutu drew on the colonial legacy of imposed categories of "ethnicity," "race," and "tribe." In their response to earlier episodes of terror, Hutu launched attacks primarily against those who were perceived to be ethnically Tutsi. Though they were not necessarily different ethnic groups, Hutu and Tutsi certainly came to fit into different social classes that shifted over time. Hutu and Tutsi were long engaged in patron–client relationships as well as intermarriage and exchange. Episodes of violence in the twentieth century highlight that there can be moments of rupture and fracture even in societies that value hospitality and relationship building between insiders and outsiders. During the genocide, large groups of refugees spilled across borders into Tanzania, Zambia, Congo, Uganda, and even as far as Malawi. Overwhelmed with refugees, many of these nations were anxious to repatriate those who had fled. In the aftermath of the genocide, Nyerere's powerful words did not necessarily guide decisions by the post-Nyerere state. Tanzania allowed small numbers of Rwandan refugees to settle in western Tanzania. Yet this more limited assistance should also be placed in the larger context of Tanzania's longtime, consistent support to exiles and refugees. These included South Africans who were provided land in Morogoro, Tanzania, from the 1970s through the 1990s; 100,000 Burundians throughout the 1970s to the present; and Bantu Somalis granted citizenship and land in Tanga, Tanzania, in the 2000s. Over the last six decades, Kenya, Tanzania, and Uganda have created spaces for refugees from surrounding nations but have also worked as the East African community, with uneven success, on a number of issues to facilitate migration across all three nations. Although it is continually transformed and perhaps under greater threat as societies become more urban and commercialized, hospitality as a value does continue into the twenty-first century to hold import within many Bantu speech communities.

---

[19] Rwanda and Burundi have three primary communities differentiated historically by economic practices and social status. They are Hutu (agriculturalists), Tutsi (pastoralists), and Twa (gatherer-hunters). They all speak the Kinyarwanda language.

FURTHER READING

Ellis, Stephen, and Gerrie Ter Haar. *Worlds of Power: Religious Thought and Political Practice in Africa.* Oxford: Oxford University Press, 2004.

Fourshey, Catherine Cymone. "Stranger Come Heal Thy Host." *African Historical Review* 44, no. 2 (2012): 18–54.

Klieman, Kairn. *The Pygmies Were Our Compass.* Portsmouth, N.H.: Heinemann, 2003.

Nurse, Derek, and Thomas Spear. *The Swahili—Reconstructing the History and Language of an African Society, 800-1500.* Philadelphia: University of Pennsylvania Press, 1985.

Parker, Shipton. *The Nature of Entrustment.* Princeton, N.J.: Princeton University Press, 2007.

Ranger, Terrence. *Voices from the Rocks: Nature, Culture, and History in the Matopos Hills.* Bloomington: Indiana University Press, 1999.

Vansina, Jan. *How Societies Are Born: Governance in West Central Africa Before 1600.* Charlottesville: University of Virginia Press, 2004.

Whitaker, Beth Elise. "Refugees in Western Tanzania: The Distribution of Burdens and Benefits among Local Hosts." *Journal of Refugee Studies* 15, no. 4 (Dec. 2002): 339–358.

Wilmsen, Edwin N. *A Land Filled with Flies: A Political Economy of the Kalahari.* Chicago: The University of Chicago Press, 1989.

Index

Adaptation, 51, 69, 72
Advanced, 68
    development, 68, 141–143,
        152, 154
    learning, 90, 104–108
Aesthetic, xxvi, 3, 115, 128, 132, 134,
        137–8
Affine, 56–57
Afrasian, xxii, 157
Al-Masudi, 160
Altar, 61, 159 (*see also* shrine)
Ancestor, 43–56, 57–62, 64–67,
        80–81, 85–86, 96, 111–112, 128,
        137, 139, 141, 147, 148, 153–160
        (*see also* *-*dimo*)
Ancestorhood, 44
Angola, xxvii, 18–19, 41, 49, 58, 76,
        93, 101, 104, 148, 164
Anthropomorphic, 152
Archaeology, xv, 1, 7, 16, 19, 25,
        32–33, 39, 44, 124
Architecture, xvi, xxvi, 133, 144
    building technique, 23
    conical roof, 133
    flat roof, 135
    gabled roof, 133–135
    house, 133–34 (*see also* *-*umba*)
    thatched roof, 133–134
        (*see also* *-*bimb*-)
    woven roof, 133
Arrow, 11, 53
    poison arrow, 11
Arrowroot, 122
Asian Crops, 119–122
Asu, 128–129

Atlantic, 92, 101
    coast, 10, 16, 19
    era, 104
    ocean, xxvi, 22, 91, 101
    slave trade, 93, 101, 122
    trade routes, 155, 161, 165
Austronesian, xv, 120
Authority, 23, 36, 44–45, 49, 56,
        66, 68, 76 n. 39, 103, 107, 125,
        155–6, 161–165
    complimentary, 63
    gender, 45, 70–74, 151
    generational, 74–75
    matrilineal, 78–81
Axe, 7, 117, 125, 130

Babessi, 129
Bafia, 129
Baka, 156–157
Bakutu, 138
BaMbwidi-mbodila, 49
Banana, xv, xx
    cooking banana,
        119–120, 123
Bangando, 156–157
Bantu defined, 2 (*see also* *-*ntu*)
Banuunguli, 95
Basket, 7–8, 140
    ceremonial, 99
    fishing, 90, 94, 118
Batibo, H. M., xx
Batwa, ix, xxii, xxix, 4–5, 13, 15, 30,
        32, 42, 49, 51–54, 100, 107, 117,
        132, 147–148, 155–158
    trade with, 117–118, 132, 156

Bayeye, 94–95
Bead, 107, 110, 122, 124, 132,
  136–137
Bed, 136
Beekeeping, 8
Belonging, xxvi, 18, 43, 94,
  151–155, 159
  histories of, 48, 153
  lineage, 56–58, 155
  social, 47, 70, 84–85,
    147, 159
Bemba, 13, 37, 53, 81, 86–87,
  98–99, 104
Bilingual, 109
Black-eyed peas, 6, 11
Body art, 137–138 (*see also* henna)
Bolia Kingdom, 157
Borneo, 119
Botatwe, 13, 17–18, 20–21, 84, 87,
  125–126
Botswana, xxvii, 148
Bow, 11, 113
Bride, 76 n. 39, 78–8
  bride price, 72
  bride service, 70, 73, 79–81
  bride wealth, 71–72, 74, 141
Bumbudye, 106–108, 110
Burundi, xxvii, 90 n. 1, 165–166
Bushongo, 59, 86
Bwami, 106, 108

Cameroon, xvi-xvii, xxvii, 16, 38, 43,
  90 n. 1, 116, 129, 166
  Bantu homeland, 3, 5, 7
Canoe, 7–8, 10, 118–119
Capoeira, 41
Catholicism, xv
Cattle, 15, 17, 19, 21, 40, 89, 118, 120,
  123–125, 157–158
  inheritance, 72
  raising, 61, 64–68, 118, 120, 123,
    137, 157–158
  sleeping sickness, 123
Central Savanna, 20, 32, 48
Central Sudanian, 15–16

Ceramic, xxvi, 34, 52–53, 99, 104,
  114, 126–130
  kiln, 60, 62, 128
Ceremony, 53, 81, 83–84, 147
  female initiation, 98–99,
    101, 142
  graduation, 95, 103
  marriage, 101
Chaga, 76, 83, 90 n. 1, 99–101,
  110, 122
Chewa, 63, 81, 84, 86–87, 94–96
Chicken, 119–120
Chief, 70, 85 n. 47, 100, 106,
  124–125, 135, 150–156
  death of, 111
  implement of, 112
Childbirth, 76, 139, 142
China, 135–136
Chisungu, 52–53
Chokwe, 86
Circumcision, 83
  female, 66
  male, 82, 84 (*see also* *-*alam*-;
    -*alik*-; -*túá*; *-*nkunka*)
Citemene, 53, 125
Clan, 35, 97–99, 104, 107, 111, 125,
  153–155 (*see also* kinship)
Clay, 126–129, 134, 137
  item, 110, 127, 140
  ritual of, 129
  unfired, 99–100
Cloth, 103, 137
  bark, 104, 137–139
  cotton, 141
  currency, 104–105, 140–141
  raffia, 104–105, 113–114, 123
Communication, 89–90, 93, 105,
  107–112, 114
  spirit, 47, 103, 146, 159–161
Congo, xiv, xvi, xvii, xxvii, 7–8, 18,
  30, 33, 49, 93–94, 104–105, 108
  basin, 13, 111, 113, 119, 122,
    125, 164
  river, xxii, 5, 19, 106, 112, 140, 142,
    156, 164

Copper, 125
  copperbelt, 31
Coral, 134–136
  reef, 23
Cosmopolitan, 120
Crop, 5–8, 10–11, 15, 18–19, 72,
  95–96, 116–125
Cultivation, 10, 15, 17, 40, 72,
  121–124, 157
Cultural hybridity, 22
Cushitic population, 134–136
  Cushitic language, 17
  Southern Cushitic, 32, 55, 66, 83
  Tale Southern Cushite, 158

Dance, 39, 41, 47, 49, 77 n. 41, 81,
  138 (see also *-bIn; *-bInà;
  *-goma)
de Maret, Pierre, 33
Desch-Obi, M.T. J., 41
Design, 34, 51, 54, 127
  art, 115, 128, 137
  geometric, 51, 137, 140, 142
  symbol, 131, 141
Drum, 92–95, 111 (see also ngoma)
Dula, 159
Dzilo, 159

Education, xix, xx, xxvi, 1, 53,
  66, 89–94, 96–99, 101–107,
  109–110, 113, 128
  teaching, 91 (see also *-dag-)
Egypt, 137
Ehret, Christopher, xxv
Elder, 45, 52–53, 63, 66, 70–72, 74,
  75–83, 85, 91, 97–98, 100–103,
  107, 151–155, 160
Engineering, xiii, 60, 133, 141
Epistemology, 112
Esoteric, 89, 102, 109, 113
Ethnography, xv, xxv, 1, 7, 11, 25, 30,
  44, 46, 48, 51–54, 57, 61–63,
  68–69, 72, 74, 76, 79–83, 89, 91
Evil, 47, 55–56, 86, 162–163
  (see also *-dog-)

Farming, 8, 11, 39, 68, 73, 89,
  116–120, 155
  farmer, 82, 121–125, 132
Father, 62, 68, 70, 72–73, 79–80, 82,
  101, 108
  fatherhood, 82
Female husband, 72–73
Fetus, 100–101
Ficus, 139
Finger millet, 122–123
Fipa, 131, 149–157
Firstcomer, xxvi, 4, 13, 40, 46,
  51–52, 59, 64, 67, 145–151, 156
  (see also *-túá)
Fishing, 10–11, 21, 68–69, 116–119
  basket, 90, 94, 118
  hook, 7–8, 118
  pool, 94
  trap, 7–8, 90, 96
Friendship, 158, 162
Funeral, 95–96
furnace, 130–133
  gynecomorphic, 131

Gabon, xxvii, 7, 51, 59–60, 87, 118
Gatherer-hunter, 10, 12, 17, 126, 148,
  155–157
  trade with, 13, 15, 25
Gathering, 51, 53, 89, 123–124,
  155–158
Genocide, 165–166
Gikuyu, 60 n. 22, 83, 158
  Agikuyu, 72
  Kikuyu, 35–36, 72 n. 35, 86,
  90 n. 1
Glottochronology, 26–27, 29–30, 33
Goat, 11, 15, 19, 89, 116, 120
God, 5, 23, 30–31, 55, 67, 86–87,
  112, 126, 128 (see also *-amb-;
  *-ded-; *-jambe;
*-lung-; *-yambe)
  Creator, 55, 67, 86–87, 115, 128,
  130, 143
Gogo, 38, 65–67, 77, 83, 90 n. 1,
  153–155

Gold, 23, 135–136
Gourd, 11, 138
Grassland, xxiv, 118, 123, 129
Great Lakes, 60–61, 77, 87, 94–95,
    118–121, 126, 130–133, 136–137,
    159, 164
Great Wedding, 101
Great Zimbabwe, 125, 164, 112
    great enclosure, 135–136
Greed, xxiv, 37, 146
Greeting, 146–150
Groundnut, 11, 116
Guinea fowl, 11, 116, 120
Gusii, 90 n. 1, 158

Haya, 36–37, 131
Headrest, 136–137
Healer, 56, 86, 95, 105, 162 n. 16
    (see also *-ganga)
Henna, 138 (see also body art)
Herbalist, 113
Heterarchy, xix, xxvi, 43–45, 64, 70,
    75, 79, 84–85, 153
Hierarchy, 107
High veld, 125
Historical linguistics, 54
Hoe, 130–132
Homestead, 133, 141
Hospitality, xiii, xvi, xix, xxvi, 145
Huambo, 158
Hunting, 11, 20–21, 51, 53, 89–90,
    95–96, 101, 111, 116, 123–124,
    150, 156
    hunter, 82, 95, 113, 126, 148, 160
Hutu, 166

Ibn Battuta, 135, 160
Identity, 30 n. 30, 45, 50, 57, 58,
    70, 72, 80, 95, 107–108, 138,
    154–155
Ideogram, 110
Ikoku, 94, 96
Ila, 18, 60 n. 22; 67–68, 87, 90 n. 1
Indian Ocean, 14, 20, 23, 69, 119,
    133–136, 149, 164

Indonesia, 119–122
Initiation, xxvi, 36 n. 17, 44, 74, 76,
    78–83, 101–102, 109–111, 142
    female/women, 49–54, 57,
    66, 71, 80, 93, 95, 98–100
    (see also *-nyamkungui;
    *-simbi)
    male/men, 82–84, 97
    (see also *-alam-; *-alik-;
    *-kunk-; *-tib-)
    masked dance, 81, 95–96, 102–103
Innovation, xvi, xxii, 3–4, 8, 16, 31,
    40, 46, 49, 55, 64, 67, 78, 116,
    120, 163
Intercropping, 121
Iron, xvi, xxvi, 10–11, 59–60, 62, 82,
    104, 110, 112, 113, 126–127
    ironworking, 16, 19, 124
    blacksmith, 104, 112, 132
    smelting of, 15, 62
    smithing of, 16
    tool, 22
Islam, 67, 84, 109, 134
Ivory, 101, 124

Kagulu, 155
Kalenjin, 158
Kamanji, 107
Kanda, 70–71
Kasai River, 18, 20, 23, 101
Kaskazi, 16–17, 20, 24, 47, 49, 55, 76,
    77 n. 40–41, 83, 86–87, 98 n. 11,
    119, 125, 132
Katanga, 18, 20, 33–34, 90 n. 1, 105,
    108 n. 25, 125, 139
Kenya, xxvii, 3, 17, 20, 35–36, 72,
    83, 90 n. 1, 166
Kerebe, 146, 149–150
Kezilahabi, Euphrase, 146
Khoekhoe, 17, 123–124, 157
Khoesan, xxii, 14, 16–17, 19, 32, 40,
    123–124, 157
Khwe, 158
Kikuyu, (see Gikuyu)
Kilwa, 135

Kinship, xxvi, 45–46, 63, 71, 73–74,
    81, 87, 107, 146, 158 (*see also*
    clan; lineage)
Kiswahili, ix, 14, 16, 77 n. 41, 90 n. 1,
    93, 150 (*see also* Swahili)
Kitara, 164
Kitomi, 161
Klieman, Kairn, xxv, 4–5, 9, 59–60,
    123, 156
Kongo, xv, 24, 49, 70, 93, 112, 140
    KiKongo language, 86–87
    Kongo Kingdom, 70, 160–164
    Mani Kongo, 70
    mwissikongo, 70–71
Kuba, xvii, 38, 86 n. 39, 105,
    140–142, 149, 157
Kumbi, 84
Kunda, 112
Kunene River, 19, 164
Kusi, 16–17, 20, 23, 32, 47, 63, 87,
    98 n. 11, 123–125, 132
Kwadi, 158

Lake, 106
    Bangweulu, 157
    Kivu, 108
    Mweru, 53, 106
    Nyanza, 61, 9 n. 1, 123, 149
    Tanganyika, 12, 16, 19–20,
        154, 163
Lamu, 134
Lega, 59, 86, 106, 108
Legume, 121, 157
Lenje, 13
Leza, 30–31, 55, 87 (*see also* *-*ded*-)
Life stage, 57, 74–84, 97–98, 100–101,
    103, 138 (*see also* *-*yadi*)
Limpopo River, 23, 124
Lineage, xvi, xxvi, 38, 43, 97, 99,
    101–102, 104, 125, 137, 154–155
    (*see also* kinship)
Loango Island, 161
Longue durée, xx, 46, 58, 64, 79,
    84, 86, 104, 115, 120, 126, 145,
    147, 165

Lualaba River, 18, 20, 164
Luba, 13, 18, 20, 24, 33–34, 48,
    106–107, 110, 138
Luena, 158
Lukala, 107
Lukasa, 107, 110
Lunda, 24, 69–70, 86, 90 n. 1,
    101, 107
Luyia, 83, 158
Lydenburg, 128

Maji Maji, 67 n. 28, 159
Makishi, 102 n. 17, 103
    -*kishi*, 102–103
    likishi, 102–103
Mako, 81 (*see also* mother;
    mother-in-law avoidance)
Malagasy, 119–120
Malawi, xxvii, 17, 52, 54, 59, 81, 84,
    94, 166
Malebo Pool, 161
Mangrove, 134–136
Marriage, 57, 63, 65, 66, 78–81,
    101, 103
    intermarriage, 66,
        157, 166
Mashariki, 13–20, 22, 32, 97, 98 n.
    11, 125, 132–136
Mask, 39, 81, 95–96, 102–103,
    141, 143
Math, xiii, 110–111
Matopo Hills, 159
Matrilineal, 36, 48, 57–63, 95, 99,
    101, 124, 127, 139, 154 (*see also*
    *-*cuka*; *-*gàndá*)
    matriclan, 68, 70–71,
        73, 85, 87
    matrilineage, 45, 50, 58–64,
        68, 75, 78–81, 84–87, 151–155
        (*see also* *-*bIn*)
    sororal group, 78–81(*see also*
        *-*bumba*)
Mat, 136, 138
Mbandwa, 159
Mbira, 112

Mbundu, 86
  Kimbundu (speaking people), 41
  Ovimbundu (southern Mbundu
    people), xxiii, 158
Mbusa, 99
  Nachimbusa, 99
Meinhof, Carl, xvi, 28
Menstruation, 98, 103, 130–131
Migration, xv, xix, xxi-xxii, xxix, 3,
  6, 32, 36, 39, 62, 150, 166
Mitochondrial DNA, 62
Mlao, 84
Mombasa, 134
Mongo, 10, 59–60, 86
Monsoon, 20
  wind regimen, 119
Mother, 62, 66, 68, 71–73, 76, 78–80,
    99–103, 108 (*see also* *-*nya*)
  grandmother, 48, 62, 78,
    129, 138
  motherhood, 30 n. 10, 62–63, 66,
    71, 76–78, 94, 100, 138
  mother's brother, 36, 68
  mother-in-law, 63, 71, 80-8
  mother-in-law avoidance,
    (*see also* Mako)
  pregnancy, 138–139, 142
  queen mother, 85
Mother language, 27
Mozambique, xxvii, 17–20, 58, 69,
    73, 84
Mrego, 100, 110
Mukanda, 102–103
Mukumu, 153–154
Multilingual, 109
Music, 37, 41, 91–96, 104, 111–113
  musical instruments, 96, 141
  sing, 92 (*see also* *-*yimb*-)
  song, 91, 92 (*see also* *-*dag*-;
    *-*yimbo*)
Mutualism, 148, 156
Mwadi, 95, 98, 101, 103 (*see also*
    mwali; *-*yadi*)
Mwami, 154

Mwari, 23
Mwene, 23
Myth, 35–36, 60, 91–92

Nakabumba, 129
Ndop, 141–142
Network, xxvi
  economic, 23–24 119, 122, 164
  social, 4, 19, 36, 43–45, 75, 106,
    148, 154, 161
Newcomer, 107, 147–149, 156
Ngoma, 93 (*see also* *-*goma*)
Ngulu, 108
Nguni, 69, 83, 98, 124–125
Niger-Congo, 54, 86, 126, 139, 147–148
Niger River, xxii
Nigeria, xxii
Nile River, 118
Nilo-Saharan, xxii, 40, 136
  speaking people, xxii, 14–15, 17,
    32, 118, 133, 137, 157–158
Njila, 13, 18–19, 20, 32, 41, 76 n. 39,
    98 n. 11, 159
Nkáni, 161
Nubia, 137
Nyamwezi, 152
Nyandarua Range, 122
Nyanja, 76 n. 39, 87
  Manyanja, 86–87, 90 n. 1
Nyanza, 77
  east, 78, 90 n. 1
  north, 77–78
  proto-north, 77
Nyau, 81, 95–96
Nyerere, 165–166
Nyong River, 5, 8, 40, 118
Nyong-Lomami, 8, 9–10, 82
Nyumbu yu misambwa, 52
Nzadi-Kwa, 48

Oil palm, 5, 11
One-hundred-word list, 34
Oral tradition, xv, xxv, 7, 11, 13, 16,
    34–39, 42, 46–47, 52–61, 63,

66; 82, 85, n. 47, 89, 91, 94–95,
    107, 109–112, 129, 150–156
Orange River, 40
Ostrich shell, 124

Pare Mountain, 128
Patrilineal, 35–36, 57–58, 63–74, 77,
    83, 99–100, 124, 159
    patrilineage, 61, 63–66, 68, 72–73
    (*see also* *-lòngò*)
Patron–client relations, 158, 166
Pearl millet, 15, 19, 122, 124
Persia, 136
Picasso, Pablo, 143
Polygyny, 72, 74
Porcupine, 95–96
Potting, 8, 10–11, 115, 127–128, 131
    potter, 99, 104, 113, 127–128
    (*see also* *-bumba*)
    pottery, xvi, 33–34, 60,
    104, 126
Proto-language, ix, 27
Proto-Bantu, xxii, 2–5, 7, 20, 38–40,
    43–49, 54–58, 64, 82, 86–87,
    90–95, 97, 101–103, 109, 116,
    126–127, 133–134, 153
Proto-Botatwe, 31
Proto-Kaskazi, 76
Proto-Mashariki, 14–16, 97
Proto-North-East Coastal
    Bantu, 65
Proto-Sabi, 30–31
Proto-Savanna, 48
Proverb, 35–37, 47, 57, 91, 108,
    148–151, 162–163
Punu, 94, 118

Rainforest, xxvi, 3, 5, 8, 10–11, 13,
    15, 17, 19–29, 32, 38–39, 42, 51,
    55, 104, 116–120, 156–164
Reciprocity, xxvi, 148–149
Refugee, 69, 165–166
Renfrew, Colin, 29–30 n. 10
Riddle, 36–37, 91

Rock art, 51–53, 100, 114, 142
    figurative, 107
    schematic, 51–53, 109–110
Rozwi, 160
Rufiji River, 40, 133
Rukiga, 77 n. 41, 162 n. 16
Runyankore, 162 n. 16
Ruvu, 77 n. 41, 78, 83–84, 98, 154
Rwanda, xvii, xxvii, 90 n. 1, 165–166

Sabaki, 23
Sabi, 13, 17–18, 20, 30–31, 33–34,
    52–53, 55, 61, 69, 79–80, 84, 87,
    98, 101, 107, 125, 129, 157
Safwa, 92, 138
Sagala, 155
Samba, 93
Sangha-Kwa, 60, 76, 87
Sangha-Nzadi, 9–13
Sangha River, 6, 9, 40
Sankuru River, 10, 140
Savanna, xxvi, 6–7, 10–11, 13, 15–17,
    19–20, 32, 39, 65, 84, 104,
    116–117, 156, 158
Savanna Bantu, 12–15, 17–18, 20–21,
    32, 47–49, 59, 64, 66, 76 n. 39,
    78, 82, 87, 97–98, 101, 154, 158
Scarification, 138–139
Schoenbrun, David, xii, xiii n. 2, xxv,
    30 n. 10
Science, xxvi, 16, 115–119,
    124–128, 131
Secret society, 81
Seniority, 45, 74–75, 79–80, 103
Sexuality, 72, 74, 103, 130
Shambaa, 90 n. 1
Shame, 162
Sheep, 19, 120, 123
    sheep raiser, 17, 19, 123
Shona, 23, 90 n. 1, 110, 112, 125, 128,
    135, 138
Shrine, 46, 51–52, 159 (*see also* altar)
Sleeping sickness, 123
    (*see also* tsetse fly)

Smithsonian, 143
Snake, 95–96, 150
Sofala, 135
Sona, 111
Songye, 48
Sorghum, xvi, 15, 19, 122–124
Sotho, 83, 92, 113, 124–125
South Africa, xxvi, 17, 20, 40, 143
Southern Nilotic, 55
Spirit, 46, 50, 52, 54–57, 59, 67,
    78, 81, 92–93, 95–96, 99,
    102–103, 107–108, 112, 114,
    127, 143 (*see also* *-dedia;
    *-kitI; *-simbi)
  ancestral, 38–39, 46–50, 52, 54,
    56, 59–60, 62, 64, 78, 85–86,
    99, 146, 161
  territorial, 11, 13, 23, 46,
    50–56, 59–60, 64, 67, 102,
    118, 159–161
Stephens, Rhiannon, 3 n. 10
Stool, 136, 150–152
Story, 39, 49, 52, 90–92
    (*see also* *-gano)
  storyteller, 91, 93
  storytelling, xxvi (*see also* *-gan)
Stranger, 36, 129, 147–152,
    163–165
Sugarcane, 119, 122
Sukuma, 86, 90 n. 1, 94–96
Swadesh, Morris, 26–29
Swahili, ix, 14, 16, 23, 77 n. 40,
    90 n. 1, 93, 134–135, 149
    (*see also* kiSwahili)
Swazi, 112
Symbol, 51–53, 76, 142

Tabwa, 90 n. 1, 138 139
Tanzania, xxvi, 17, 20, 36–38, 40,
    52, 58–59, 65, 69, 77, 83, 84, 92,
    94, 98, 100, 129, 131, 138, 149,
    152–153, 165
Taro, 119, 122
Tato Southern Nilotes, 158

Technology, xvi, xxvi, 15–16, 19,
    39–40, 104, 115
Tetela, 59, 90 n. 1
Thagiicu, 92, 122
Tonga, 13
Topoke, 138
Torwa, 160
Trade, 13, 24, 93, 109, 113,
    117–119, 156
  Atlantic, 41, 93, 104, 122, 155, 161,
    164–165
  Indian Ocean, 22–23, 69, 164
  interior, 104, 119
  river route, 19
  sixteenth century, 70–71
  nineteenth century, 73, 101
  Swahili, 160 n. 13, 164
Transition, 31, 36, 46, 66, 68, 72, 74,
    77, 79, 97–103, 137
Tsetse fly, 123 (*see also* sleeping
    sickness)
Tuber crops, 15, 119
Tumba, 141
Tutsi, 166
Twacii, 150–151
Tyo, 164

Ubutwa, 106–108
Uganda, xxvii, 30 n. 10, 51, 52, 92,
    111, 164
Ukule, 102–103
Unilineal, 58
Unqangala, 113
Upemba Depression, 33–34

Vansina, Jan, xii, xvii, xxv, 34–35,
    38, 42, 123
Vidunda, 77 n. 41, 155

Weaving, 104, 137
Wedding, 138
Western Savanna Bantu,
    76 n. 39
  western savanna region, 32

Witchcraft, 56, 86 (*see also*
  *-dog-; **-log-*)
Womb, 63, 102
Woodland, xxiv, xxvi, 123, 137, 164
Worldview, xv, 1, 4, 30–31, 34,
  36–37, 50, 75, 76, 93, 96, 98,
  145, 147
  Bantu, 1, 4, 43–44, 49, 54–56,
    90–91, 115, 129, 142, 158, 162–163
  matrilineal, 64, 66, 71, 78
  non-Bantu, 3
  patrilineal, 72
Wumbu, 59

Xhosa, 86
  isiXhosa, 123
Yam, xvi, 5, 7–8, 11, 15, 116–120,
  122–123

Yao, 73, 84, 86, 87, 90 n. 1
Yasayama, 138
Yombe, 138

Zambezi River, 19–20, 135, 158
Zambia, xxvii, 18–20, 31, 33–34, 37
  n. 19, 51–54, 67–69, 81, 84, 85,
  98, 115, 125, 157
Zimbabwe, xxvii, 23–24, 110,
  138, 160
  zimbabwes, 135
Zulu, 3, 86, 112
  isiZulu, 123
  KwaZulu-Natal, 125
  Zulu kingdom, 125
*-alam-, 83 (*see also* circumcision;
  initiation; **-nkunka*)
*-alik-, 82 (*see also* circumcision;
  initiation)
*-amb-, 31, 86 (*see also* God;
  *Nyambe)
*-bimb-, 133, 134 (*see also*
  thatched roof)
*-bɪn-, 92 (*see also* dance)
*-bɪnà, 92 (see also dance)

*-bumba, 78–79, 128–129 (*see also*,
  potter; sororal group)
*-cuka, 59, 62, 87 (*see also*
  matrilineage)
*-dag-, 91 (*see also* music; song)
*-ded-, 31, 87 (*see also* Leza; God)
  *-dedia, 31
*-dɪ́mù, 15, 38- 39, 46, 49, 60,
  86–87, 160 (*see also* spirit)
  *-dímo, 38 n. 20, 87 (*see also*
    ancestor)
  *-zimu, 67, 86
  zimu, 21 n. 28, 86
*-dog-, 86, 162 (*see also* evil;
  witchcraft)
*-gan-, 90–91 (*see also* storytelling)
*-gano, 90–91, 161 (*see also* story)
*-gàndá, 60–62, 86–87 (*see also*
  matrilineage)
*-gàngà, 56, 86 (*see also* healer)
*-gole, 76–77
*-goma, 92, 93 n. 3 (*see also* dance;
  ngoma)
*-jambe, 86 (*see also* God)
*-kitI, 102 (*see also* *makishi*; spirit)
*-kódò, 47–48, 58, 87 (*see also*
  ancestor; matrilineage)
*-kólò, 48–49, 65 n. 26, 87, 154 (*see
  also* matriclan)
*-kud-, 102 (*see also* initiation,
  male/men)
*-kúdà, 97
*-kul-, 82
  *-kula, 82
*-kunda, 112
*-kung-, 98 n. 11, 154–155
*-kunk-, 98 n. 11 (*see also* initiation)
*-log-, 56 (*see also* witchcraft)
*-lòngò, 64–66 (*see also*
  patrilineage)
*-lung-, 55, 67, 87 (*see also* God)
*-nkunka, 83 (*see also* circumcision)
*-ntu, 28 (*see also* Bantu)
*-nya, 101 (*see also* mother)

-nyamkungui, 97 (*see also* initiation, female/women)

-simbi, 49–50 (*see also* spirit; initiation, female/women)

-tib-, 82 (*see also* initiation, male/men)

-túá, 13, 155, 160 (*see also* Batwa)

-umba, 133 (*see also* architecture; house)

-yadi, 76–78, 95, 98, 101–103 (*see also* life stage; mwadi; *mwali*)

-yambe 86 (*see also* God)

-yímb-, 92 (*see also* music; sing)

-yímbo, 92 (*see also* music; song)

bu-logi, 56 (*see also* evil; witchcraft)

li-uba, 55, 87 (*see also* Creator)

Mu-lungu, 55 (*see also* God)

Nyambe, 30, 54, 86 (*see also* God)